Ellen Foy

FROM THE INSIDE OUT

AND OTHER METAPHORS

FROM THE INSIDE OUT

AND OTHER METAPHORS

Creative and Integrative Approaches to Training in Systems Thinking

By

Bunny S. Duhl, Ed.D.

Co-Director, Boston Family Institute

BRUNNER/MAZEL, *Publishers* • New York

Library of Congress Cataloging in Publication Data

Duhl, Bunny S., 1931–
    From the inside out and other metaphors.

    Bibliography: p.
    Includes index.
    1. Family therapy. 2. Thought and thinking.
3. Interpersonal relations. I. Title.
RC488.5.D83 1983   616.89'156   82-24428
ISBN 0-87630-328-9

This book is dedicated . . .

To my families, past and present, extended and over-extended, who offered me the contexts to experience and learn what family and human systems are all about;

To Fred, husband, father, mentor, dreamer, innovator, who moves possibilities into new realities, creating contexts for exploring the unknown;

To all the trainees and faculty at the Boston Family Institute over the years, who entered into, shaped and were shaped by whatever it is we call a "training program";

To the people at the School of Education at the University of Massachusetts, who reaffirmed for me that my life need not be irrelevant to my education;

To Jack, friend, evoker, resonator, guide, who ignites creative sparks, shields them with curiosity and acceptance, and fuels them with belief and wonderment.

Contents

Prologue: What This Book Is and Is Not About

FAMILY THERAPY AND HUMAN SYSTEMS THINKING

Family therapy has become an established "field" within the larger arena of mental health over the past two decades or so. Particularly within the past 10 to 15 years, the central idea that has caught the imagination of many, many people is that individual behavior does not exist in a vacuum, nor is it created only in the inner mind of the individual. Rather, individual human behavior exists in relationships of dynamic interaction with others. Thus, if one person in a family has a "problem," all family members are seen as involved in and with the existence of that problem in some way. From this follows the assumption that one then works with the whole family, carrying a "map" in one's head about the interconnectedness of each one's part in that process, or one perhaps works with an individual, still within that "map." One does not work with isolated persons, but with persons conceptualized as in relationships.

Since this idea caught hold, more and more training programs have developed to teach ways of working with whole families and with couples—ways of conceptualizing and working with relationships.

This is not a book on marital and family therapy. Although the material in this book derives from the training program in family therapy developed at the Boston Family Institute since 1969, *the emphasis here will not be on treating families, but on drawing forth and developing the map of human systems thinking in context over time, in the mind, and in the behaviors of each trainee.* We believe it is necessary for trainees to have such a map in order to understand and to work holistically and realistically with individuals, families, and all other human systems.

Families themselves do not exist in a vacuum. They are members of interlocking networks of extended families and friends, living in neighborhoods, within larger communities, comprising states, nations and so on. If there is a Great Depression at the national level and father loses his job, that indeed affects what happens inside a family and inside the individuals in that family. Thus individuals exist in the context of families, in larger contexts, in a total

ix

ecosystem, over time. These multiple coexisting contexts influence how and what we each learn to learn, think, imagine, and enact. Trainees are individuals existing in families in larger contexts over time, who bring into a program their previously learned maps.

This, then, is a book for trainers, for teachers, for educators, for students of human systems, who may or may not be or ever plan to be family therapists. This is a book for those who would like to come along on the exploration of ways of developing and drawing forth the maps of human systems thinking in each trainee. The material for the exploration is culled from the 12 plus exciting years of experience that the author has had helping to develop and "grow" systems thinkers at the Boston Family Institute.

No prior technical knowledge of human systems or family therapy is assumed necessary on the part of the reader. However, much of the material in the book is meant to be explored with other people, and it is hoped that the reader will have some context in which to do that.

Those who were pioneers in the field of family therapy went through a variety of experiences and ways of working with individual people before they arrived at a human systems perspective and methodology. When they "bumped into" the awareness of individuals-in-context, they became explorers, eagerly charting unknown territory. Their way of thinking and of conceptualizing human systems came out of their interactions with previously known, observed, and formulated material about individuals, in conjunction with these new, puzzling questions about individuals-in-context. Many of these early explorers felt grounded in their own professional experiences with individuals, as their search for answers to questions of human interrelatedness slowly and steadily replaced earlier linear and singular individual models with human systems models.

From very isolated and sparse beginnings, training programs and courses in family therapy have mushroomed and multiplied to over 300 institutes in the United States alone, and countless numbers of courses and programs in colleges and universities today.* The growing edge involves questions relating less to how to work with families as a human system, and more to how to train trainees in generic inclusive human systems thinking.

At two major therapy conferences during 1979,** this author engaged in discussions and presentations with well-established practitioners and trainers

---

*Personal communication, James Framo, Ph.D., pioneer family therapist and information resource person in this field.

**The American Family Therapy Association, Chicago, April 1979, and the International Forum of Family Therapy Trainers, Tavistock Clinic, London, England, July 1979.

in the field of family therapy, including some of the "pioneers," as all struggled with difficult questions on training. They covered a broad range of issues and expressed a variety of assumptive sets:

- How can you train in such a way that theories and techniques are drawn forth from, and become part of, the trainees' way of seeing the world?
- How do you teach a personalized style?
- How much of the trainee's personal life is it necessary to go into, in order for him/her to be an effective systems therapist?
- How do you train people to think in metaphors and gestalts, or analogically, rather than linearly/digitally? How can you train people to recognize and tap into the analogues between their own life positions, roles, situations, and those of the people they treat?
- How do you train for continued curiosity rather than pat formulas?
- How do you train for the responsible use of influence?
- How do you guide trainees to find ways of empathizing and caring that also allow for wide ranges of flexibility in interactions with clients?
- How can you train for an integrative model of therapy without it being seen as and feeling like an eclectic lump?

And so on. Many of these questions are not singularly related to training people in family or marital therapy, but have been around a long time in the helping professions in general. These questions are generic questions of great importance. In terms of a specific helping and educational profession, they can be grouped around: *How do you "ground" people in their own lives, in becoming caring, competent, centered yet continually curious human systems thinkers and actors, in ways that enable them to help others become the same?* And that is what this book explores.

PIONEERS AS SEARCHERS, AS QUESTION ASKERS

The pioneers had been excited by their quest. They were self-selected and self-motivated in pursuing solutions to riddles. They explored from the inside out. Trainees today enter a field from a completely different base. Many entering it see it not as a personal quest with challenging questions and puzzles, but as a route to gainful employment, to provide services to those in need. They expect to learn answers and quick how-to's.

It is quite possible that the pioneers, in amassing, elaborating and organizing a large body of information and material on family systems, were so absorbed in *what* they were finding "out there" that they paid little attention to *how* they each were integrating this material inside themselves, or in their own style or way of thinking. They took their own integrative style and processes as a given base.

For many trainees today, it is not a "given base" to think integratively in human systems. Trainers, who now have a point of view and a treatment technology to pass on, are bumping into blocks in not being able to have their body of material transmitted and incorporated, integrated and used as they would like. One leader in the field* commented at a meeting that he didn't understand how some of his trainees, after four years of medical school and other clinical experiences, and after working with his team in their training program for six months to a year, "just could not think systems." What he was expressing was that *the way in which trainees think is key* to whether or not they will be capable of working with and intervening in family or other human systems.

This very question—*"How do people think and learn?"*—has been kept up-front and conscious by the trainers at the Boston Family Institute since its inception in 1969. And, from the beginning, two other key questions were present: *"How do you train sensitive, competent and creative therapists?"* and *"What are families and human systems and how do they 'work'?"*

We have gathered quite a lot of information and perhaps a few answers to those questions on training raised by ourselves and other trainers. We feel we have been "growing systems thinkers"** who think, live, breathe a systems metaphor, and who do not lose touch with each person in the larger system. That is what this book is about.

This book examines experiments done in a learning laboratory. While drawing from many diverse fields, as we do in our training, this book will, in turn, I hope, stimulate the reader's excitement in "the having of wonderful ideas" (Duckworth, 1972), with the possibility that the reader can name, locate, and organize those ideas into useful frameworks for understanding, thinking, and acting in human systems, including those that one inhabits.

This book, however, is not a book of answers. It is meant to be a dialogic sharing, in which the thinking behind, about and of training is coupled with the involvement of you, the reader. Any other way negates the way we train.

Let us turn now to what you will find awaiting you.

---

*Luigi Boscolo, Milan, at previously mentioned conference at Tavistock Clinic, London, 1979.

**This is a phrase used for an early family therapy conference title, Institute for Juvenile Research, Chicago, IL, May 1972, and by Larry Constantine, BFI graduate, in his *Family Process* article on our method of training, 1976.

AN OUTLINE

Chapter I presents a triple-decker view of three levels of systems involved in the presentation of this work at this time. In a biographical and narrative fashion, the contexts in which such training programs in systems therapy began to be developed are explored, as well as the interconnection of many of the ideas of the explorers involved. In this general systems model of presentation, the wider lens focused at the national level of mental health narrows down to focus on the next system level: the beginning of the Boston Family Institute and the particular explorers involved there. And finally, switching system levels once again from group-now-organization to the individual level, we will look at the author's involvement and interest in this way of thinking/training, which led her to write this book.

Chapter II graphically attempts to draw readers into the first BFI seminar that the author attended, as a way of giving readers a feeling for the powerful first impression experience as anlage for what followed.

Chapter III tells an analogic tale of training in a nonhuman system.

Chapter IV begins to acquaint the reader with the general systems framework for thinking, derived from general systems theory, that underscores our view of human systems and of the families, individuals, and other systems with whom we work, in their dance of "fit" with each other. Chapter IV also clarifies what it is we are talking about in training for multicentric integration.

Chapter V explores and elaborates the values held by those training at BFI, and makes the point that all educational and training programs are grounded in a value base, in a context, whether fully acknowledged or not.

Chapter VI outlines the paradigm we have adopted since 1973 to guide us in our planning and thinking, as well as in designing curricula and analogic or metaphoric exercises. Here we explore and elucidate the various types of outcome guidelines. This chapter further explores our assumptions about learning and about adult learning in particular, and begins to indicate what trainers will have to keep in mind and be prepared to do if they should want to play with training in this manner.

Chapter VII discusses metaphor, analogue and synesthetic learning, and the modalities we have explored and discovered by which to train organismically in ways radiating out to all levels of human systems. Here we begin to present some examples of types of analogues and metaphors at work, and conceptualizations about the processes involved, including Piagetian constructs.

Chapter VIII introduces the concepts of family-as-system and family-as-theater that have been operant at BFI since its inception. These two thrusts allow us to look at family from the outside in (system) via analogic exercises, and from the inside out (theater) via personal metaphor creation. Different processes of mind are involved in each of these experiential learning modes.

Chapter IX then develops the concept of family-as-system and explores analogue designing by first returning to the first-night exercises presented in Chapter II and analyzing them. The processes involved in designing and participating in analogic exercises are explored as we look at different types of situations.

Chapter X then rounds out our basic approach to generic training in systems thinking with a full discussion in metaphor creation and *family-as-theater*. The connection between theater, people, spatial metaphor, training, and systems thinking is developed. An in-depth exploration of *sculpture* and spatialization—the medium by which we can express any relational concept, or human condition—is fully explicated.

A brief Epilogue concludes this work, with some thoughts about the impact of this type of training on trainees and trainers. The results of a project researching the impact of BFI's training methods, undertaken a number of years ago, are mentioned, along with comments about generic education and creativity.

It is my greatest wish that this book will be enjoyable to read, and that the reader will find much to play with, for we have found that not only are play and humor integral aspects of learning wholly and organismically, but, without play and humor, life and learning are tedious and dull. Play involves us in ways that leave our defenses at rest and our minds open to new information and ideas.

Designed play is basic to the BFI way of training. The book will be sprinkled with many such designs, some explored in depth, others hardly at all.

It is my hope that the reader will enter this book and these ideas in a playful and explorative manner, prepared to suspend judgment for a while and to experiment with some new images and thoughts as they are conjured up while reading. With the idea of the reader entering into the book, I have also sprinkled some exercises for the reader to engage in, should that be a way to "play" for some.

For those who "read" first and play later, so be it. One suggestion would be to ignore the exercises, as participatory reading, and ponder on the designing of the exercises themselves. For that, too, is an attempt to engage you, the reader, in your own discovery processes.

A PARTIAL LIST OF ACKNOWLEDGMENTS

Many people have aided in the discoveries explored in this book, far too numerous to list here: all the trainers and trainees over the years, all the workshop participants and university course students with whom I and others have engaged. To all of them, I am personally grateful for not only participating in developing this particular way of training and seeing the world, but also for enriching my life in the process.

Of particular importance to me during the last couple of years when I was engaged in writing this book are various BFI faculty—Howard Berens, April Manganielio, Joel Neiditz, Laurie Weinman, Joe and Jane Carpineto, Lucy and Carter Jefferson, Dick Ronan, Fran Toy, Bob Keating, Jane Davis, Peggy Hughart, and Mel Bucholz, all of whom read the material in progress and commenting on it, helped me to further shape my thoughts and reflect the ethos of the program. Rosalie Brown, who also had achieved her doctorate after her BFI training, offered me encouragement that indeed there was an end to *that* path. Yetta Bernhard, Bud and Michele Baldwin, Maria Gomori, Annis Gross, and so many other good friends in the Satir Avanta network read all or parts of various versions, and checked in with me periodically and supportingly. Evan Coppersmith and Ted Slovin at the University of Massachusetts aided me in being more clear in my meanings and differentiations. Al Gurman was most important at a particular moment in time with his enthusiastic responses and appreciation.

And to Carol Holzberg, friend and typist, I can offer my honest thanks for being so tired of multiple drafts that we finally acquired a word processor to make the project more achievable. I believe Fred's excitement with this new toy when it was not employed for the book has saved our marriage. And to Arlene Clark, my typist who took over where Carol left off, I give my heartfelt thanks for her flying fingers, constant overviewing of the content for its sense, her attention to the intricacies of the word processor and printer, and her constant unflappable good humor.

And while I will mention my family and others who helped shape my ideas later in this work, I believe my children, Sara, Josh, and Dina, are due a very special thanks for their encouragement, solace, and role-reversal ministering to me at times when the going was rough, for their expressed pride, and for putting up with and joking with me about the trials and tribulations of a new-age mother going back to school and writing a book. And if it were not for Fred, who supported me fully in this venture in every way he possibly could, this book would never have materialized. As a matter of fact, if it were not for Fred, who helped start the whole BFI program, my exposure to new ways of thinking and learning might never have happened.

A SUGGESTION FOR INVOLVEMENT

Now, let us get back to the book itself and your own engagement with it. Those who "learn by doing" might want to try our associative reading and listening excerise:

Exercise: Associative Reading and Listening

Have you ever kept track, while reading a book, of where your mind goes, of what you experience as you read? You might want to write that down in a notebook or journal, with a key or page reference to locate the stimulus.

What is printed in this book or paper will stay there. One can always turn to the same page and find the same messages. What passes through your body/mind is *your* information. Each association while reading and listening is often evanescent information, glimpsed but not grasped, and not easily retrieved. Such a separate notebook or journal is often the place to keep track of *your* "having of wonderful ideas" (Duckworth, 1972).

At this point, for those interested, let me suggest that you jot down your associative ideas as they are stimulated as you read.

Your notes are then available to trace patterns in yourself, in your way of thinking, being, training, living, to record your "aha's" en route to weaving them into *your* "patterns which connect" (Bateson, 1979).

In addition, such associative tracking in reading is similar to associative tracking as a therapist, counselor, educator. "Where does my mind go while I'm listening to *them*?"

Those who lean towards a "right" brain approach to this topic of generic systems thinking might want to start with Chapters VII–X first, and then come back to explore history, definitions and the frameworks for program design in earlier chapters. Indeed, one will find oneself quite free to skip around the book, if that is preferred style, for it is my hope that each chapter will be experienced and imagined as a fragment of a holographic plate. Such fragments, or bits, according to Karl Pribram's definition, when "transilluminated by a coherent light source," reflect the whole (1971). It is my wish that I succeed in being a "coherent light source," and that I am able to illuminate the bits in such a way that the reader will find him/herself stirring with new thoughts and images which he or she will want to try out in his/her own setting.

The writing of this book has been for me a new platform experience, pushing new "I wonder if's" into the foreground of my thinking. I hope it does the same for you.

Intelligence thus begins neither with knowledge of the self nor of things as such but with knowledge of their interaction, and it is by orienting itself simultaneously toward the two poles of that interaction that intelligence organizes the world by organizing itself (Piaget, 1977b, p. 275).

FROM
THE
INSIDE
OUT
AND OTHER
METAPHORS

How We Arrived at Systems Thinking: Mental Health, BFI, and the Author | I

Life takes place in context. There is not one among us who could grow up of English-speaking parents and invent Chinese. How we think is always a combination of what is around us in all our contexts and what can be imagined.

With a general systems model, we can look at contexts and phenomena from different levels of system sequentially, while we know that all are interwoven and ongoing at the same time. As I come to explore the way of thinking about training and the methodology developed at the Boston Family Institute, it seems important to me to fill in the contextual background for these events, since this paradigm for thinking, and ours for training are relatively new phenomena. That background includes three levels of system, and at least three sets of contexts: on the societal level, the country at large in the arena of psychiatry and psychology since the mid-1940s; on the group level, the people who formed this training program, thus raising it to an organizational level; and on the individual level, the involvement and role of the author. All are equivalently parts of the whole story.

Exercise

Have you ever wondered how being born into the generation you were born into has shaped your thinking and your life? Have you ever tracked what major themes in your life reflect those ongoing in the world around you? This might be a good opportunity to let some of those questions stir, as you read this account of the beginning development of human systems thinking in the field of mental health in this country. What societal themes have influenced and affected your way of looking at and being in the world?

THE MENTAL HEALTH ARENA

Psychiatrist Theodore Lidz,* an early explorer of language transmission in families, talked of the push given to intrapsychic psychiatry during World War II, in rehabilitating to active duty soldiers with battle fatigue and nervous breakdowns. Some were physically sound and psychologically unglued. Others had physical symptoms which could be neither explained nor detected by laboratory tests. The extensive havoc that the war experience incurred, rendering many formerly functioning people psychotic, brought government support of veterans' hospitals, research in mental illness and mental health, and development of new treatment modalities for psychiatric disabilities. The National Institute of Mental Health, formed in 1949, became the arm of government which pushed and guided many of these supports. Lidz was interested in context and mental health. His early works on schism and skew in families were early attempts at defining how family contexts affected the development of the person identified as patient (Lidz, Cornelison, Fleck, and Terry, 1957).

Those who had been trained in the more intrapsychic yet evolving views of psychological man, such as psychoanalysis, came to a startling awareness in the 1950s. When schizophrenic patients in hospitals, who had been treated in an individual, psychoanalytically oriented mode of therapy and who had made progress towards adaptation to reality in this therapy, then met with their families, they "regressed" to "pathological behavior."

Elsewhere psychiatrist/researcher Murray Bowen had begun to observe that not only was that so with schizophrenic patients, but ordinary normal people, such as himself, also reverted to less autonomous, less differentiated and more child-like behaviors when with their original families for any period of time. Bowen had become aware that certain working situations could call forth the same type of less differentiated behaviors on his part, accompanied by feelings of being unable to operate independently of the others. There was something within the context of those relationships and interactions of working group and original family members that seemed to be influencing individual reactions and behaviors (see Anonymous, 1972).

Bowen and others** (later called family therapists or family systems researchers) had begun their early work with people labeled schizophrenics, in an effort to help them, and became fascinated with the implications of their

---

*Informal discussion, February 1974, at the Nathan Ackerman Memorial Conference of *Family Process* Board of Editors, Cumana, Venezuela.

**Virginia Satir, John Bell, Ivan Boszormenyi-Nagy, James Framo, Ross Speck, Carl Whitaker, Don D. Jackson, Gregory Bateson, Margaret Thaler-Singer, Paul Watzlawick, Jay Haley, Lyman Wynne, Theodore Lidz and many others.

early hunches. Schizophrenics were seen as "the growing edge" for learning, the patients on whom clinicians needed to concentrate efforts. Most such patients did not seem to respond to the various forms of treatment evolving in the aftermath of World War II. Their behaviors invited challenge, and this new discovery of regression or reverting to "sick" or "crazy" behavior when with family members stimulated puzzlement and curiosity. The various individual intrapsychic approaches of psychology and psychiatry, including Freudian psychoanalysis, did not seem to offer adequate explanations for the differences in behaviors that changed as individuals changed social and physical contexts. Nor did the pure medical model of illness explain this phenomenon.

Other clinician/researchers* also noticed contextually shifting behaviors, such as another family member becoming ill as the one labeled patient improved in functioning. Clinician/researchers began to ask new questions: What were these shifts about? What were the differences and what processes were afoot that caused people to shift basic behaviors, attitudes and logic in different contexts, and with different constellations of people? How did changes in attitudes and functioning of one member influence another to change ways of being? How did the presence of family members make a difference? What was this system of checks and balances in behavior?

With the exception of psychiatrist Nathan Ackerman (1958), who had been seeing nonhospitalized "neurotic" families since the mid-1930s while working at Jewish Family Service in New York, researcher/clinicians observed only families of hospitalized schizophrenics in any depth or for any reasonable period of time. Between 1954 and 1959, Bowen had such families live in the hospital at NIMH (Bowen, 1978). Satir worked with such families in Chicago, while Whitaker had begun seeing the families of schizophrenics with Thomas Malone, M.D., and John Warkentin, M.D., in Atlanta, as supportive of their direct treatment of schizophrenic patients. Many others worked with such individuals and families in other parts of the country.

Ackerman had approached the family slightly differently, through children. He had suspected years before, and had pioneered such work, that *when a child had problems, the rest of the family was involved in the problem,* and a family diagnosis as well as family treatment was needed. Ackerman had also studied the impact of context on families in his study of miners' families (Ackerman, 1958). Ackerman's work with families, as organic systems, was psychodynamically oriented or, in other words, was drawn from psychoanalysis.

Later, Bowen became aware that different people in his own family be-

---

*E.g., Don D. Jackson, M.D.

haved differently in combination with him alone than when more than two family members were together. Alone, each talked "straighter." He observed too that as more people were added, they tended to form interlocking triangular patterns of connectedness, with unequal bondings (Anonymous, 1972; Bowen, 1978). Or so it seemed to him. He and his research team at NIMH began to look for these behaviors in the families of schizophrenic patients.

Bowen's work combined the medical model of sickness/health with systems thinking, in comparing schizophrenic families to normal ones—in treatment and later in training. Bowen was primarily concerned with the engulfing aspects of families (their ability to be an "undifferentiated ego mass"), issues of triangulation, and individual differentiation.

Within the hospital settings, however, there were two categories of researchers: those who were clinicians first, who were practitioner/researchers, and those who were not. Bowen, Nagy, Framo, Speck, Jackson, Whitaker, Wynne, and Lidz were among the clinician/researchers. In their participant/ clinician/observer/researcher stance, they became aware that every mechanism and technique by which they had learned to work with individual people fell apart in the context of a schizophrenic patient and his/her family.

Lyman Wynne and his colleagues (1958) wrote of the "rubber fence" that such families presented. Wynne also spoke of the feeling of going crazy himself, of being drawn into the quicksand of the family's interior.* He spoke of the need to have a co-therapist with him in the room. This was unheard of in the world of dynamic psychoanalytic psychiatry, where all was confidential, hush-hush, and private. Wynne and his team's need of co-therapists revolved around the necessity of having someone "sane" to refer to, to talk to, for the communication patterns of the schizophrenic patients and their families were seen as consisting of strange usages and meanings, in unusual sequences which deviated greatly from the expected norm. Wynne and Margaret Thaler-Singer began then and have continued to study families of this type, constructing together and separately many hypotheses about the crazy-making quality of schizophrenic family communication (e.g., Singer and Wynne, 1965a, 1965b, 1966; Wynne and Singer, 1963a, 1963b; Singer, 1967; Wynne, 1977)

These early explorers, whether trained in psychology or psychiatry, were in strange territory. Psychoanalysis could not explain family phenomena. Those in psychology were aware that the behaviorist theories of stimulus-response did not account for total behaviors of individuals in context, nor did operant conditioning theory explain the switches in behavior and meanings of language when contexts switched. Neither psychiatry nor psychology had

---

*1974, at the meeting of *Family Process* Board of Editors, Cumana, Venezuela.

any full theory yet which dealt with multipersonal behavior, phenomena, communication, and interactions. It is not surprising then that these early explorers began to look beyond their own disciplines for answers.

RELATION OF MENTAL HEALTH AND OTHER FIELDS

Interestingly enough, puzzles and questions without answers in one arena often are reflections of the same types of questions in other arenas. A search for more comprehensive ways of looking at the interrelatedness of economics with technology, sciences, and politics within a full ecological map had been going on since before World War II. Indeed, in this country, the multidisciplinary thinking which mobilized, created, and coordinated war efforts could no longer fully revert to linear thinking in a compartmentalized fashion.

The same thinking that went into the technology of rocket and atom bombs also brought us computer technology, as well as information recording, processing, and transmitting devices. And as the technology of communications, especially television, developed, along with transportation technology, the world became (and is still becoming) smaller and more interrelated.

The development of computer technology lent itself as a model for cybernetic communication processes and as a model for human information processing mechanisms. And television has revolutionized our ability to see individual, multipersonal and group system patterns and interactions, including those of which we ourselves are a part. Television has helped to make multicentricity—the view from many centers—possible.

Norbert Wiener (1948, 1954), a mathematician at M.I.T. who had worked on computer technology during the war, wrote about "the Second Industrial Revolution." He coined the word "cybernetics," meaning a circular and reflexive system of information flow, in which information and control are linked together. (This is an important forerunner of how some systems therapists later began to look at human communication and systems interactions.)

During World War II, British anthropologist Gregory Bateson, then an American resident, was assigned to an intelligence team in the Pacific,* since Bateson had studied several cultures in that area. His job with that team was to transmit messages to the Japanese which would either confuse them or give them devious information. The thinking behind these types of war-time deception maneuvers emerged after the war in von Neumann and Morgenstern's *Theory of Games and Economic Behavior* (1947), Shannon and Weaver's information theory in *The Mathematical Theory of Communication* (1949), both at about the same time as Wiener's *Cybernetics* (1948). More

---

*Personal communication, 1979.

recently, Watzlawick's *How Real Is Real?* (1977) delineates in anecdotal form some of the same issues.

This cerebral, logical approach to communication was investigated by Bateson after the war, when he met Wiener and began between 1948 and 1950 to work with psychotherapist and psychiatrist Juergen Ruesch on communication and therapy. He then began to look at communication processes, humor, play, and metamessages or contextual messages about messages.

The Palo Alto Group: Bateson and Team

Between 1954 and 1956, while therapists like Wynne, Satir, Whitaker, Bowen, and others were caught up in the direct "feel" and confusionary process with a schizophrenic member family through their clinical work with them, Bateson, Jay Haley, and John Weakland began observing the communication of schizophrenic families at the Palo Alto V.A. Hospital in California. Psychiatrist Don Jackson joined them as a consultant. Of this group, Jackson was the only clinician at that time. The others came from diverse fields: mass communication (Haley), anthropology (Bateson), and chemical engineering and anthropology (Weakland).

This group began to look at the shift in the logic and type of communication patterns of the schizophrenic with his family in the light of cybernetics, information theory, and levels of logical type (Bateson, Jackson, Haley, and Weakland, 1956). These researchers tracked the families' communications through levels of logical types and the self-regulating feedback loops of cybernetic theory. Clinician/therapist Don Jackson brought in the term "homeostasis" (Watzlawick et al., 1967) from medicine, linking cybernetic and information theory to the emerging epistemology of general systems theory.

As it pertained to schizophrenics and their families, this group's non-evolving, non-developmental, and homeostatic, cybernetic model of closed systems of information flow was reflected in "Towards a Theory of Schizophrenia" (Bateson, Jackson, Haley, and Weakland, 1956). In this research, Bateson et al. formulated the theory of the double bind as explanatory of the schizophrenic family's interaction and the etiology of schizophrenia. In a double bind, the patient is seen as damned if he obeys messages, damned if he doesn't, without an ally and unable to comment on, leave, or escape the field of messages. At the time this was an extremely important shift in ways of looking at family communication and at schizophrenia. In 1969, Bateson wrote again about this double bind theory, labeling it too limited in scope to explain the full complexity of schizophrenia (1972, pp. 271–278).

Jackson's adding the word "homeostasis" to Wiener's cybernetic model of non-living systems rendered the concept applicable to biological subsystems, communication, and families of schizophrenics. The Palo Alto group found that in some families, when patients got better, another family member often fell apart, thus keeping the homeostasis or balance of process in the total group, even though the particular roles of individual persons changed. These investigators became pioneers in looking at the interactions of family members, and describing this homeostatic mechanism largely in terms of communications of power and control, logical type, and paradox. All communication was regarded by the researchers as geared to maintaining each such system the way it was, repetitively patterned and unchanging.

Thus, in psychiatry and psychology, much of the investigation of families as human systems whose members were capable of creating and regulating impact on each other's behavior began with an explanation of those families which contained at least one member considered furthest from society's norm. It was as if by defining what was abnormal, normality of a family system in interaction could be inferred. Additionally, such investigative findings in these extreme families began to lead to guidelines, parameters, and "rules" for clear communication.

Group Researchers

The phenomena of related and non-related groups began to be explored and researched following World War II, which had given a push to group therapy (Ruesch and Bateson, 1968). Social psychologists, including Sprott (1958), Corsini (1957), and Bradford, Gibb, and Benne (1964) began to look at natural primary groups and special groups with changing membership. Psychiatrist Eric Berne (1963, 1964, 1966) began to explore and write about therapy groups, as did others in the field. Anthropologists Bateson, Margaret Mead, and earlier, Ruth Benedict had already done much to illuminate patterns of interrelatedness of groups in other cultures. Their influence began to be increasingly felt in psychology and psychiatry.

MacGregor and Team Family Methods

Other realizations of the concept of human systems in the mental health arena came in other ways. Clinical psychologist Robert MacGregor, working with a team in Galveston, Texas,* became involved with children of "multi-

---

*Harold A. Goolishian, Ph.D., Alberto Serrano, M.D., Agnes Ritchie, M.S.W., Franklin Schuster, M.D., and Eugene C. McDonald, Jr., M.D.

problem families" who lived in rural areas and who were involved with several different agencies (see MacGregor, Ritchie, Serrano, and Schuster, 1964). Team members began seeing all family members on the same day, then combined the information and impressions they had at team meetings. They realized that the information from all was different from information from one or two family members, as a cell is different from an organ. They also realized that piecemeal information, being colored by each team member's view, led to divergent ideas and solutions. Sharing information and views aided the team in finding convergent solutions. They soon began inviting all involved agency members to the same team meetings. They realized that only when members of all involved and influencing systems participated in sharing the same information and forging a common solution would any total solution be possible.

Later, psychiatrist Ross Speck developed similar ideas when he began to work with total family networks, including all those people a family felt to be important to them, as the milieu of and for problem-solving (Speck and Attneave, 1973).

Virginia Satir

Of the early pioneers, social worker Virginia Satir is one of the very few who began seeing families in private practice in 1951. Her anecdotal tale* relates that it was "an accident." A mother of a disturbed young woman Satir had been seeing, who had been improving, called her and threatened to sue Satir for alienating her daughter's affection. Satir asked her to come in with her daughter; she then saw the same behavior between the girl and her mother that Satir had originally experienced between the daughter and herself. She soon asked for the husband and son to join the mother and daughter, and from then on began seeing families of people with many types of problems, from learning disorders and somatic illness to schizophrenics. As she explored family life histories, she began to find that "sickness was a result of imbalances in the family." In 1951 she began to work with hospitalized psychiatric patients and their families.

In 1955, Satir was asked by Kalman Gyarfas, M.D., at the Illinois State Psychiatric Institute to set up a training program for residents, based on her health model rather than a psychopathology model. (Psychiatrist Ivan Boszormenyi-Nagy, a well-known family therapist, was a resident in that program!)

---

*Virginia Satir, personal communication, 1980.

The Beginnings of the Mental Research Institute

In 1959, Don Jackson invited Satir to join him and psychiatrist Jules Riskin to do research with families in California, at Jackson's new Mental Research Institute. Satir, within a year, got a grant to do training and became the first Director of Training at MRI, where she stayed until 1966, when she left to become Director of Esalen Institute at Big Sur, California. Satir's groundbreaking book on family therapy, *Conjoint Family Therapy* (1964) was based upon a communications model combined with issues of self-esteem.

Bateson, Haley, and Weakland were brought together with Satir and Riskin for discussions of family interactions and communication by Jackson. Jackson invited linguist Paul Watzlawick in 1962, and Jay Haley in 1963, to join Riskin and himself at MRI in doing research. Out of this work came a basic text in the field, Watzlawick, Beavin, and Jackson's *Pragmatics of Human Communication* (1967), which analyzes normal and pathological communication.

Dick Auerswald and Sal Minuchin

Information and its role in human systems interactions and mental health became a key concept and arena of concern for psychiatrist Edgar "Dick" Auerswald. While working with juvenile delinquents of minority background at the Wiltwyck School for Boys and later with Puerto Rican individuals and families in New York City, Auerswald became increasingly aware that access to and availability of contextual information and cognitive information processing skills were necessary requisites for competence in living and self-esteem (1966).

He began looking at individuals and families in the total context in which they lived, which he termed the "ecosystem," and discovered, for instance, that the behavior of many Puerto Rican immigrants diagnosed as psychotic was contextual; i.e., they were isolated strangers in a strange land. Auerswald and his team discovered that when these "psychotic" people were 1) given information about their new surroundings, 2) connected with other immigrants in a networking fashion, and 3) given telephones, the psychotic behaviors disappeared. Each of these processes constituted a way by which these rural people could orient themselves and connect with other Spanish-speaking neighbors in a strange and frightening city. Auerswald (1975) determined that the people weren't crazy, in and of themselves; rather, the situation they were in was disorienting or "crazy-making."

Auerswald also differentiated a systems view from the concept of interdisciplinary approaches to people in his work with the crisis intervention team at Gouverneur Health Services Program in New York City. An interdisciplinary approach leaves each one still looking through varying lenses of meaning. An inclusive ecosystemic approach to individuals and families includes all information under one inclusive umbrella, emphasizing how sense can be made of all contingencies operating in their interrelationship. In other words, how do all important factors and phenomena from all levels of system fit together?

Psychiatrist Salvador Minuchin, who worked with Auerswald at Wiltwyck, had brought a variation of the team approach of MacGregor et al. to the Wiltwyck School. There he also began to observe family members through a one-way mirror. As he began to experiment and rotate different family members behind the mirror, he began to notice that different interactional patterns and sequences occurred within different family constellations. In focusing on the effect and impact of these different structural arrangements of members, Minuchin, Braulio Montalvo and others, first at Wiltwyck and later with Haley at the Philadelphia Child Guidance Center, began to explore the process of change in family members by changing their structural patterns. Minuchin in his work also "saw" human systems interactions as relating to their context. *Families of the Slums* (Minuchin, Montalvo, Guerney, Rosman, and Schumer, 1967) elaborates many of the ideas which grew out of Minuchin's work at Wiltwyck. His later book, *Families and Family Therapy* (1974), elaborates many of the awarenesses of family structure and context.

FAMILY THERAPY TRAINING

Regarding the natural group called 'family," there are to date very few studies which begin to explore the range of variations of normality of families in context, in all their complexity as interacting systems. Thus, for training purposes, deviants and deviancy comprised the norm.

The work by Kantor and Lehr (1975), in which researchers lived with a small group of normal and schizophrenic families, as well as the more recent comprehensive studies of normal families by Lewis, Beavers, Gossett, and Phillips (1976) and Walsh (1982), are among the few major research works in psychiatry expanding our awareness of the range of variation of interactions in normal families. Such works are critical for training, for tilting the balance concerning the normal range of variation in families.

Thus, there have been a variety of ways in which human beings began to be conceptualized as in dynamic interaction with others and with the environment. The family, as the smallest natural human system at the group level, became the focus for much attention and description.

Once the family had been looked at as a human system, many people said "of course!" and were quite aware that no one had ever been known to grow up by him- or herself without something resembling a family group influencing him/her. The idea that one perhaps impacted upon or influenced other family members while growing up—that was a much more difficult idea to conceptualize.

HUMAN SYSTEMS AND FAMILY THERAPY TRAINING

Virginia Satir had developed the first training program in family dynamics in Chicago in 1955, and expanded her concepts and her training approach as Director of Training at MRI from 1959 to 1966. Her 1964 *Conjoint Family Therapy* contained a brief description of using certain communication "games" and action exercises in training, which she had developed while training at MRI and many California hospitals.

Murray Bowen had begun teaching his approach to family systems at Georgetown in 1956 to medical residents and in 1960 Ackerman started the New York Family Institute around clinical case conferences.

Of these three generative settings and approaches, Satir's was the only one to include play in training at that time, through the use of role played families and other games as a training technique. She introduced these new ways of training in cooperation with other new approaches to training in doing therapy: observed clinical interviews, videotapes, feedback, and live supervision. In addition, her approach to training was also the only one at that time to center attention on trainees' researching their own families for a three-generational chronological and factual history, as the matrix of family influences by which the trainees were themselves shaped. Bowen later had trainees explore their own family history and genealogy.

The family movement had begun, as well as the search, research and re-search for ways of describing family interactions, for ways of influencing them and intervening in them, and for teaching about these new concepts and practices. The various elements for an integrated general systems approach to people in context had begun to appear.

PSYCHOLOGY AND GENERAL SYSTEMS THEORY

Ideas, those ephemeral products of human minds, like their creators, grow in context and, like dandelion seeds, seem to be carried by the winds to distant places, germinating and creating new flowering fields. Sometimes dandelion seeds are joined by those of milkweed pods, and they grow in the same soil, side by side. And so it seemed with the humanistic psychology seeds, which also began germinating after World War II, as they joined those of living systems theorists.

Perhaps the heightened consciousness not only of man's symbolic capacity for discovery and creation, but also of man's horrendous capacity to destroy himself through the evil of genocide and atomic holocausts brought forth the corrective humanistic psychology that psychologist Abraham Maslow termed "a revolution" (1968, p. iii). This "Third Force Psychology" created "new ways of perceiving and thinking, new images of man and society, new conceptions of ethics and of values, new directions in which to move" (Maslow, 1968, p. iii). This last is important, for this *humanistic psychology was not just descriptive. It was generative, suggesting choices and actions and implying consequences.*

> It helped to generate a way of life, not only for the person himself within his own private psyche, but also for the same person as a social being, a member of society (Maslow, 1968, p. iii).

This Third Force Psychology, then, referred to man as a social, interactive being, and openly sanctioned values and processes towards an image of man Maslow had already found through his research. These ideas took root and spread throughout the country. America was also the nurturing haven for a horde of psychiatrists and psychologists, including Erik Erikson, Felix and Helene Deutsch, Kurt Goldstein, Fritz Perls, and myriad others, who had fled Europe before the war. Thus, humanistic psychology included Jungians, Gestaltists, Adlerians, existentialists, Rogerians, psychodramatists, and many, many others—all of whom held as a basic tenet the idea that man had the potential to be a humane, responsible, actualized creature, conscious of his self and others, and tending eventually towards the transcendental.

Maslow actually conceptualized his "hierarchy of needs" (1946) towards self-actualization as a stage progression (and as such, as a biological contextual given) of individuals in interaction, over time, with other human beings and the environment. Thus Maslow's theory, like Piaget's stage theory of cognitive development, embodied concepts of living systems, as von Bertalanffy's theories embodied the concepts and values of humanistic psychology.

Von Bertalanffy had come from Europe to Canada in 1949, and later moved to the United States. Von Bertalanffy and Maslow both had been concerned with values in science and society, and appeared on the same program on values in 1957 (Maslow, 1959). Maslow's humanism and interest in creativity fit with von Bertalanffy's recognition of man's ability for "play, exploratory activity, creativity and self-realization, etc." (von Bertalanffy, 1968).

By 1953, the Society for General Systems Theory had been formed by thinkers from diverse fields, from mathematics (Anatol Rapoport) to sociology (Walter Buckley). These thinkers had begun to cluster around von Bertalanffy's ideas. In 1954, the name was changed to the Society for General Systems Research (von Bertalanffy, 1968) and the annual meetings and yearbooks of papers attracted people in many fields.

During the early 1960s, the subject of families, family systems, family therapy or conjoint therapy, as it was first titled (Jackson, 1959; Satir, 1964), began to appear on the programs of national organizations, such as the American Orthopsychiatric Association, whose membership spanned the fields of education, nursing, social service, psychology, and psychiatry. Those disparate lone-wolf explorers in the emerging field began to find each other and excitedly share their discoveries. This excitement of exploration and discovery mushroomed—and clinicians and researchers alike searched for integrative models to deal with this new inclusive way of understanding human beings.

In 1966, spearheaded by psychiatrist William Gray of Boston, the American Psychiatric Association held two sessions on general systems theory in psychiatry. The climate was ripe. By 1967, psychiatrist Frederick J. Duhl and psychologist Nicholas Rizzo aided Gray in organizing the next two APA general systems meetings.

When a room holding 1,500 people is so jammed that hundreds stand through an entire morning session, the subject must be one in which the audience is keenly interested. This was the situation which took place at the symposium on the use of general systems theory in psychiatry at the Detroit meeting of the American Psychiatric Association (Damude, 1968, p. 7).

A BIT OF LOCAL HISTORY: BFI IN FORMATION

Exercise

At this point, as we move "down" in system levels, and into a narrower context, I invite you to let your thoughts wander to the various work settings and contexts that you have experienced. What were the qualities of those contexts that nurtured or informed your work and thought? What happened in each that was important to you in shaping how you now think and act?

The founders of the Boston Family Institute coalesced around Fred Duhl and David Kantor and their innovative teaching program in Family Therapy at Boston State Hospital. Duhl and Kantor had each brought to a set of programs at Boston State their not inconsiderable talents and experiences, as well as their already established friendship of three years.

An Aside on Innovation and Creativity

Innovations and inventions do not happen by pure magic very often. They usually occur as the result of a confluence of factors, people and ideas in the environment at large. Usually, there have been many smaller innovations and inventions along the way, and the one that emerges at the noticed nodal point is a new juxtaposition of previously available components. The inventions of thought that move an entire field an inch forward are those that offer a new way of seeing, of imaging reality, that many can grasp. Creativity or genius is the new way of *seeing* of the inventor. The components are known in another form already.

The innovative Residency Training Program at Boston State Hospital developed by Fred Duhl and the new Family Therapy Training Program there evolved by Fred Duhl and David Kantor came out of such a confluence of the times, the people, and the ideas in the environment at large.

Fred Duhl

Fred Duhl had been brought to Boston State Hospital in 1966 as Director of Education to head the Residency Training Program and, subsequently, the in-service educational program. Kantor, already at Boston State Hospital, was Director of Research. The openness and innovations in the larger social context of the 1960s were reflected in the arena of mental health by new programs, more community control of local services in new mental health centers, and the closing of state hospitals.

By 1966, in other contexts, Fred Duhl had developed innovative team appoaches, creating therapeutic milieux on psychiatric wards through enlisting staff members and patients, regardless of degree, status, or condition, in contributing their skills and talents cooperatively. At Massachusetts General Hospital, in the early 1960s, Psychiatry Professor Erich Lindemann's crisis intervention and community mental health program allowed for the integration of system levels. As a resident, and later as assistant head of the outpatient psychiatric clinic, Duhl's interest in individual learning, development, and psychoanalysis came together with interests in people in context. Duhl and several others began to explore how patients' complaints fit within their contexts, and they began to see couples and families. Families, they realized, were the link between individuals and the community.

Fred Duhl's meeting with psychiatrist Bill Gray in the early 1960s provided him with his first awareness of general systems theory, which seemed to make room for an integration of his range of concerns and interests. He became an active explorer of general systems theory (Gray, Duhl, and Rizzo, 1969), examining concepts in dialogue with psychiatrist Edgar "Dick" Auerswald, from 1961 on.

When Duhl came to Boston State Hospital, he spent one year meeting and conferring with other training staff, discussing what resident psychiatrists needed to learn to be prepared for the world of the mid-1960s and the future and how they could go about learning those things. Out of those meetings emanated a general systems model for residency training (Duhl, F.J., 1971).

Duhl insisted that residents take courses in and be involved with all levels of system at one time: psychopharmacology, neurology, individual, group and family therapy, and community psychiatry. His goal was to train residents so that each could assess treatment or intervention by assessing which level of system might be the most effective choice for the particular issue, given the particular people, context and resources available, including those of the resident. To make "the best assessment" meant that residents needed to know that there was a map, that there were different options at different system levels, and that each option affected the whole in varying ways and degrees.

Several months after this model for residency training was put into operation, Duhl, with the cooperation and agreement of other staff, opened all residents' courses to other hospital personnel, including aides, nurses, social workers, occupational therapists, and pastoral counselors. This unusual move cut across the well-entrenched medical hierarchy. The beginning attempts at a cooperative systems care model, based on task and skill rather than on status and ownership of knowledge and information, was set into motion.

In the midst of such an overall general systems training model was to be a family therapy course, to be dreamed up by both Kantor and Duhl, neither of whom had ever taken such a course or had any direct training in family therapy, although Duhl had been going to whatever family therapy workshops or presentations were available at psychiatric conventions for several years.

David Kantor

David Kantor, meanwhile, had been interested and involved in Moreno's psychodrama (1946) since the late 1940s, when he had studied it at Brooklyn College with Paul Covnyetz, trained by Moreno. By the mid 1960s, Kantor had finished his graduate degrees, and was involved in exploring innovative therapeutic milieux from a more sociological view. He had completed some basic research mixing the "world cultures" of college students and schizophrenic patients at Metropolitan State Hospital (Umbarger, Dalsimer, Morrison, and Bregin, 1962). He was now involved with a project in which volunteer college students and former mental hospital patients lived together in a "halfway house" called Wellmet.

In 1965, Kantor had begun his pilot *in vivo* family research, in which university student researchers lived in the homes of a small group of normal and schizophrenic families as participant observers for a month. During that time, all rooms of the house of volunteer families had tape recorders working all the time. Kantor's research aimed at investigating what ordinary family life was like, in both normal and schizophrenic families, in their own environment, day after day. His theory of family and findings from a subsequent grant study were later presented in *Inside the Family* (Kantor and Lehr, 1975).

Additionally, Kantor had been working with groups, and was very much interested in the liberalizing impact of the 1960s, and moving with that impact. Although he had never been to Esalen, Kantor was intrigued with their emphasis on active communication modalities, into which psychodrama also fit. While Kantor and Duhl collaborated at Boston State Hospital on creating a joint family systems therapy training program, Kantor was simultaneously involved in "an elaborate communications center, comprised of artists, dancers, theater people, electronic wizards, poets, called, 'The Readeasy.'"*
His interest in psychodrama and Moreno's action approach had continued (see Chapter X). Kantor conducted psychodrama and other therapy groups both at Boston State Hospital and at the Readeasy, experimenting with the special use of drama, analogue and action in effecting change in interpersonal behaviors within the group.

The Beginnings of a New Way of Training

When the training program in family therapy started at Boston State Hospital in 1967, Fred Duhl and Dave Kantor gave a series of lectures and discussions on "family." They found that "nobody listened." Assuming that they knew themselves to be less than boring people, they discussed and then bypassed self-recrimination and blame on a variety of levels, from personal to theoretical and speculative. Neither did they blame the trainees. They settled on a new set of questions.

---

*Personal communication.

If trainees didn't "hear" trainers, was that process in any way analogous to families in which people do not "hear" each other? If trainees don't listen to trainers, how do they listen to or hear anyone? Trainers were sending messages. The messages were not being "taken in." How did each person take in messages?

They then designed an experiential exercise based on: "How do people 'hear'?" "How do you hear another?" This time, instead of no one listening, their training group was alive, involved, curious and working hard.

The trainers had completely shifted the focus in a major way: Instead of concentrating on the content about family processes, they focused on the processes in, between, and among trainees as real and as analogous to those that occur in families. In addition, this particular phenomenological question (how do people hear?) was by analogic extension related to family problems requiring treatment, where people are disconnecting, disqualifying, and non-hearing of each other. Indeed, was there a connection between how trainers sent messages and how families send them, which are not heard?

"How do you hear another?" in your family is usually asked and seen in its negative version, meaning, "Why is he/she not listening? What is he/she blocking?"

In the seminar, the question focused not on the trainers' expectation or status issues, but on the processes of hearing or message intake. There were then some 16 different composite ways of "hearing" or "taking in informa-tion" in the room. What were each person's ways of hearing? The questions later arose: "What constituted the range of styles or ways of hearing? What must the range be for all people? What might the critical elements and limita-tions be? What did hearing have to do with message sending?"

In discovering self-in-context in the hearing exercise which involved at least two people together, trainees began to learn at various levels simultane-ously. Each was exploring "hearing" in dialogue with others! In addition to each trainer's conjuring up multiple contextual images of other "hearing" or "not hearing" encounters in his/her life, each trainee began to learn that each had an idiosyncratic way of "hearing," just as family members might have. Later, trainers and trainees began to find that similarities of character-istics among individual ways of hearing could be seen as fitting into a larger grouping, called "hearing styles."

These hearing styles were again seen as part of a larger metaconcept and set of processes, called cognitive styles, learning styles, or, perhaps more correct-ly, "information processing styles." Trainees "had" them, trainers "had" them, children, parents and firemen "had" them. Everybody "had" such a phenomenon, and each person's hearing and information processing style could be different, with varying types of impact and influence.

Styles of hearing, of attending to input, as analogous to styles of learning, were felt to have something to do with *fit* between message sending and message receiving. When trainees discussed their own hearing/learning styles with each other, they understood the points being made about message sending and message reception "from the inside out." They had just experienced the contrast. The trainers' original lectures had been passively received, if at all. "How do you hear?" activated an active search, which they found exciting. The trainees' learning had involved their participation.

From that very first "How do you hear?" exercise, Duhl and Kantor created the challenge for themselves, of creating processes in and of teaching that were congruent with processes of learning. These processes of training were later recognized as being congruent with processes of application in therapy and other settings. Any process in training could be looked at for its analogic fit in a therapy or other human system setting.

Other Team Members at Boston State Hospital

Sandra Watanabe, occupational therapist, was a participant in that first set of seminars that Kantor and Duhl taught. She had been hired to work at Boston State Hospital in 1965 on a hospital/community grant funded by NIMH.*

As a person of wide-ranging interests and concerns, Watanabe's task was to explore the role of occupational therapy in generating new living experiences for formerly hospitalized, now heavily medicated outpatients living at home. As part of this Home Treatment Service project, Watanabe did many home visits and immediately realized that dealing with patients at home involved dealing with total families, in their own contexts. Watanabe began to meet with Kantor and talk about how families lived their lives in their own environments. Later, when Duhl came to Boston State and began the family therapy training program with Kantor in 1967, Sandra Watanabe asked to join it. Her particular fascination with how different people learn, how they use time, space and energy, and how they make themselves known to others coincided with Kantor's and Duhl's interests in "How do you hear?" as analogue to "How do you learn?" Watanabe took the seminar and, afterwards, began to teach with Kantor within the hospital in the fall of 1968.

At that time, Duhl, Kantor, and Watanabe were joined by nurse Madeleine Gerrish, who had worked at Boston State with psychiatrist Norman Paul. Paul, who was also working with families, had not wanted to join forces with Kantor and Duhl at that time. Gerrish subsequently worked with terminally

*Personal communication, March 1981.

ill patients and their families at the Lemuel Shattuck chronic disease hospital, in addition to working at Boston State.

The Educational Techniques Lab

As a core group interested in family therapy, systems and training, they began their Educational Techniques Laboratory, a long-talked-about fantasy of Duhl's and Kantor's. The group of artist and theater people joined the family therapy and systems people, in exploring drama and image, action and analogue, as they began to create innovative ways of working with groups, with teaching, with families, with understanding relationships and change processes.

While Kantor and Watanabe taught one course in the hospital, Duhl and Gerrish taught another to hospital personnel and Northeastern University graduate students. Key themes began to emerge: Kantor's interest in family-as-theater, Duhl's interest in family-as-system and as learning environment for its members, Watanabe's in family-as-living-space and learning environment, and Gerrish's in family-as-context for illness and death. They began to invent ways to work with and present these themes in training and to explore systems issues.

The Birth of an Institute and the Involvement of the Author

In the fall of 1968, Duhl, Kantor, Watanabe and Gerrish began to talk of creating a training program in family therapy outside the hospital. Jay Kuten and Alan Sheldon, both psychiatrists, expressed an interest in the new project. Kuten was Duhl's Assistant Director of Education at Boston State and Sheldon, a friend of Duhl's, was involved in community psychiatry and mental health and interested in the family/community level of system interface. In the spring of 1969, this group of six started The Boston Family Institute.

The author became a trainee at BFI in the fall of 1969, interning at Boston State Hospital, and graduating in June 1971. All new faculty were chosen from graduates of the program, following Sandra Watanabe's move to Illinois in 1970 and Madeleine Gerrish's decision to leave BFI at the same time.

In 1971 David Kantor in BFI and Jeremy Cobb, of the Boston State Hospital program, asked the author to teach with each of them, which continued for two years. In 1971 also, Fred Duhl invited her to work with him as cotherapist in private practice, as well as a co-seminar and workshop leader. During the busy next two years, the author concurrently worked alone as well as with these three different co-leaders, and has been consistently involved with the program from that time. The overlapping faculties of both the BFI and hospital program then met weekly, evolving similar formats and processes, though adapting to the different conditions and issues that each training context brought. Both programs were co-directed by Fred Duhl and David Kantor, until the summer of 1973, when Duhl left Boston State Hospital, and Kantor left BFI.

Since the decision was made early not to run a clinic, but to be connected with other clinics where trainees worked or had clinical placements, faculty members have been free to conceptualize and experiment broadly for training in thinking as well as training in intervening at varying levels and types of systems. There have been many types of "target populations," such as school systems, hospitals, agencies, and businesses, in addition to individual people and families in distress.*

The images drawn on in this work, then, come out of 14 years of the author's continual excitement and interest from the beginning in an organic process and open systems model for training. Over time, the faculty realized that to help develop competent, caring, and creative therapists, such a training program needed to put its prime investment in the persons of the trainees, and to focus on developing integrated multicentricity in each person. How to do that has been a continually stimulating and inventive challenge for more than a decade. For the author, this challenge seems to have tied in with lifelong interests.

AN AUTOBIOGRAPHICAL ACKNOWLEDGMENT: HOW I CAME TO THINK SYSTEMS AND TO WRITE THIS BOOK

I believe that our ways of thinking, acting, and writing emerge from our whole life in context, and you will find this a major theme throughout this book. I believe in this theme so fully that I have convinced myself that as author I am probably not immune from its rigors and surprises. So as I begin to present some of my thinking to you, it seems appropriate to offer to you my autobiographical acknowledgments as fairly as I can construe them in the hope that they may contribute to your understanding of this endeavor. I also hope that my woven story will invite or evoke your own parallel and complementary acknowledgments and appreciations of the autobiographical contexts for your own ways of thinking and being.

Ever since I can remember, I have been thinking, observing, and wondering about people, relationships, ideas, and connections between them. I be-

---

*In 1971–72, the BFI way of training was researched as an agency level intervention, concerning workers' openness and competency in seeing alcoholics and their families. The positive results gave us new information about generic systems training. See Epilogue and Research Grant Report by Hoffman and Hoffman, 1974.

came aware rather early that I didn't fit some expected mold. When I was 11, a college friend of my older sister's asked me to take a preference test. She wanted me to name my one favorite male, and my one favorite female movie star, and my one favorite hero and heroine in other categories which would tell her who I most wanted to be like. I said I didn't have one favorite movie star and starlet. She told me *every* young girl did. I said that there were things I liked about lots of movie stars and other people, and that I really would like to be like the best of each of them. She looked dismayed, as if my answer was going to earn her a flunking grade in her psych course. I reluctantly put aside my ideas about preferences and played the game for her, so she could tally the test and fit me into some preselected category to meet her course requirements. I was aware of feeling different from this category of "every young girl," and was somewhat bothered, as if there were something wrong with me, for I seemed to know then on some level that I was a part of all that I had touched and that had touched me. Not that I knew then what to do with that awareness. Absorbing and integrating that awareness in ways that I could and can use have taken me the rest of my life thus far. Yet, how many of us have ever escaped the experience that how we perceived, thought, and experienced the world or some course did not fit a prescribed category or curriculum or way to be? This book, then, like the theories created by so many in the field of human relations, is the web spun of the totality of all that I have touched, the threads of my life experiences and integrations.

Certain central threads of thought, whose origins long predate this work, seem to be tugging at me and asking for recognition here. They have been ongoing and recurrent ones, dipping in and out of sight at different times in my life. Perhaps mentioning them here will shed some light on my interest and involvement in the arena of thinking about thinking, human systems, and training.

When I was a junior in college at Brandeis in 1951, I got caught up and dragged down by a series of questions that seemed to me crucial and very private, for I seemed to think/feel/believe that everyone else had the answers to them, and that I was the only one who didn't. There was something of the flavor of "I should know already" in my sureness that others already *knew* what I was struggling to figure out. The series of questions had to do with questions of identity, of relevance, of how I was to judge the value of my life and the way in which I lived it and looked at it.

I had spent two years at Oberlin, once a pioneering school as the first white college to accept Negroes and now a traditional, almost super conservative school in the McCarthy era of the late 1940s. And I had now been at Brandeis for one year, as a transfer student into the "pioneering first class," where so many of the events we enacted would become tomorrow's traditions. I had been with all kinds of students and professors, during those three college years when one is most open to exploring one's sense of place and purpose. I had been subject to a contrasting and varied range of values and experiences, and I felt that by now there was some definite way that I was supposed to be, or to choose to be—some particular and settled way in which I was supposed to look at myself, the world, and the wide variety of life experiences that I had had to date which would fit together, rendering them meaningful and connected, giving me a sense of clear, goal-directed purpose. My life experiences seemed divorced from any schooling I had, as well as divorced from any frameworks for understanding them in a coherent way. Feelings, actions, thoughts, relationships, in daily life seemed to have little to do with college studies, important ideas and ideals. I guess, in the early 1950s, before everything became politicized, I was looking for a form of relevance and coherence.

I had grown up in a rural area, about an hour outside of New York City, in a Jewish family, among non-Jews. We were part of a minute Jewish community of six or seven families who lived there year-round, while during the summers there was an influx of several hundred "bungalow" families. I experienced the dramatic seasonal feast or famine of friends, and nine months of the year had lots of alone time for thinking, exploring, wandering and wondering about. I became a kind of self-referent. I was bussed to school, as were all rural school children. I experienced anti-Semitism young and felt the pangs of expressed racism towards the Negro children on the bus. I learned about cultural, ethnic, racial and other differences early. I was a good student, as were my older brother and sister. In 1943, during the Second World War, we moved to New York City, where I went to junior high and to the High School of Music and Art, where I met people who were excited about and involved in doing, in ideas, in creativity and new possibilities.

By my junior year in college, in addition to being a good student, I played flute well, I modern danced, I'd been in amateur theater off and on since the age of four, I'd been in summer stock, been an arts and crafts counselor two summers, and had spent a summer at Alfred University's ceramic engineering department where I learned and loved to create wheel-thrown pottery wrapped in glazes I had formulated. Nobody else I knew in college seemed to have such a peculiar background. I didn't feel like anyone else. And I was still very much a people-puzzle person, curious what made people "tick," trying to connect how people thought with how they lived, connected, created their lives. I read and talked ideas about life, and wondered how these ideas and living could move closer together.

I had left Oberlin because I found that psychology there was rat psychology, and because I couldn't decide on any other major. I had discovered that interest followed work, that anything I studied, as long as it had to do with some aspect of how people fit together, or how people thought and lived was interesting to me, and anything I got interested in carried an excitement with it. That covered a pretty wide range and made deciding on a specific topic major impossible for me.

By an accident of communications on transferring into the first junior class of a new university, I ended up majoring in the history of ideas of Modern Europe instead of majoring in people psychology. I loved this major, for it allowed me to explore how ideas had changed, and how other people had made sense of the world, and our behaviors in it over time. Yet that too was a problem, for the views and ideas changed contextually, historically. Professor Frank Manual, whom I credit with giving me several vital process frameworks for how to think, used to say to us, "When you read, read between the lines, and ask what this writer is against. In that way you will discover what he is for." What a wonderful dialectical way to read! Frank Manual believed in ideas, not psychology, which he called "Alchemy 102" and "Witchcraft 304." He believed in the world of the mind rather than experience, as if they were separate, and in a passionate way delighted in discussing great concepts that emerged from the tenor of historical contexts, not individual lives. Yet there were so many "isms" and "ists," so many ways to look at how human beings made sense of themselves and the world they lived in, how was one to find *one* way that integrated one's personal life and experience with the many ways of understanding? What was the "tenor" of our historical time and context? My inner voice was asking difficult and badgering questions that I couldn't answer. There was no one framework, no one way with which I felt comfortable. Each one seemed to leave something else out which was of importance to me.

I remember one day taking a walk by myself and allowing these nagging questions to come to the surface in full awareness. I remember feeling the aches of struggling with them as I walked, and writing them down later, somewhat self-consciously, in a once-in-a-while journal that I kept. The questions and inner dialogue went something like this:

How do I make sense of my life? By my emotional ups and downs, in feeling and exploring the widest range of passions and intensities possible? Or by living an even keel, rational existence? Am I a romantic or a rationalist? I can experience both aspects in myself. I can get wildly fired up about some event, some idea, some creation, and I can sit back and think things through. I can feel and argue for both sides. Yet, I often feel a pressure to declare myself, to choose either/or, with no middle ground. There must be some way to put them together. Yet, I hadn't heard of any.

How do I look at and judge, understand my life? From myself as center of the universe? In terms of my personal connections with others? For after all, if I wasn't here, I wouldn't matter, and I wouldn't know, and I wouldn't care. Do I look at myself in terms of the continuity of my personal family? I mean, from my parents' parents, to my parents, to me, to the children I will have? Do I look at my life in terms of myself in my extended family, my place among and relationships with my brother and sister and parents, all my aunts and uncles and cousins on both sides? Or should I look at my life in terms of my relationships to friends, my place in the community, in the flow of events of local history, in terms of whatever roles I take? Do I look at my life in terms of the long flow of Jewish history, and where I fit there? American history? The history of Western civilization? The history of the world? In each of these, I feel myself getting smaller and smaller, with personal meaning of less and less importance. Finally, do I look at my life in terms of evolutionary time? When I find myself imagining that and seeing myself as a speck in the universe, I feel somewhat eerie.

Each of these stances was "valid," with a field of study, of expertise attached, if only I left me out of them. Yet they stopped on the edge of combining, as if facing and repelling each other like the negative ends of magnets. Each was valid, yet they all had to do with me, and each registered different feelings and meanings. It was very confusing. And I didn't know how to feel or think, and I didn't know what to do with what I felt and thought. Psychology professor James Klee told me that what the world needed was generalists. At the time, that was of no help either. I didn't know how to go about being a "generalist," nor did I know what one did being one.

In actuality, I survived, and the questions went underground. I thought of them as I moved to New York City and entered the worlds of work, pottery, dating and psychoanalysis, as if they had been those kinds of ethereal questions that indeed one asks oneself in adolescence, before settling down to *real* life. Perhaps I was looking for some of the answers in psychoanalysis, for I was certainly into another level of self-viewing, self-valuing, and self-appraisal, and looking for connections. I learned a lot and even changed somewhat, yet there seemed to me to be so much more involved in what life was about than that vantage point allowed.

I found humor in the desire of my analyst to look at my completing a pottery assignment of throwing (forming) 12 " tall vases on the potter's wheel as evidence of severe penis envy! I remember laughing and saying that I would explore the meaning of clay to me, of making something out of nothing, of giving form to blobs, but since the forms it was possible to shape on the wheel were rather limited to variations of penises, wombs, and breasts, I thought it was a rather sterile and futile idea to discuss shape as meaning. In addition, I found technical skill development, by assignment in a class, hardly worthy of being the place to look for hidden motivations and covert issues of me with myself. (I used to wonder what category I would have fit when my assignment was throwing flat dinner plates!)

I think the most important aspect of the analysis was the general process of having a space to wonder out loud, to give voice to those thoughts that I had hardly let myself hear, to become a less afraid explorer of my inner territory, and to have a place to report and evaluate new behaviors enacted in other contexts. Equally important was the person of the analyst and the particular way he was, the particular counterpart he allowed himself to be, and the particular way of putting things he sometimes had, when he wasn't hiding behind techniques and party-line jargon. One throw-away line he said to me one day, "You're only vulnerable when you want something," became for me a self-in-context organizer. I turned his phrase around to a directive for myself: "When feeling vulnerable, ask myself, what is it I want?" It was a very important phrase for me, offering me new information each time, with lifelong ramifications extending to this day.* I checked with him some three years after I finished analysis. He never remembered saying it or thinking it special.

At that time, I also learned about the world of work in New York City, as a woman college graduate with a magna cum laude, humanistic and artistic interests, and no specialty. Nonprofit organizations loved such young women, and I did my share of community organization, writing brochures, planning conferences, and writing newsletters. And although I didn't know it at the time, I was learning how organizations and businesses worked.

So some of the old questions were possible to ponder and figure out in analysis. But what about the rest of them? They didn't seem to have a place to rise and be tussled with. The ordinary world did not seem to value women with questions and ideas who wanted to use their minds beyond the college environment.

In 1955 Fred Duhl and I were married, after some four years of knowing each other and trying to iron out those interpersonal issues which I later realized people who get married right away struggle with also. Fred was the only person I'd ever met whose wide range of interests, abilities and curiosities matched my own and with whom I could discuss ideas. Some of the old questions about how to view self in the world popped up now and then, and were

---

*In 1974 I developed a *Vulnerability Contract* (1976b) in our seminars. The seeds for it had been planted some 20 years before.

discussed, but mostly they stayed inside at the underside of awareness. I was busy living, getting on with it. I was a young wife, working at a variety of jobs and learning a lot as writer, assistant occupational therapist in a state hospital, clinical psychiatric research assistant, and project summarizer. I was busy helping to support us in the days when psychiatric residency paid $2400–$3600 a year. And I studied pottery.

By 1969, when the Boston Family Institute started as a training program in family systems therapy, we had been married 14 years. I was 38, and we had three very special and different children, not only in their own personal idiosyncratic ways of being, but also in their method of arrival: one by adoption, one by "normal" birth, one by cesarian section. I'd been learning a lot about how differently little people learned, grew, changed, and interacted, and how we as parents changed in the process. I found I was thinking and learning family systems from the inside out. Being a mother allowed for exciting and wonderful observations, interventions, and experiments with ways of being, connecting, getting messages across and interpreting. And I had my pottery studio at home. I had stopped working as a research assistant at the Putnam Children's Center, when our first child arrived. I considered myself a professional (if somewhat nonprofit) potter and sculptor, who had exhibited nationally and sold her work. I also had helped organize, found, and run the grass-roots Brookline Arts Center, and become surrogate mother/advisor/counselor to a myriad of adolescent cousins or "adopted" cousins who went to school in the Boston area. And, somewhere around 1962, with Fred's meeting of Dick Auerswald, another part of me had relaxed.

I think it was in 1962 that Fred went to some national meeting and came home saying he had met this brilliant guy with whom he could discuss something called "general systems theory." I asked what that was, and Fred explained that one could look at all levels of human activity, at all *living* systems, by this systems concept, as if in concentric circles, and that they all existed at the same time while they all kept changing; that there were ways of looking at each level of system and finding the same types of processes operating. And he went on with his description, using at times some technical words. If he was really saying what I thought he was saying, this was very important. I stopped him and asked, "Are you saying that this general systems theory is an umbrella theory, that all fields relating to human beings have to fit under it in some way, in some ordered fashion, and that all ways of looking at human beings can exist simultaneously, in some connected fashion?" He answered, "Yes." Something in me relaxed at a very profound level. "Oh," I remember almost whispering to myself, "I have always thought that way." Now there was some sort of framework, outside of myself, that seemed to fit the way of thinking, seeing the world, I had struggled with. How this framework fit, and how people in daily life fit within it, became the next very large set of questions.

We and the Auerswalds became friends. We shared children and ideas up at their farm in New York State. All together, we talked about our kids, about how they each approached the world differently, and seemed to process information differently. And we discussed how people's ways of processing information affected interactions and coping skills. I listened, questioned, and discussed for hours over several years as Dick talked about his applications of general systems theory to the clinical and community practice of psychiatry. Dick's basis was very much rooted in what was real and how people lived, and how their customs and context shaped their thoughts, images, feelings, experiences, and behaviors. For instance, I have never forgotten his telling the story about the Puerto Rican woman in New York City who was seen as crazy by her husband and others, several months after arriving from her warm and tropical island. She was talking to herself, and her husband was sure she was "loco," and the doctors at Bellevue did nothing to change his mind. Dick's team saw her and said that she was isolated, that she knew nobody here, and needed a telephone and a network of other Puerto Rican women to call. Her husband was never home, she was alone all day, frightened of the non-Spanish-speaking neighbors and this foreign and alienating city environment, and she knew no English. Dick talked with much feeling and dismay about how his team had not been heard, that there was no money to supply this woman with a phone. Instead the woman went to the psychiatric ward of a state hospital. Dick told many similar stories, and in some he was successful in his endeavors to have people seen in the light of the real contexts and fullness of their lives and not the narrow lens of any one particular psychological theory. I guess I listened and talked a lot, because the ideas fit a way in which I saw the world. Yet the map was very large. And I later first heard of Gregory Bateson from Dick.

Somewhere in the mid-sixties, I still wanted to go back to school and get my long-put-off advanced degree. I wanted to go to graduate school in psychology, or social work, and looked into the latter as more practical. I had just helped a younger cousin get through the emotional part of social work school as well as helping her with her papers. So much of what she was learning seemed irrelevant to understanding human beings in connection with each other, though the course work was a way of getting into clinical positions with real people. However, when I looked into schools of social work in the Boston area, I felt I could not learn that way, that I needed to be put on line and then I would find out what I didn't know. And so when 1968 rolled around, and Fred, our neighbor David Kantor, and several others started talking about a family institute, Fred and I started talking about my "professionalizing" that which I seemed to be doing already: my working with people on a community basis with the arts center, my "working" with the cousin group, my previous jobs in psychiatric settings, my interest in the different ways in which our own children and others seemed to learn and process information, and my lifelong interest in how people worked and fit together, and how ideas fit together.

I thought that the either/or question of working with my hands with clay or with all of me with people could be made into an "and." I was ready to tackle new arenas. For between 1962–69, a lot of living had gotten done. By then, we had had our third child, and I had watched how all our relationships had shifted as we incorporated her into the family. We had survived Kennedy's death and survived, barely, the death of Fred's mother, learning first-hand, with death, the impact of unfinished business on the living. By 1969, we felt our marriage was in a place where we could tolerate, enjoy, and survive a situation in which I was a trainee in a place where Fred was an instructor. It was very important for me to go through the experience as student, as learner, and not as Fred's wife. And we thought our marriage could stand two of us in the same field (although I had always felt myself to be in this "field" of people-connection exploring all my life) and I decided to give it a go. By happenstance, when BFI began, the first exercise planned, about which I knew nothing, was a nonverbal one. No nametags were used, no names were mentioned. When we did start on names, they were first names, for a while. In addition, without specifically talking about it, Fred and I had cut down all those nonverbal cues of connection that connected and married people generally use in groups. As a result, I found out a year later that there were three people in that first year seminar who had not realized for some three to four months that Fred and I were married.

At home Fred and I talked a lot. I found this particular program and way of learning one of the most exciting experiences of my life. Many of those piercing and tormenting questions of my junior year began to have a way of coming together, from the inside out. Yet I still had many questions about the connection between personal experience and theories.

As a student, then trainer/co-experimentor/conceptualizer, my own education at BFI became a platform experience against which to bounce new thoughts, ideas, feelings, and "I wonder if's. . ." about training in systems thinking, as well as about daily life and therapy. I was personally excited by the possibility of aiding in creating a climate for a collaborative and open search for innovative and integrated learning, in which trainees could indeed include their own experiences, information, and world view as resources for finding answers to their questions about people and families. It is unusual but validating when what you know from life itself is deemed worthy data in seminars concerned with overviews of the human condition.

And I went to meetings, talked to others, began writing and putting my ideas down on paper, gave papers, believing that as a woman I could still think and use my head even without the proper initials after my name. I read Bateson and began to realize that he said a lot of things I thought and a lot of things I struggled to think. He also left out arenas I thought about. And I read a lot of others on systems, yet there were big gaps between theory and life as experienced and lived. More answers, more pieces of the puzzle, and still more questions. And at home, we struggled with new and ongoing issues in our marriage, raised by my increasing involvement and creativity in the "field."

I had thought of going to graduate school after BFI. This plan was thwarted by the death of my father, when, through my mother's way of being, I learned about the ownership of grief by one member of a family. My mother's impending death of a slow-growing brain tumor taught me scads about finishing business with her during her life, which we did and helped others do. And after her death, I knew I had to go through a year as an orphan, at 44, to experience each season and anniversary date when there was no longer a generational buffer between me and my death, before embarking on new and important ventures.

Meanwhile, I had done a lot of teaching and therapy in different contexts, alone and with different co-leaders and co-therapists. I had gotten very excited at BFI exploring how people learn and think. I had begun to invent other processes for teaching and for doing therapy in an interactive way so that trainees could discover, utilize and integrate how and what they felt, thought, imaged, and brought with them while they also learned to think systems multicentrically. We had begun to put together my old questions, in action, from the inside out. Life experience finally had a place to connect to ideas.

I explored schools, and then applied to and was accepted in graduate school at the University of Massachusetts, Amherst. I started there in the fall of 1977, in the School of Education, following Fred's close brush with death through coronary bypass surgery that spring. There were many gaps I wanted to fill, many bridges I wanted to find.

There, and here, 80 miles apart, the dialogues continued. Through my contacts in the Human and Behavioral Science Cluster at UMass, I began to find new ways to put together my range of interests. It was interesting to go to graduate school at this point in my life. I now had had all kinds of experiences and a general map. I was still looking for more connections within this map, into which life experiences fit. I also wasn't trying to prove anything to anyone, as one often has to do earlier in one's life. I wasn't looking for a career, or for particular skill development. And I had purposely chosen a place, which also chose me, in which I would be free to learn, to fill gaps, to struggle with integrations and combinations in ways that had to ring true to some inner part of me. Of all the wonderful schools in the Boston area, UMass was the only one which did not insist that I fit into some pre-packaged program.

I became more and more puzzled and curious about how and why the BFI "home developed" way of teaching "worked" with adults in such an exciting and holistic fashion. I was looking for underlying and integrating frameworks for understanding what we were doing in practice. I felt every course I took, every person who taught, every other classmate, had something to offer me in my search. Klaus Schulz, who taught a course in Piaget, didn't look at me cross-eyed when I started raising questions about how adults learn through sensorimotor activity as well as cognitively, and how adults continue learning, integrating, in new holographic ways not talked about in Piagetian stages. I knew it was so because it had been my experience, and I had seen it in others. And I wondered what were those adult stages for that learning? And I dialogued and experienced Gerry Weinstein, "Mr. Humanistic Education," and gained more insight and awareness of what we were doing at BFI. We grappled with learning styles, which I first became aware of through our own children, and wondered if this concept fit with the stage development models of different learning theorists.

Ena Nuttall grounded me as we discussed cognitive and emotional psychological testing as relevant only contextually, as pieces of a whole story, a whole system or set of systems. Every child in the neighborhood became my WISC-R subject, and I fed back my thoughts and impressions to the parents and children as I put my awareness of them in context together with testing results and impressions about learning styles. I delved further into Piaget with George Forman, an authority on Piaget and children, who was a planner/advisor for the grade school attached to UMass. George Forman did not turn off when I still raised questions about adult learning. The more I learned about Piaget, the more I felt something was missing in Piaget's material concerning learning that we were doing successfully with adults. Piaget seemed to be an excellent cartographer of the left brain. George Forman pointed me in the direction of Jacques Jimenez, W. J. J. Gordon, *Synectics,* and metaphor, and I discovered more connections. This time I was able to make integrations of a special nature: right/left brain type integrations with external maps to begin to put them together, as I began to reread Ornstein, Pribram, Bogen and others, with new awareness.

And I explored issues in intimacy, again picking up on ideas, a model and a paper written years earlier. How people connected, how we taught at BFI, how we did therapy, and how people learned, changed and grew began to take on added dimensions as I began to integrate them more fully. My way of writing expanded, and I became more comfortable expressing the images in my mind on paper. Ron Frederickson asked the right questions, and when the images did not come across clearly to one who did not think that way, he said so.

In addition, I took group courses, family therapy courses, statistics and more. I felt like an amoeba, constantly expanding, constantly absorbing, comparing, contracting and connecting, always coming back to central questions and issues.

In 1979, participation in the two family therapy meetings of trainers (see Prologue) here and in England, where important questions were raised about training issues and methodologies, spurred me to think seriously that perhaps what we had discovered and evolved could be of interest to others.

And then, the time came to put together a dissertation. I decided to try to pull together experience and concepts, to combine the "research" I had been involved in for years on learning/teaching systems thinking with adults, with the conceptual underpinnings I'd begun to weave together that seemed to shed light on what we were doing. I chose Jack Wideman as chairman, for his breadth and scope, for his amazing capacity for caring and inclusive listening and thinking, for his sensitive tuning in to help me find out what I was struggling with and trying to express, and for his delightful ability to speak in illuminating images. The dialogues continued. Jack's concept of "reflexive coherence" seemed to capture what personally mattered to me, what we did at BFI, as well as to offer me another framework for thinking about those original nagging questions. I got to wondering: How did each question shed reflexively coherent light on the whole? How did people fit together in ways that expressed their *own* reflexive coherence? This is a generic systems question—another way of asking a question I had asked myself: How did each person's way of being lend form to a larger system?

Jack's willingness to help shape the banks so that the river could flow included getting permission for me to do my dissertation my way, in book form. As such, this was perhaps an attempt at the impossible—to describe a dancing hologram and one's own experience of it at the same time. Like a hologram, ideas about events occurring in training conjure up images whose edges are not sharp, and which cannot be boxed and contained. Any linear description, then, is, as Bateson says, a punctuation of experience (1972, p. 288–292). I would also call such descriptions choices, simplifications, bracketings around ongoing phenomena, but never the whole image. Like holograms, processes and ideas about a reflexively coherent approach to training are projected in space and over time, and exist in the minds of those involved with them. All this notwithstanding, I wanted to give it a go.

Dialogues ensued with Jack, with Fred, with Esther and Howie Scharfman. Occasional conversations with Dick Auerswald, Larry Allman, Len Duhl, Virginia Satir, and Carolyn Attneave connected me to a more distant thought network. And so, with all the support from outside, most continually from Jack and Esther, underpinned at home by the super support of Fred, Sara, Josh and Dina, who it seemed, slipped meals to me under the door of my third-floor study, the dissertation version of this book was completed.

And now this book, with some rearrangement of chapters as well as some new material, and careful, sensitive editing by Susan Barrows at Brunner/Mazel, is the momentary result of all those questions which began stirring so many years ago. While many, many people have helped shape the BFI program, this work will not be an historical account of each one's contribution to the hologram, nor will this book be a full account of the total ongoing program itself.* This book will hardly even mention our second year program in family therapy, yet everything here pertains as much to therapy as to any other human systems situation. The images drawn here are those of generic approaches to training and systems thinking, colored by my lenses, and painted with my brushes and palette. They are approaches which catch my imagination as the exciting ones on which to focus in this volume. Like the laws of nature uncovered, this book explores the thinking and processes in training, which, when pulled together, seem to create new "patterns which connect" (Bateson, 1979).

Susan has enthusiastically urged me to publish now. Yet while she says this book is finished, the subject isn't. There's a lot more to say, to describe, about how people fit together holographically, and ways to help trainees integrate the internal sense of self with one's contextual interactions with others, which is already under way as a second volume. If I can keep my dialogues and energy going, and round up my network, I'll get to finish it sooner.

In any case, while I give grateful and appreciative thanks for all the help and thoughts along the way, I'm the one to fuss with should there be errors and disagreements to the ideas expressed in this book. After all, they're my answers to my own plaguing questions and those of others I've taken on which, it seems, I've been struggling with and researching in one form or another all my life.

---

*There have been several earlier attempts to describe our training program. See Duhl, B. S., and Duhl, F. J., 1974b; Duhl, B. S., 1978; and Duhl, F. J., and Duhl, B. S., 1979.

First Impressions and Afterthoughts | II

When I walked into the room, the chalkboard said, "SILENCE! DO NOT TALK." So the group of some 14 adults sat and looked around, uncomfortably, smiling awkwardly. Some stared at the floor, others examined the peeling pale green paint, the steel-meshed windows. Eyes searched out the inanimate, moving upwards to investigate the four-sided balcony with slatted railing in this mammoth two-story room in an old Boston State Hospital building. Stark bare light bulbs hung in the center of the room, casting soft shadows under the balcony. Eyes scanned each other fleetingly, and then shifted away. One woman rummaged in her pocketbook for something. Anything so as to pass the time in nervous silence, wondering what this was about and trying to look casual.

If we had been younger, the chances are we would have giggled and whispered and hidden behind our hands. I knew two of the 14 people. They were a couple—friends through children who were friends. He was a businessman, she a homemaker. They were each interested in family and human systems and had just joined the Boston Family Institute (BFI) course as I had, during its initial seminars. It was September 1969. The leaders had had a first spring semester. Now they were going to start with a new group of trainees, while the first group "waited." After three months, both groups would be joined together—to continue a two-year, part-time course.

So there we were—no names, no talking, no exchanges of the usual social and verbal information. We were left without our usual tools of establishing our places vis-à-vis each other. Without such tools, we were amorphous. We were left to deal with information and communication with our first and earliest preverbal skills, and we were uncomfortable using or interpreting this language, directly, in conscious awareness.

I was reminded of sitting in doctor's offices, waiting rooms, the subway, airports, and all those similar places where you are supposed to pretend that you are the only person in the room, or else that you and "they" are invisible. The chalkboard only said: "Silence, do not talk." It did not say, "Do not notice each other. Do not communicate." Yet we acted as if it did.

35

The leaders of the seminar arrived. I knew them. One said something like: "We want you to meet each other without words. We are going to divide you into two groups and those halves into two smaller groups and give you each instructions as to what to do. After you receive your instructions, you will mill about—using no words—carrying out those instructions. When we say 'switch,' you are to switch to the second instruction we have given you. Then we'll talk about this. Remember—no talking."

At this point, the leaders arbitrarily divided the group down the middle and then again, in quarters. Each leader spoke to each of two subgroups, telling them what to do and in what order. Each small group knew only its own two instructions. Mine was to first be a "positive responder," who, when the signal was given, was to become a "negative responder." These ways of being were to be carried out completely without words, solely with movement, facial expressions and gestures. No matter what others did, one was to stick to one's instruction, one's role, and not speak.

We began to move: awkwardly, avoiding, then tentatively towards each other. Some people looked "pleasant." Others looked "mean." All of a sudden, someone pushed me hard, looking quite angry. Automatically, I felt like pushing back. My instructions, however, were to be a "positive responder." I smiled and tried to take the person's hand. She shook loose abruptly, turning quickly towards another person whom she purposely bumped into. There was so much going on. I smiled somewhat rigidly, and nodded nicely no matter who did what with me. I noticed a woman slumped down by a pole. I saw others smiling, bumping, moving abruptly. One felt the sense of awkward tension, of restrained energy, in the room. My muscles were tight.

The command "switch" came from the leaders and I became just as fixed as a "negative responder." I was aware for the first few minutes that it was a relief *not* to be nice, to shrug others off and turn away, to give a push back when pushed. My own tension and held back energy felt released. This situation, however, was awkward. We didn't know each other. We didn't know who we were pushing or avoiding. We were just "roles." We were grown-ups and strangers, not children. We were enacting these behaviors in awareness, and we "knew better." It was both fun and freeing, and equally uncomfortable and tense.

The leaders said "stop" and asked us to come sit down and debrief what had happened. They asked each person to mention his/her first name as each spoke and began by asking us, "What did you learn? What did you find out?"

What did I find out? What did I learn? What interesting questions! What did they mean, "What did I find out and learn?" About what? Myself? This place? Others? Leaders? Impressions? Thoughts? Feelings? On what level?

How does one answer? I had a zillion associations and I didn't know where to begin. *What did I learn?* I had to think about that.*

WHAT DID I LEARN?
A REVIEW A DECADE LATER

Thus began for the author in 1969 a whole new venture and adventure into the reflexive land of learning/teaching/learning/therapy/learning—an adventure that continues to this day. For that first question, *"What did you learn?"*, which opened practically every debriefing session, also threw the door open to individual exploration. It was then and still is a radical question.

Such a question led trainees to ask themselves, "What *did* I learn?" One has to pass the experience and the resulting information evoked through the filter of the self, that personal screen of meaning, in order to come up with any answer to that question. And trainers must also have a way of thinking about answers that admits to and allows for a wide range of possibilities.

Though that may not seem startling to the reader, it was very startling to the author. By the time we have each reached adult life in this culture, and have gone through our customary schools and universities, we are quite well educated in being told what we have studied and learned, or should have learned. We are not accustomed to reaching inward for our answers. Rather, we have become habituated to accepting information, ideas, and techniques as prepackaged commodities, compiled by "the experts," either the ones who originally explored and discovered the concepts, or those who compiled what is being taught. Indeed, especially in those human service programs and training seminars which lead to or towards a profession dealing with people, we become skilled followers and users of other explorers' discoveries, often denying our own perceptions and our own sense of coherence, of how people "fit" with each other.

What did I really learn, indeed, in that total training context from such exercises and questions?

I learned that the primary locus for knowing about the world and for the integration of that knowing was based in my own experience, a discovery that I had truly suspected for a long time, but that most of my life contexts and schooling had not guided or encouraged.

I learned that there were many levels of answers to match the many levels of questions I had. Over time I became aware that all levels of answers were relevant, depending upon which level one focused on. I found out that the

---

*For a thorough examination and discussion of this exercise, and its implications, please refer to Chapter VIII.

contextual answers I discovered within myself were important for me to pay attention to and important to discuss with others. I discovered again that *the mind is timeless and analogic*, hoarding events and thoughts and awarenesses long ago perceived, and flashing them as if they were current.

I learned that happenings in my own life were illustrations of observations discussed in larger theories.

I learned over time that "What did you learn and find out?" covered a wide range of data and meant, translated: What did I experience? What did I or others do? How am I feeling and thinking about these experiences, these events and my perception of them right now? How am I sensing, perceiving the world? What are my sensations, thoughts, ideas, images of what just happened? What does it remind me of? What core images, what screens-of-the-past, do I bring to bear on this material, this scene, this situation, this theory, this idea, this action, this family? What associations does this stir up? What information from other sources—from books, from other fields, places, theorists, courses, therapists, films, television—seems to connect with and inform my reactions and thoughts? How does what I am thinking and feeling fit with what others think and feel? What larger maps about human responses and interactions can we draw upon to make sense of all the data? What data do those larger maps ignore or leave out as well as include?

I learned to use everything I had.

I learned that every exercise created an opportunity for a far-ranging search, along many avenues simultaneously. I realized that whatever I found out during an exercise could become data, just as whatever others answered became data. There were no right answers; there were only personal, individual answers, from different people, representing different contexts, backgrounds and images. Responses were "diversities of instances" (Bruner, 1973a), all parts and pieces of answers to larger, wider ranging and open sets of generic questions. I felt all answers to the same questions could be organized somehow in some connected and coherent scheme. Where did they fit? How did they fit?

These questions about "fit," old and familiar to the author as very private and personal questions, were now being elevated to another overt level for legitimate, open search and research: How do people fit together? How do things fit together? How do ideas fit together, and how do they all interrelate? What are the dynamics of relationships—the "betweenness" of people? Very private curiosities were now open for public inspection and discussion.

Was there really a way to make coherent, living sense of personal answers and larger maps that were inclusive of life as experienced, life as observed and reported, and life as conceptualized? Here was the rare opportunity to connect events, responses, ideas, to make hypotheses, and even theories.

The first evening's exercises in 1969 set the tone for what to expect in this new learning context: adventure, involvement, and the search for personal relevance of one's experience with more formal concepts about human systems. They also highlighted that a new framework for thinking *about* training in this new paradigm of systems thinking was being developed.

The new way of learning was as exciting as the new concepts being learned! As trainees, we could not predict in advance the specific content or processes a seminar might include. We expected that learning about families, other living systems, and family therapy was not going to be passive, removed, and left only to one's cerebral imagination. Rather, learning about family interactions in context gave evidence of being alive, active, and different, involving all of oneself. Like children playing charades and pantomime, we would be calling upon parts of ourselves not usually acknowledged in adult life. It was strange to play and to have fun in the process of discovery and learning about human systems. Yet it seemed to make sense to be active, in exploring family and other living systems, since people do live their lives interacting in real time and space. Ideas about interacting are not the same as the interactions themselves or as the experience of being an interactor.

These first exercises, along with myriad others that followed in the training program, stimulated me both as a trainee and later as a trainer to think about how learning and change takes place in adults. Over time, I began to observe and think about the processes by which data are evoked: the design of exercises, the climate or ambience necessary and elicited, the content, the processes, and particularly, what aspects of trainees' capacities, information and skills were called upon in any particular situation.

I realized over time, as I participated in and debriefed many exercises as a trainee, that the thoughts, images, perceptions, and feelings evoked in experiential metaphors were analogic and isomorphic to other realities experienced. I began to think about and pay attention to the range of possibilities inherent in each exercise. I became aware of the rich mix that action and analogue seemed to create, calling forth learnings never approached in other settings.

My exposure to such learning from the inside out began a continuing journey for me, a search for bridges integrating experience with theory, integrating epistemics (one's private theory [MacLean, 1975]) with epistemology (formal and public theories), and integrating systems concepts across ordinary and different human contexts. So few of the written theories that we read in 1969–71 seemed to have any way of connecting with daily life. The original team of BFI trainers themselves were in the midst of searching for comprehensive connecting maps, for none existed.

The basic issues in training people to become systems therapists were both simple and complex: a matter of finding ways of integrating one's sense of being a human system with being an actor in larger human systems, while learning to be a facilitator and intervener in still other human systems called families. What an intricate tangle!

The context of the training program then became a laboratory, in which all participants, trainers and trainees alike, searched for paths through this intriguing maze of learning and of changing. Issues in training seemed to be analogous to those in therapy. Therapy, too, is an "exercise" in how different people learn and change. Integrations about learning and changing in training and therapy would need to fit in some larger metamap, some huge umbrella, inclusive of basic frames of reference about how people process information, about context, and about patterns. Such a larger map seemed possible to find within general systems theory, yet we had no way in the beginning of being specific and of tying it all together.

THE IMPORTANCE OF GENERIC QUESTIONS

Beginnings in themselves are interesting. New starting moments are "system precursors, system formers" (Gray, 1981), wherein random possibilities can become organized by the larger contexts, the events themselves, and the people involved. The system formers in 1969 were questions, curiosity, personal exploration, and discovery.

While one could predict that discoveries would take place in a program where so much was uncharted territory, no one could predict the way in which those discoveries would take place nor what those discoveries would be.

While content and specific emphases within the program may have changed over the years as it evolved, what has remained constant is the manner of training through "structured spontaneity* (Duhl and Duhl, 1979), the manner of goal-directed training through metaphor and analogic exercises which allows for the exploration of inner and outer contextual components at all levels of human systems.

A beginning is just that—a beginning. Yet, if the questions asked in the beginning of a training program concerning human systems are generic ones, if they relate to the "how" of adult learning, as well as to the "what" of process and content, and if they are asked continually, the training program always stays open to new answers and to seemingly subsidiary information being raised to focal attention (Polanyi, 1958). Such an approach to human systems also stays open to the focus that among the key issues in training are

---

*Sal Minuchin, M.D., well-known family therapist, visited the BFI program in 1974 and bestowed that label on our approach to training. We later used that phrase in the title of a paper on training.

those concerned with the integration in the trainee of his/her life experiences, his/her ways of thinking and being, with theoretical constructs concerning specific processes and arenas of application. We are concerned with exploring the coherent relationship between one's epistemic world view and one's epistemology, That is, we are interested in exploring the implicit maps that each trainee brings which seem to bear upon the way in which trainees interpret and act within more formal theoretical maps. How one looks at one's own family and life contexts seems to be part of how one looks at all families and life contexts and a part of the aesthetic preference we each have for certain theories.

Thus, the generic questions—"How do people, children and adults, learn? How do you train competent and creative systems thinkers and therapists? How do family and other living systems work? How do people change? What did you learn? What did you find out?"—have been continually asked, as other generic questions have been added over time.

All the "answers" gleaned over the years establish a broad "data base" of knowledge generalized into constructs and conceptualizations, woven into and with other theory. *Yet, in order to integrate them, each person must explore and answer these particular questions for him/herself.* The learnings then are grounded not just in one's own experience, but in the *evocation of new thought* about those experiences in each person and the fresh generalizations made by each group with the trainers. Integration is a process, requiring activity on the part of the integrator.

Although there have been times when particular questions of "What did you learn/find out?" have been in jeopardy of being overcome by "Here's what you learned, or should have learned," or "Here's what you're supposed to know," the original questions have been kept alive.

The search for "the patterns which connect," for "new information, the difference which makes a difference" (Bateson, 1979) in training and therapy, has been and continues to be ongoing, with new discoveries always folded back into the program, in feedback, feedthrough and feedforward fashion (Richards, 1968). Such a process is akin to kneading clay. BFI then is akin to a large and constantly changing clay sculpture, and all who have been part of it have helped shape it. As anyone who has ever sculpted with clay knows, the forming, the shaping, the detailing of nuances, are never accomplished in one move or plan. The sculptor has an image and creates it in time and space, adding on bits or bunches, sometimes delicately carving away small lumps or masses until, in her interaction with the clay, the sculptor achieves her image. As with a sculpture in formation, one monitors what is happening against some ongoing mind's eye aesthetic image that considers relationships of the parts, form, and balance, a feeling of rhythm, a sense of wholeness and movement, and a watchful eye for the unexpected creative accidents. In that sense, the image of clay sculpture is limiting. It is solid. Training rather evokes an organic aesthetic image of evolving processes, more akin to creating and projecting a dancing hologram, a multidimensional image projected and moving in space, defying linear description (Pribram, 1971).

The program thus has been kept an open systems one, evolving and allowing for the coming together of experience and thought in a coherent, organismic and integrated fashion. Theory-as-espoused continually grows closer to theory-in-action (Argyris and Schon, 1974), as theory-in-action is tried, debriefed, analyzed, feeding data into the metamap of our theory-as-espoused.

The reflexive coherence (Wideman, 1970) resulting expresses and reinforces our belief that trainees must be empowered, aided and reinforced, like Taoist students, to draw their thinking from themselves, within a connected and empathic metamap. We believe it is important that each trainee learn to trust that all his/her personal experiences and knowledge are rich resources for and in understanding human systems and human systems theories. We insist that trainees must explore aspects of original questions so that they are centered in and in charge of the answers, the theories they adopt.

After all, it is US *they* are describing in those theories!

An Analogic Tale | III

Exercise

You have carte blanche to design a program to explore human systems that includes all aspects of a family's life, as well as all aspects
of the lives of each individual in the family. How will you go about designing such a program? What will you include? Exclude? Which factors and arenas do you see as important? Unimportant? How will you
go about thinking about this?

Indeed, if BFI were beginning such a program from scratch today, with no
previous history, I am not sure how I would or could answer these questions.
They boggle the mind.

What would one include? What does one think of when one thinks of "all
aspects of a family's life"? What about the persons "inhabiting" family?
What can we say about them?

Several images flash on my mind, drawn from the pictorial archives of
families: photographs. The first is of a young woman, captured in a snapshot
laughing and playing with three children. Another image is of several old
brownish very formal portraits, in oval wooden frames, hung on a wall. The
people stare out, looking quite distant in dress and expression. Still another
image is of a wedding photo, on a piano, surrounded by individually framed
photos of each child, each chosen at an arbitrary moment in the child's life,
and destined to become the remembered photo by others in the family. What
would we say about the people behind those photographs, who lived real
lives, day in and day out, year after year?

Exercise: A Fantasy

Or suppose we had the task of conveying our knowledge and assumptions about human systems to beings who had no experience
with systems or humans? Imagine, if you will, that we have taken these

photographs with us on a space voyage, and we have landed on the planet Clonem, where friendly English-speaking extraterrestrial beings live. Each being in front of us is identical to each other one. We are curious, and so we ask about them.

The Clonems tell us that on their planet, every new member is an adult replica of the peer who produced it. Each member produces four other replica members at exact intervals during a Clonem's "being-time." All beings exist for the same amount of "being there" and each instantaneously dematerializes when the "being there" is all used up. All new members perform like those who produced them immediately upon formation, and members cannot distinguish the one who produced them from the ones they then produced. Each Clonem is the same in all ways. Speaking to one is the same as speaking to another. That is the way it is, always has been, and always will be.

They are very aware that we are *not* exact replicas of each other, and they ask us how it is where we came from. What would we tell them?

How can we explain how human beings work? How can we get them to understand about the issues of history, of developmental time, and bonding, the issues of form and fit when Clonems reproduce by binary fission and have no past or future, and no group forms? How could we tell them that in our world everyone has a history, that families beget families; that the beginners of a new family always come from two other and different families? And how can we explain that no two human beings or families are exactly alike, as no two countries or eras are alike, though certain forms and processes may be alike?

"But what are these things called families?" they ask.

What would you say to them? How would you make yourself understood?

OUR STORY

What indeed would we say?

Well, as I imagine it, we answer, first, that families are not exactly things, but are groups of living beings who are all different ages and connected to one another by mysterious and special bonds. These bonds seem to call forth special and singular meanings and behaviors among those members who belong to a family and those who do not.

Can we see those bonds? No, these bonds between members are invisible and intangible, yet are felt or experienced by all members, who usually know by a certain *age* who belongs and who does not.

Age? Yes, different amount of years lived. No, the members are not replicated adults. They each have to be *born*. Born? No, not materialized like here. . . . Born means that the new member has finished *developing* inside the mother, and has come outside to continue developing, and forming, until each dies. How does one get to develop? Each new member is formed by seeds from two different members, a man and a woman. No, not every man and woman put seed together to make new members, called babies. Can they? Yes, they probably could, but they don't. Why? Because there are certain customs and *rules* about that. Why? Because, unlike here on Clonem where you are all the same, people on Earth *live in groups, within larger groups,* and making *rules* keeps them clear who goes with whom and who belongs where. Why does that matter? Because it does. Why? Well, human beings assign *meaning* to and try to *make order* of everything they experience or perceive. Thus, they experience, assign meaning, and make order of the bonds of connectedness and caring which they have with other human beings, making some bondings more important or more meaningful than others.

Are there rules for caring and connectedness? Well, there are "rules of order" for *belonging,* and there are customs and rules about how people are *supposed to care* and make *connections* with each other as family members, in each grouping. And there are personal preferences, personal aesthetics.

The Clonems ask: Are all the rules the same for each group? We wonder: How can we talk and explain ourselves to beings who cannot conceptualize difference? However, we continue. No, different groups have different rules. Why is that? Well, because a long time ago people in groups that got started in different places developed different ways of being with each other and then made rules to continue the ways they had developed. A few groups still exist, with the very definite and clear *rules of order* and *rules of access* that their *ancestors* evolved long ago. However, in many places on earth, lots of these different groups of people have gotten combined, and *intertwined* with each other and so have their rules, and ways of doing things and being together.

Rules of order and *rules of access*? Yes, those are the ways that each group derived to deal with that sense of belongingness, to provide for how the group as a whole was to be *organized* and *survive* physically. For unlike here on Clonem, where life or being there is supported by the atmosphere, on Earth human beings have to find food and to provide for the physical survival of their group, for the ongoingness of it. The rules of access, which relate to who can get to know whom, and who can be with whom, how, when, and under what conditions, used to be part of those rules of order within each group. In a very few groups that haven't mixed with other groups, more unified rules of order and rules of access still exist.

What happened to the groups that got mixed up together? Well, they developed individual, personal, and particular rules of access to add to the more general ones in the larger group we call the "society." The unified rules of order and access used to allow people more of the sense of similarity, of sameness, closer to what you have here on Clonem. But here on Clonem, you don't seem to have any sense of meaningful belonging, or bonding, which all human beings can have. You are all the same to each other.

How does one get to belong and be bonded meaningfully? Well, new members are usually *born into belonging,* into a family, or clan, with the *capacity* to bond. Then the new ones, the babies, and the older and more capable people who take care of them, become bonded to one another through their involvement with each other. Why this bonding happens is a wonderful mystery of human life. Some adult members have a sense of bonding without caretaking simply because the new member is from their seed or the seed of other family members. The new members are *helpless* when born, and must be taken care of until they are each *mature* enough to be able to take care of themselves.

Mature? Oh good grief! Never mind. This is endless. We'll have to think of some other ways to get these ideas and images across to our Clonem hosts. How *can* we tease apart what is so woven together as the fabric of our reality?

Indeed! What can we tell them? And how? How can we explain to them what families are about? How do we say they are made up of individuals who belong but then go on to belong to other units but never stop belonging to the first group? How do we explain that, while each belongs, at different points in life, within other groups of members and assumes multiple roles, each member is also a separate, unique, and special entity, encased in one continuous skin? How do we explain the affinity and the bonding of belongers, and the exclusion of non-belongers? How do we explain the separate/connected aspects of all human beings?

How do we look at and explain what we all take for granted as a given, which has been in front of us—no, which we live in the midst of—in some form or other, each day of our lives?

How shall we say what families and human beings are about, when *THEY are US*!

The Clonems become a little loud and active. They would still like to know what a "family" is and what an individual is and how life is lived on earth.

Maybe the Clonems will understand through specific stories, rather than all this general "talking about." We take out the photos we've brought with us and we ask the people trapped within the paper to tell their stories to our strange new far-planet hosts, for on this planet, photos can speak. We ask that each "tell it like it was" in their lives as a family, before, during, and after the chemicals froze their likenesses on paper at particular moments in each one's life's flow.

What story will each tell us of their lives? How will each tell it? What will they emphasize?

We are curious. Which events will be selected by each to grace with focus and meaning? Which moments drawn from the infinitessimal number possible for people in a family will appear highlighted and illuminated with those particular emphases that make each person's story his/her own and unique? Which inner snapshots and movies, registered on the film of each one's mind, will punctuate and illuminate each one's presentation of the flow of life as lived?

For each one's story contains the "I-Eye" of the individual. One's story is the thread in one's life, containing and locating one's sense of bonding and belonging, of continuity, fit, and coherence. That sense of bonding, belonging, continuity, and fit resides only in the inner world of each storycreator/storyteller.

Let us ask those with stern and formal countenances encased in the oval frames to speak first.

The story starts with the oldest photoperson, a man who tells us that he was born in a place called Russia, just before the beginning of this new century, in a family of many children. There was a leader there called a Czar who did not like the group his family belonged to, called Jews.

His father died when he was six, and his mother became busy running the dried fish business that supported the family. His uncle helped his mother. He tells the story that he left and came to a place called America by himself at age 12, because he knew, as a Jewish boy, he would not be allowed entrance into the gymnasium in Kiev. He had heard that America was a "land of opportunity," and he wanted to become a doctor. So he came to where some cousins had previously come, to America.

And then we hear from another portrait, a woman. Her family was originally from Austria, also Jewish. Her parents had come to America with their six children when she was very young—just three years old. The man and the woman speak of how they met at a skating rink, and "fell in love"—a type of strong invisible connection and bonding of each to the other. They tell of their courtship and their story together, and we have a beginning sense of how it was for them. We learn how the father became a salesman and not a doctor, and how the mother had worked before she married, after her father died when she was 14, and how *her* mother lived with them after they married.

And as we ask them to elaborate their story for the Clonems, we ask what each did, and about the births of their children, and how they each fared in life. We learn that one child was stillborn. The parents tell how that left a hole in their family that never closed over. We hear how they "got on with it," and how they as a family managed to struggle, doing whatever they could, to survive the Great Depression so that they could send their children to the colleges they had never gone to. They were very proud of what they had been able to do and thought they had a fine family.

Each photochild then talks, describing the family differently, each from his/her own time and context of entry. At this point one could almost believe each talked of a different family!

Our Clonem hosts are interested in the stories, and ask to hear some more. They say they are not sure they grasp the idea and meanings yet. And so we ask the next photofamily to tell their story, and we find that their stories of the way it was to be quite different than that of the first family.

The parents in this photo were each born right before World War II, in America. Neither had ever known struggles for food or money. The man who is now the father had moved around quite a bit as a young child, living in many places, while *his* father was in the Army. He had never stayed in any one place long enough, until he was 11, to make any friends, and by that time, he didn't know how to. He learned to be on his own a lot.

The family of the woman who was photographed as the bride in the wedding picture had lived in the same town in upstate New York for three generations. Her father had a bad leg and had not been in the Service. She was a rooted, church-going and socially capable person who had at first felt attracted by the man's shyness, and the excitement of his knowing about so many different places. They married when he was in engineering college.

Then they moved a lot as he pursued his engineering career. This father earned a good living, yet he and his wife battled regularly about their type of invisible bonding and who made the rules. The wife/mother did not like the moves and her husband's travel. It took her from her sense of bonding to and belonging with her earlier family, friends, and relatives in her community. He said he had to travel and to move because of his job and she was supposed to go with him, to be behind him. One child hated her father's traveling so much because her mother made her stick around when he was gone. Another teenage child enjoyed her father's absences, saying he was very strict; when he was not there, she had more leeway to be with her friends, to whom she felt more bonded than to her parents.

The Clonems get very confused at this point. They say they are having trouble understanding about rules, bonding and belonging, developing. They cannot grasp what all these "things" mean. Is there some way the photopeople can tell them more about that?

The photofamily members start to talk together about what actually happened among and between them, and what it felt like to be a part of each family, and what they thought bonding and belonging and rules meant.

While they all agree on certain "facts" or events, there is hardly any unanimity on the meaning of any events. One talks of belonging, meaning that inside a family one can do anything and still be loved. Another says that's not so—not in her family. A third says he never felt especially loved, yet he feels connected to other family members, that family is family, and that family means obligations!

This then provokes arguments, and we begin to hear tangled voices: "That's not what happened," "You never asked how I felt," "You were always a bad child!" "Funny what kids will think," "I always loved you even if you didn't feel it!" "Yes, I remember that! You were wonderful to me," and other mixed impressions. Soon, everyone is jabbering all at once to tell how it *really* was, what the rules were at any moment in time, and how each experienced the sense of connectedness and his/her world. Each seemed somehow to want to be acknowledged in the family by each of the others as important enough to be heard and known.

We wondered whose story our foreign hosts would believe, for each member's story would be his/her "true" account, yet incomplete as part of a whole. What sense could they make of these accounts?

The Clonems say they do not understand why everyone was talking all at once and they do not understand why the stories of the photopeople in the family groups were *different*. They don't understand what a Depression or a World War II is and why any of these would matter. They are confused by the wide range of voice tones and don't understand what the different speeds and loudnesses of talking are about and why people move in certain types of ways. In addition, they really do not see why the photopeople emphasize and make much ado about where each grew up and who died, and whom they married, and *why that seemed to make a difference with how people were with each other*. Could we please find a way to help them understand why all these "things" seem to be important to us earthlings?

And so we think and think. How can we get our images and messages across about differences—about families and the very unique individuals who comprise them—to a group of beings who see everyone alike and interchangeable? How can we convey to beings who have no sense of differences the specialness of situations, bondings, and contexts which shape human beings and by which people help shape each other? Was there a way to present the "whole picture" of what being human encompasses?

We then ask ourselves, can we find a way in which we can use their way of understanding as the base from which to draw comparisons? Could we go from what they *did* know and lead them into some new territory to a new way of seeing and understanding? Could we take them through a "paradigm shift'' so that they could not only understand us cognitively, but comprehend us wholly, so that feelings, images, thoughts, sensations, actions, and context were all interconnected in that comprehension?

What if we were to say to our hosts, "Would you be willing to play with us for a while?" And what if they then said, "Yes!"

And what if we then said, "OK then. We are going to "play house." Please, you there, come over here. Now, you must be the woman/mommy, and you must be the man/daddy. And you must *make believe* that. . . . " And off we would go.

Just think of the fun we could have, inventing so many ways of informing the Clonems about us and our world. Imagine! What a range to choose from! Why, we'd have to reinvent theater! And pantomime! And storytelling. We'd have to become playwrights, choreographers, directors, actors, role players. Why even to do a role play, we would be free to invent all the possible scripts we could think of for them to play out. We would be free to remove the dialogue and to portray the dynamic pulls and pushes of human bondings in pantomime, in dance, in movement. We would be free to explore the essentials of relationships between human beings, in varying cultures. What wonderful fun we could have telling the Clonems what gestures to use, what stances to take, what words to say in what voice tones, in order to express certain Earthling ways of being!

What a delight it would be to watch them evolve into new ways of seeing and thinking!

But wait. Would they *be able* to evolve new ways of seeing and thinking? Could we *ever* get our images, ideas, and messages across? I mean, would the Clonems be able to develop that very special structure of mind that human beings have—that ability to see differences? To think anew, and to "go beyond the information given"?* Would they be able to fill in the "space" *between, to connect by a process of mind, separate phenomena*? Would the Clonems be able to have an "aha"—that external expression of an internal integration that proclaims "Yes, I see! I know! I understand what you mean!"?

Or, with the Clonems would we just have to hope that after myriad exposures to many, many ways of presenting the holography of human and family life, each Clonem could create the images, ideas, and connections we human beings so take for granted? As Earthlings, all our sensings, imagings, thoughts, feelings and behavings over time fill our well of tacit knowing,** upon which we constantly draw. Our past knowing informs our present, and guides us, as our new and now experiences inform and are added to the well.

---

*Bruner, 1973a
**Polanyi, 1958

Indeed, with Clonems, we would have to hope that they could *learn*, for Clonems have no comparable experiences against which to reference so many ways of being which are so different from their own. Clonems would have to believe on "faith" that everything we say is "true." They would have to learn expressions, feelings and ways of being by rote, as the only way to "know what they can't know." Their impoverished base of comparison gives them so few or no *ways of approximating* by which to extend and transform images of their world into a sense of or comprehension with ours. Would their mind structures enable them to bring from inside themselves metaphors and analogues, those leaps of generalization from one particular experience to other experiences which create connection and relationship between phenomena?

How else, except by those analogic and metaphor-creating structures and *processes of mind*, could they grasp the *idea* of patterns, connection, flow, and relationship in human life? How else could they become cognizant of the co-evolving ongoingness of individual persons, families, and larger groups? How else could they conceptualize multifocal *relationships* over time, wherein, for instance, one person can *simultaneously* "be" many people? That is, one can be a daughter, a niece, a wife, and a mother, with different behaviors and sense of bonding in each "position." That same person can simultaneously be a sister to four, and an aunt to yet another six, while currently being a supervisor of a work team, on a community council, as well as a neighbor and friend to numerous others.

We could present many types of experiences for our Clonem friends to try, but we would doubt from the outset that they were *educable*, that is, *capable of being "drawn forth."*

POINTS OF ENTRY, POINTS OF DEPARTURE

Let us leave the Clonems and draw our fantasy story to a close now, as we come back to Earth. Let us talk about training programs for human adults in exploring human systems, including exploring families and the individuals who make a human system what it is.

My version of the space travel fantasy above expresses the general framework in which we look at both individuals and families—as part of and shaped by the patterns of the larger contexts of which they are a part, while interacting, changing and co-evolving over individual developmental and historical/contextual time.

Our educating attempts with the Clonems also reflect our sense of what training is about.

However, the differences between Clonems and adult earthling trainees is enormous. Here on Earth, we do not have to hope that comprehension can somehow find a way and a place to jell inside adult human beings, for each one comes to such an exploring/learning experience with the available mind structures and vast numbers of comparable daily life experiences, as bases against which to bounce one's sense of similarities and differences, that is, one's sense of patterns.

Each adult trainee brings with him/herself into a seminar a completely equipped transactional and analogue-forming human systems laboratory. Unlike Clonems, adult human beings can already think, feel, image, sense, and act in context in relation to other human beings. Each adult trainee knows at least one variation of the first human system larger than self, i.e., family. Each has experienced some version of those intangible essences I am calling bonding, which, when combined with our human capacity for meaning-making, creates uniqueness and differentness in relationships, in intimate and non-intimate ways of grouping and belonging. Each trainee knows something of the rules of order and the rules of access by which each has survived and navigated in the varying systems of which he/she has been a part. Each adult has an awareness of the differentness and the importance of personal stories, especially one's own.

There are available to adults in a seminar many points of entry and points of departure into and through the holography of thinking about human beings in relationship. What better and easier way to explore the experiences of these entities called systems, and the concepts about those human systems, than by *capitalizing on all the resources and data already present and available to be tapped*? How better to explore theories of human organization, behavior, experience and interactions than by drawings on the differences of trainees' live families, home, and work settings, contextual cultural influences, and individual idiosyncrasies?

How better can one's way of thinking about human relationships, and one's way of behaving be interlinked than by having to experience theories of human behavior in action? Each then has to pass it through the filter of the self, adding to one's explicit and tacit well of knowledge. When each person's thoughts, actions, images, senses, and experiences of self in/as/and system are drawn forth and are received by others as valid data, several other conditions follow: 1) It is very difficult to think in right/wrong terms when all experiential data are affirmed as being valid! 2) Categories must be found inclusive of all these different types of processes and phenomena. 3) The maps evolved must have a way of connecting all such categories.

In so doing, we are saying, "There are larger weavings into which the fabric or metamap of our lives fit. Look at the threads in the fabric of which you are a part so that you may *know, recognize, and approximate* those threads in the designs that you and others make. Know how to connect the experience and raw data with the metamaps.''

Unlike trying to reach and teach Clonems in what human beings are like, here on Earth we can use each one's epistemic territory as the base for the epistemological map about all such human territories. The more experientially one owns, walks, explores, and expands one's "territory," the easier it is to extend one's personal understandings to new epistemological constructs that then feel old and familiar. Such acceptance of each one's epistemics takes the meanings given experience out of the realm of context, or the realm of "what," and into the realm of *types of fit-in-context* by which we define relationship and system.

With such a way of exploring and learning, former paradigms shift out from under oneself in a series of exciting aha's which mask the movement of the moment, which only later are recalled as the context markers of a change in perception.

Let us now turn to exploring how we approach the phenomena of fit-in-context or living systems here on Earth in ways that we'll never be able to try with Clonems . . . whoever they are and wherever they may be!

Training for Integration in Multicentric Human Systems Thinking

Exercise: Training in What?

I am supposing that the language used in the title may sound strange, even confabulated, to many readers. And yet, I feel sure that each reader has already stirred in his/her mind many of the ideas I am attempting to integrate here.

Thus I will take the liberty of introducing my subject as I often do at Training-for-Trainers workshops, by inviting each reader to pause and reflect on the title of this chapter, to "brainstorm" with yourself what comes to mind and to jot down whatever ideas, images, words this phrasing stirs in you. It is my hope that your thinking, writing, then reading what I have written might resemble aspects of the active component present in our workshops and seminars. Such activity creates more of a dialogue, which I have grown to prefer and trust.

WHAT'S OUR DEFINITION?

When a chapter announces that its contents will be devoted to exploring "training for integration in multicentric human systems thinking," some furrowed brows and quizzical expressions can well be expected. Whatever it is that is being referred to in this grouping of words does not conjure up everyday images. And the reader cannot be sure if what he or she conjures up matches anything the author might have in mind.

Let me see, then, if I can clarify ideas and images by presenting some definitions and descriptions to bring us to a more common understanding at the beginning.

From Ground Zero

What are systems? Dictionary definitions for systems cluster around familiar concepts, like "an assemblage or combination of things or parts, forming a complex or unitary whole . . . any assembly or set of correlated members . . . an ordered and comprehensive assemblage'' (Random House, 1967). These definitions do not inform us greatly, nor do they bring us to any advanced level of thinking. One might well ask, then, ''Do we mean to train people to think about assemblages of parts?'' The answer, of course, is, ''No.''

However, if we ask ''What are living systems?'' of which human systems are one form, we are in a different metaphor, for which we find not a dictionary definition of several succinct phrases, but volumes. The most recent one on this subject by psychiatrist James G. Miller, *Living Systems* (1978), is a not inconsiderable 1051 pages of micro-definitions.

Briefly, living systems were defined by Ludwig von Bertalanffy, the original conceptualizer in this arena, as ''*a complex of components in dynamic interaction*'' (1967, 1968). The key words here are ''dynamic interaction,'' meaning that active components *inform, impact on,* or *exchange with each other.* That has quite a different feeling to it than ''an assemblage which forms a whole.'' Implicit in this too brief definition of living systems is a suggestion of reciprocity of impact. And that begins to hint of something even more interesting.

The umbrella that these formulations group under was called by von Bertalanffy, a biologist, *general systems theory,* and later by Miller, *general systems behavior theory.* Both relate to living systems. Miller (1971b) is particularly concerned with the behavior of each of the seven levels of living systems, which he differentiates in hierarchical ordering: cell, organ, organism, group, organization, society, supranational system.

Ideas are getting a little more complex now. Here we have at least seven levels of system, all containing component parts which impact on, inform, or exchange with each other. Before referring back to training, let us examine what some of these concepts are and mean.

Miller, elaborating some of von Bertalanffy's original premises, expands this definition in describing living systems as:

- Existing in time space;
- Made of matter and energy;
- Exchanging matter and energy;
- Organized by information; and
- Exchanging information (1971b).

This implies that living systems are growing, evolving, changing over time, eventually dying. They are *open systems*—exchanging energy, matter, and information. That *exchange* of energy, matter, and information is the dynamic interaction of component parts. And importantly, such systems are susceptible to *change over time*.

It is this type of change over time that differentiates living from non-living systems: living systems contain the capacity for the self-organization of progressive differentiations. They co-evolve. In other words, there are mechanisms which trigger, receive, and organize new information (messages) in living systems, which cause them to change form, stages, and processes in some recognizable progressions in what we call a "life-cycle."

Information here means: biological messages, such as those carried by DNA; physiological messages, such as nerve impulses; verbal and paraverbal messages or data imparted by human beings to one another.

Open systems, according to von Bertalanffy, also contain the capacity for self-generated activity. Again, that could mean DNA in action or someone's "aha!" or new idea.

In comparing the levels of systems from organ to human organism, or evolutionarily, from animals to human beings, man and mankind are markedly differentiated from all other living systems by von Bertalanffy. This differentiation is based on the human capacity for symbolic activity—the ability to create symbols—to imagine, hear or feel "something" and represent it in a mode that is not the thing itself. Ideas, images, words stand for and are symbolic representations of, yet are not experiences or things. And human beings manifest that amazing capacity to create meaning, to create and transmit connections about the self and world, to one another through those symbols.

If one thinks about thinking, one becomes aware and conscious, or knowing, of one's own symbolic activity. What we are doing right now—my writing and your reading—is based on this capacity for symbolic activity. Von Bertalanffy is passionately adamant, particularly in his *Robots, Men and Minds, Psychology in the Modern World* (1967), that this capacity which distinguishes human beings from other life forms and systems, this capacity which *is* the stuff of being human, not be reduced by human beings to seeing themselves, or others like themselves, as robotic. He appeals to man, who can create ideas, not to create the idea that man is a machine and dispensable.

Miller, cooler and analytic in style, states that human beings contain the capacity for symbolization, including the ability to create conceptual relationships of meaning, which he calls "conceptual systems" (1971a; 1978). Man thus has the ability to "think" and to create symbols to represent that thinking, imagining, sensing, hearing, feeling. He also has the capacity to create those symbols outside himself—to string symbols of letters, words, hieroglyphics, metaphors, images, together in interrelated patterns creating written or spoken meanings.

Miller further differentiates conceptual systems from living systems. Living systems are concrete, existing in time-space, made of and exchanging matter, energy, and information, whereas conceptual systems exist in the "minds" of human beings and nowhere else, and are composed of information and ideas, also symbolic.

Now we are speaking of sets of ideas *about* living systems, and of human beings as the creators, retainers, and users of these sets of ideas. This gets more intriguing.

Von Bertalanffy also drew upon his extensive background in biology and the physical sciences and proposed that, almost without exception, the same structures and processes (relationships) are manifest at each system level, from cell to universe, in some isomorphic (similar) form, and involve energy, matter, and information exchange (1967, 1968).

In other words, the same types of processes could be found operating in some analogic or corresponding form in a society-at-large as in a small group or cell. This is where living systems definitions and conceptual systems begin to be intertwined. In order to translate the isomorphic or analogic forms at different levels of living systems, one has to be able to "see" and recognize configurations or patterns of relationships. One has to be able to look at form, derive function, and make the active perceptual leap which compares and connects.

How does one begin to look for and to recognize these patterns, these analogues? "Analogue" refers to associative and comparative images, patterns, and metaphors. Even if one does find analogues, how does one make sense of them and utilize those conceptions, given that a cell is not a person and a person is not a society? These are the types of generic questions that are addressed in our training for integration in human systems thinking. Now let us continue.

At every system level, according to von Bertalanffy, there is "immanent activity" (1967), which means thoughts and processes indwelling (Polanyi, 1958), or inherent within the organism, having no effect outside of it. One can solve an entire problem entirely within one's mind, without any external representation of that activity. Additionally, activities can start inside an organism which are not necessarily in response to an outside event. For instance, one's heart has its own idiosyncratic beat and rhythm. One can think about a frightening dream and increase one's heartbeat, devoid of any immediate "outside" stimulus. This "immanent activity" forms the basis of the "functional autonomy" (Laszlo, 1972a) of each organism at each system level, and is at the root of creativity, play, exploration, and fedforward ideas and images. The "decider" in each person is a functionally autonomous entity.

That raises some more questions. How, then, can one put together "dynamic interaction," which implies reciprocal impacting, and "functional autonomy," which implies acting alone? These are the wave/particle questions of the life sciences, the separate/connected questions that apply to all levels of living entities.

Von Bertalanffy expands on these issues when he states that *organisms are directed by internal phenomena, though they are influenced, affected, and impacted upon by external forces. Context is always implied.* For example, he states, "the developing embryo is not directed by outside forces" (1967). Yet we know that poor nutrition or measles can affect its development.

One's racing heart and one's sense of self-protection are directed from inside, yet can be influenced from outside: Another person's startling entry into the room can evoke a loud scream and self-protective behavior—or not, depending on each individual's tolerance for abrupt behavior. In addition, the same scream response could be evoked by a nonhuman stimulus from the ecosystem, such as by an abruptly and loudly slammed door. Thus, each system is conceptualized as functioning autonomously within a level that can be influenced by sub- and suprasystems, or by internal and external contexts or events in an ecological fashion.

And every living system, though open, has equilibrating processes, which tend to keep it in balance, as it evolves from germination through death and disintegration. Such balance is maintained by feedback, feedthrough and feedforward processes at each level of system, which become pattern influences. Without the self-regulating processes of a living system, it would soon not *be* a well functioning system.

For instance, all the systems in the human body are in a delicate "checks and balances" relationship. Too much hormone from the pituitary gland and one grows to gianthood. Too little and one does not grow enough to be normal size and is called a dwarf. Without certain other hormones, food cannot be digested. These types of checks and balances are said to be isomorphically represented at every level of living systems.

Thus, *constant evolving change or morphogenesis and self-regulating processes create the dynamic homeostatic balance, the earmark of open, co-evolving living systems.*

Like Russian nesting dolls, each system level is conceptualized also as existing simultaneously and as subsumed within successive levels of system, in hierarchical order. Unlike the wooden, nested dolls, however, each level of living system is but a "hypothetical 'whole'" (Grinker, 1967)—a *convenient metaphor*, for each level of a living system is at the same time linked to, part of, and formative of the next "larger" or higher level of a living system. After all, individuals in families are also members of classrooms, neighborhoods, businesses and the society. And each living system always exists in context (time-space) with other living systems at the same level as well as those of supra- and sublevels, and with non-living systems. The totality is often referred to as the ecosystem (Auerswald, 1969).

Larger living system units are conceptualized as functioning differently together than each of their parts separately. For example, lung cells separately cannot create a sac nor perform the expansion/contraction function of breathing. A person acts differently by him/herself than when with other people, especially family members. Which "units" we draw a boundary around, declaring them "system," is often arbitrary, an agreed-upon convention. Boundaries, like cell membranes or that metaphorical boundary around a family, are implied at each level.

These, then, are some of the broader descriptions, some of the agreed-upon conventions (though scarcely all!) of living systems. Yet as we stop and think about these statements, we realize that they are conceptualizations, ideas, theories, metaphors, constructs, hypotheses, conventions—whatever symbolic word we choose to assign here—for ordering our understanding of the world we inhabit and observe. The human mind strives to create order (organize and be organized by information), weaving data into ideas and theories. Theories are mind-made.

These theories (ideas, constructs) form a conceptual system, an epistemology (Bateson, 1968), a formal way of seeing the world and everything in it, a world view, a formal and public organization of knowledge.

We now have a conceptual system of ideas about living systems. However, a symbolic conceptual system is not the thing itself. As Bateson attributes Korzybski as saying (Ruesch and Bateson, 1968), "the map is not the territory!" A conceptual system *about* a human being is not the same *as* a human being, nor is it the same as the experience of *being* a human being.

We are now talking about ways of thinking, about a particular way of conceptualizing the world, called human systems thinking, and about people who think in this particular way, called systems thinkers. We are also talking about the way human beings in this world think, talk and write about, and experience themselves and others as functionally autonomous and dynamically interconnected with others.

WHAT IS SYSTEMS THINKING?
AND WHAT DOES ONE NEED TO DO IT?

Unlike "systems" there is no dictionary definition of "systems thinking," nor is there the equivalent of Miller's work. Here we shall have to construct a definition that will serve as the backdrop and reference point for our image of the meanings, as they relate to the way of training we are describing. Thus, I will explore a range of generic definitions and models and attempt to delineate the ones BFI seems to have evolved.

Systems thinking, as an internal mode of "seeing" ordered patterns of relationship, processes, and interconnectedness in and between objects, phenomena, and people, has perhaps existed forever in the minds of various disparate individuals. As a particular way of looking at the world that when extended becomes a shared total world view of a dynamically interacting model of the universe, it is more recent. And the body of conceptualizations about living systems has just begun to be put together since World War II.

Thomas Kuhn (1962), in discussing the history of science and scientific "revolutions," refers to the paradigm or framework shifts, which have occurred when those in the scientific tradition asked new questions and unearthed new data, or dislodged old data and juxtaposed them in new combinations. What resulted from these processes were new images, new patterns woven into new ways of looking at and understanding the world. The shift in ways of looking at the world to systems thinking with ecological models (although not named such by Kuhn) is the most recent of those *paradigm shifts.*

While Kuhn basically limited his exploration to natural sciences, the same paradigm shift was occurring in the human sciences, economics, and other disciplines. For instance, those influenced by Whitehead and Russell's *Principia Mathematica* (1910–13) and the Theory of Logical Types, such as Bateson (1972), have postulated conceptual systems of hierarchical levels of messages, logic, meanings. Systems theorists in other human sciences, such as Piaget, Loevinger, Kohlberg, Perry, Alschuler, and Erikson, emphasize and highlight the developmental progression toward higher levels of organization and differentiation in people, from birth to death. In such stage theories, each progression is seen as irreversible, in a fixed hierarchical ordering, with each new level or stage incorporating the preceding ones.

These are ways of ordering our understanding. Not everybody, however, is born thinking systems—conceptual or otherwise. Nor do all people necessarily automatically "grow into" or learn to think this way over time.

Variables in Systems Thinking

There are many people today who would label themselves "system thinkers," yet who have widely different conceptions of what that encompasses or implies. If we apply a Miller-like microscope to the range of variation in systems thinking, we would find that what is being talked about breaks down into several variables:

1) Different aspects of systems themselves
2) Different models of systems
   a) Living and non-living
   b) Conceptual and operational
3) Differences in location of the speaker when describing a living system
4) Differences in agreement as to what are considered data and their location
5) Differences in the private world views of different observers-speakers

Let us take a closer look at these variables.

1) *Different aspects of systems.* This variable can refer to highlighting or focusing on different phenomena within a living human system. One person could be concentrating on sequential or hierarchical ordering, i.e., who is in charge, when; another could be focused on similar structure of different systems levels, called isomorphisms, i.e., the father's relationship to the mother is the same as the brother's relationship to the sister; and a third on processes between members, i.e., communication between members is unclear and fuzzy. Like figure-ground arrangements, each person could be seen as ignoring the other's area of focus, though all are phenomena of fitting within living human systems.

In any living system, and particularly any human system, there are so many phenomena going on at one time that the human mind can neither focus on nor grasp them simultaneously. Choices of focus must be made for any semblance of ordered understanding to take place. These choices are based upon personal aesthetic preferences (Kuhn, 1962) and theoretic leanings. While preferences then cause us to narrow the focus, all other phenomena continue to occur, focused upon or not. Different models of human systems focus upon different aspects of the human condition and ways of being organized, productive, healthy, separate, and connected as human beings go about ordinary daily life. All models are useful, all are interesting, none are complete.

2a) *Different models of systems, living and non-living.* This is somewhat more complex. A mechanical engineer can quite accurately describe himself as a systems thinker. A computer programmer could do the same, as could a physicist, biologist, or family therapist. The first differentiation that would need to be made would be whether living or non-living models were being talked about.

Even with agreement on living systems as the overall model, within the family systems arena, there are variations of models which are often confused. The two main such models are the *living systems* model, already discussed and the *cybernetic* systems model. Let me say a little more about this second one. In the arena of human services, and particularly family therapy, there has been confusion between definitions and operational models, between understanding human beings in context and implementing change.

In *cybernetic theory* as originally expounded by Norbert Wiener (1948), the basic concepts are feedback, information, and control. According to von Bertalanffy (1967, 1968), cybernetic systems are essentially closed systems of information exchange, whose feedback loops render them self-regulating and circular, such as in thermostats in both living and non-living systems. A thermostat is set for a particular temperature. When the heat goes down, the thermostat registers that information and clicks on the heater. It keeps it on until the appropriate temperature is reached, and maintains it at that level. Such signaling feedback loops regulate the temperature of the system.

Von Bertalanffy found the cybernetic model applicable to a wide range of biological regulations, subsumed under the term of homeostasis (1967). Homeostatic means, like the thermostat, self-regulating and circular and staying within the same range, yet subject to a variety of influences. The same can be said for interpersonal transactions in any system that tend to stay within a known range.

However, this cybernetic model was felt by von Bertalanffy to be incomplete in describing or representing all the phenomena evidenced in living systems. As we mentioned before, general systems theory delineates a living system as open, in which there is the dynamic interaction of many variables, with certain patterns of relationships, susceptible to change over time. Living systems co-evolve, influencing each other. A thermostat, to stay with that type of cybernetic system, does not meet these requirements. For instance, it does not change over time, evolving in form or process. It does not co-evolve with any other system or entity.

In addition, other variables of living, open systems include the capacity of self-generated activity (the ideas that pop into your head), the self-organization of progressive differentiations (DNA "programs"), and the evolutionary capacity for developmental growth and for higher levels of organization (we all grow up and change over time, whether we want to or not, and as we grow our capacities increase). The original cybernetic theory of systems, upon which several versions of family systems therapy were based, did not allow for these phenomena. Rather, cybernetic descriptions of living systems focused on these aspects of information and feedback wherein each member's contribution acts as a control upon the others, no new information is generated, and the system seems closed, automatic, and unchanging.

For instance, certain "automatic" types of information exchange are conversations likened to circular cybernetic system patterns. Consider the following two dialogues, each at a very simple level of depth and complexity: "Hello, how are you?" "Fine, how are you?" and "What's new?" "Nothing much, what's new with you?" "Not much, really." "Well, it's good to see you and catch up with you." Such a sequence is conducted automatically, without thought, each comment cuing the next from beginning to end.

A slightly more complicated example, implying repetition over historical time, might be:

Son: Dad, let me tell you . . .
Father: You don't have to tell me anything. I know all about it.
Son: But Dad, I didn't tell you . . .
Father: There's nothing you can tell me. I know what you're going to say!
Son: But Dad, I didn't say anything yet . . .
Father: You don't have to. I know you. Now *you* listen to me!

These are simple examples of behavioral patterns and conversations which tend to stay the same, which, like tape-recorded announcements, are automatic, wherein no new information is generated or exchanged. In addition, a fixed level of relating is indicated.

While the focus on cybernetic aspects of systems helps us make sense of the impact of such patterned sequences, it is not sufficient to explore or explain the whole.

General systems theory then subsumes and includes cybernetic theory as belonging within and descriptive of important aspects of living systems, having to do with information exchange and regulation, but does not see cybernetic theory as a complete or inclusive theory of human behavior.

2b) *Different Models of System: Conceptual and Operational.* The cybernetic model indeed influenced some early family therapists and researchers (Bateson, 1972; Haley, 1971; Jackson, 1957; Watzlawick et al., 1967; Watzlawick and Weakland, 1977) in their original operational models of family interaction and family therapy. Their theories of family and of therapy do not consider the interlocking multigenerational and contextual levels of living systems. The individual person is not focused upon as a functionally autonomous person at the same time he/she is an interactive member of a larger level of system, i.e., a family. The emphasis in cybernetic theory of human behavior centers around systemic information, power, control, and feedback mechanisms. Under information would also come Bateson's (1972) analysis of communication by levels of logical type. There is little attention paid to individual developmental processes, the impact of the context and events in one's life on the timeless mind, or individual attributes such as differences in information-processing styles and the issues of subsequent fit between members.

Let us look more closely at how conceptual and operational models fit together.

While a theorist's view of a human being in and as a living system may belong under the general systems theory umbrella, his/her theory of implementing change as a therapist may purposefully narrow the range of that focus. He/she may find a narrower focus more useful and effective in implementing change in a system. This latter, perhaps narrower view is called an operational model, while the full conceptual model may or may not be wider. However, understanding systems fully and implementing change in therapy are different cups of tea.

THE BFI FRAMEWORK

At the Boston Family Institute, our preference is for the fuller general systems theory model as both the conceptual and operational model, for both teaching systems thinking and for systems therapy, and perhaps for life itself. We feel there is a reflexive coherency in such an approach. When we think and work with such a model, no aspects of being human need be left out—neither the influence and impact of larger societal contexts nor the genes and biology of individuals who comprise families. It allows our approach to be an anthropological one, in which different clusterings of systemic phenomena emerge as being most relevant within different systems. We are free to inquire about all.

As therapists or human system facilitators, our range of options is far greater when all aspects of life and of persons are available to be connected in a coherent manner. For us, the cybernetic model is exceedingly useful, but incomplete.

Our framework includes the awareness that human beings are developmentally shaped and influenced by the tumbling processes of their life events, in the world at large as well as in microcosm. Some of the events by which we are influenced and which *we* influence are our other family members! People learn to learn patterns by the ways in which the information of their lives is communicated in larger contexts, family contexts, as well as by the personal and idiosyncratic meanings each brings to the same information. As developing and open living systems, one makes meanings out of the totality of the context one lives within, given one's developmental stage and style in fit or relationship to others in one's context. Our framework gives weight to the capacity for exploration, self-generated activity, play, and creativity that is fundamental to our human condition. We move towards drawing forth those aspects in people that allow them to generate solutions to their own issues.

Lastly, our preference for a wider training and operational model is set in a historical context. The models of therapy and change techniques derived from cybernetic theory were developed in the context of viewing schizophrenic families (see Chapter I). Cybernetic models seemed useful and effective since the fixedness of patterns in psychotic and/or schizophrenic families seemed mechanical. However, methodologies derived to work with these families with members so far from normal are rarely the methodologies of choice for working with all types of families and other human systems with widely varying issues and levels of inner and outer competence. Our bias is for a wider model, offering us a range of generic ways in which to approach and understand families, groups, institutions, and cultures. Individuals and families often need to become aware that they did not create themselves. They seek a sense of coherence of their past learning-to-learn their inner world of experienced meanings and their present arrangements, called systems.

A fuller general systems model allows us to be curious about and to work with all systems interfaces—between family members, family and community, agencies within the community, business institutions, and so on. It is also our strong belief that the tools for change must be put into the hands of the people needing them most, which does not follow naturally from the way cybernetic theory has been utilized in family therapy. Information about people belongs and needs to remain in their hands. A full discussion of these issues for family systems therapy could well be the subject of another book and is beyond the scope of this work. However, we will discuss further certain aspects of our bias and preference for the fuller general systems model in Chapter V, wherein our concern with values is raised.

Let us continue now to look at the types of variables that play into the *concept* of systems and systems therapy—words that are used by so many with different meanings and images.

3) *Differences in the location of the speaker or reporter when describing a living system.* This variable relates to the artificial or convenient boundaries of inclusion or exclusion around the components to be labeled system, as determined by the speaker/observer. This then locates the speaker's position: the location of the "I" who is speaking.

The differences mentioned in 4) and 5), i.e., *differences in agreement as to what are considered data and their location,* and the *differences in private world views,* will be included here in our discussion and in our diagrams, since these variables are interrelated.

Human systems thinking, for some people, refers to that ability to be a sys-

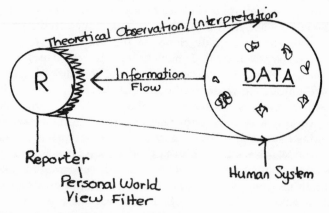

1) Location of reporter: outside, fixed distance
2) Movement of reporter: none, or in fixed orbit
3) Theoretical world views: stated/not stated
   Personal world view: not explored, not stated
4) Information flow: one way, to reporter
5) Information source: observed system, noted by observer/interpreter
6) Interactional impact: none usually stated
7) Control of interpretation: observer/reporter

Figure 1. The Outside Observer

tems describer of other people as if that group were a kind of "outside" event or phenomena. In this model (see Figure 1) the human system, being observed, be it an individual or a family or classroom, is seen as if the observer were a fly on the wall. Or else the group is seen as on the other side of some impermeable boundary, at a fixed distance, without the observees being aware that they are being observed. What is often presented, then, by the observer is described as pure, objective data, from "out there." There is no mention of data emanating from inside the observer, no "I" position of reference.

Usually, the pronouns used are third person singular and plural. The observed have no input on which data have particular meaning to them. The epistemics (MacLean, 1975) or personal world views, biases, and reactions of the observer are not taken into account as lending weight to the meaning of what is observed.

Thus, in this view of systems thinking, there is an ability on the part of the describer to note the phenomenological interconnectedness and interrelationships, as if he/she, the observer/describer, were not in or part of the process or system, and as if he/she had no preferred theory or idiosyncratic way of "seeing." This model treats the human observer *as if* that observer were an invisible recording computer, with data falling onto a *tabula rasa,* like sounds on a magnetic tape.

As the Heisenberg Principle states, the presence of the observer already changes the "experiment"—not necessarily because people suspect themselves of being described and therefore are influenced, but because the observer/describer is not a *tabula rasa,* but brings his internalized context, his entire world view with him, which organizes and gives meaning to the data. Each observer brings to his/her experiment (experience) not only that conceptualized world view (a theory-as-espoused), but also a private, epistemic, idiosyncratic world view, built out of the experiential fabric of one's life, one's theory-in-use (see Argyris and Schon, 1974). Thus the same data can be interpreted differently even by people within the same general theory.

> Though values are widely shared by scientists and though commitment to them is both deep and constitutive of science, the application of values is sometimes considerably affected by the features of individual personality and biography that differentiate members of the group (Kuhn, 1962, p. 185).

The second model of human systems thinking (see Figure 2) is one in which the observer announces his/her position as capable of moving from outside the external boundary of the larger system, into the system as one of its components, and moving outside again, so as to impact on it.

This model is not an unusual one in many forms of consultation and therapy, including some types of family therapy. In this view, there is recognition of and description of the actions of the reporter only insofar as he/she notes their impact on the observed human system as data, according to the held theoretical world view. A private, idiosyncratic-learned-to-learn world view may have been utilized, but is not stated in its relationship to weighting and interpreting data of the observed system.

A third model of systems thinking is one in which the range of location of the reporter can also vary from any position and distance outside the system to any position inside, in which the source of data is both those externally observed and described as well as internally evoked from the reporter him/herself (see Figure 3).

And, of course, there are different combinations of the same variables. This last model is the one maintained and taught at the Boston Family Institute, and is the image referred to in this work when I speak of "human systems thinking." It is a holistic, and holographic model, allowing the widest range of exploration and options.

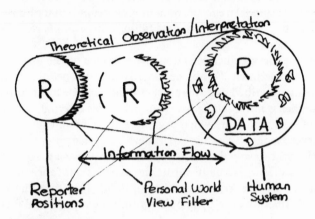

1) Location of reporter: inside—outside
2) Movement of reporter: variable
3) Theoretical world view: stated
   Personal world view: not necessarily explored or stated
4) Information flow: both ways
5) Information source: observed systems—noted by observer
6) Interactional impact: reporter on system noted by observer/interpreter
7) Control of interpretation: reporter/observer

Figure 2. The Inside/Outside Observer

The same "universe" has been here all along. We understand it differently and interact with it differently than did the cave man. Thus, both the vantage point and the personal view of each observer within a larger world view, plus the location and interpretation of data, change the description and meanings of the human systems in question.

For this author, then, the characteristics or definition of integration in multicentric human systems thinking begins to emerge as those described by Figure 3:

a) An innate or learned ability to see and to conceptualize aspects of behavior (thinking, imaging, sensing, feeling, talking, acting) between human beings as being functionally autonomous *and* in dynamic interaction, in context and over time;

b) The ability to locate and conceptualize units, as interfacing with other units, in differing contexts and levels, never forgetting that all are present simultaneously, though constantly, slowly, and progressively co-evolving and changing;

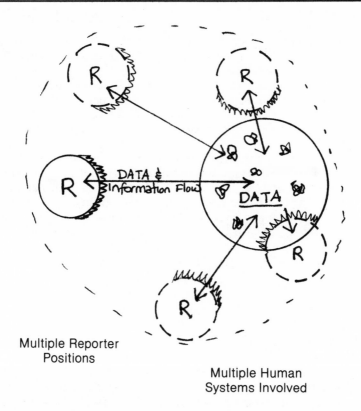

Multiple Reporter
Positions

Multiple Human
Systems Involved

1) Location of reporter: all positions/distance possible
2) Movement of reporter: variable
3) Theoretical world view: stated
   Personal world view: explored and stated
4) Information flow: both directions
5) Information source: reporter, observed systems, varying interfaces,
   their self-report
6) Interactional impact: all directions, shared
7) Control of interpretation: consensual

Figure 3. The Outside and Inside Observer

c) The ability to conceptualize oneself as an active and reactive part of the systems one is in and describing;

d) The ability to conceptualize those actions, reactions and interactions as data;

e) The ability to recognize, depict, and describe one's idiosyncratic or epistemic world view (MacLean, 1975), as well as one's formal frameworks, or epistemology;

f) The ability to locate and conceptualize and describe oneself in a wide variety of positions, from within different parts of the context and larger systems, to distant points and meta levels; the ability to move from egocentricity to multicentricity and back, and to know which is which;

g) The ability to know that "the map is not the territory" and to realize that *it is the human mind that conceptualizes patterns.* The *map* is in one's head and the people aren't. Maps are conceptual and ephemeral. People are concrete and real, experiencing physical and psychological joy and pain in their search for survival and meaning in worlds they never made.

The complex work and goal of training at the Boston Family Institute since 1969 seem to have been to develop and enhance these capacities in trainees en route to their becoming sensitive, caring, differentiated and skilled assessors and facilitators of change in human systems.

Exercise: Matching Images and Definitions

At this point, I invite you to look at your brainstormed list of thoughts and images of integration in multicentric human systems thinking. Is there any matching between what you wrote and what I wrote? What new thoughts do you have now? What new questions do you have? What new connections have you made? That is, what new sentences, ideas have you generated for yourself? You might want to jot those down now.

Beliefs and Values, Ethics and Training | V

Exercise: Who Owns the Information?

If we were engaged in the kind of workshop or professional training experience that I have grown to trust and prefer, I would ask you to pause at this moment and to imagine yourself talking to someone about your personal life. Consider what kind of person you would choose. Whom would you trust? Even jot down thoughts about what would enable you to trust. How would you want him/her to handle the information you impart? Who owns that information?

INFORMATION AND IDEAS

When I was in high school in the 1940s, a self-proclaimed "genius" student continually interrupted all eager, earnest, and intense budding philosophical discussions in our groups about education and life with, "Well, answer this one: Who's supposed to decide who will teach whom and about what?"

It was and is a niggling question. I wrestled with it then, and I wrestle with it still—for whoever shapes and dispenses information, ideas, and frameworks helps shape the microcosms and the macrocosm of the contexts we inhabit.

The control and ownership of information are perhaps the biggest political and economic issue in this 20th century world. Information is a powerful commodity. Nations rise and fall based on who owns, dispenses, and controls information.

The coin of the realm in therapy, teaching, training, counseling, and medicine is information. Who owns it, interprets it, dispenses it, uses it, controls it—indeed, even labels what is information and what is not—controls how we live our lives and perceive ourselves and others. Training (in some form of psychological thinking and skills), therapy, and teaching are mind shapers,

71

fitting data and information into existing conceptual systems and/or creating revised or new conceptual systems.

Information and ideas are not exactly the same. Information is what is exchanged between people or between systems units or what is perceived by people in relation to nonhuman things, such as books, television, and objects, or nonhuman creatures. Information comprises the bits of which ideas and images are made. Information is always *now* and *current*. Information is present tense. Ideas are many informational bits strung together and are the templates which shape our understanding of information. When someone talks to a therapist, that is happening now. It is current information, data without value and meaning unless and until it is shaped by the ideas, theories, images, or metaphors which both client and therapist bring to it. The power of the therapist as "expert" to shape the information that clients bring is enormous.

IDEAS IN THE MARKETPLACE

Ideas and the information which "feeds" them play a definitive role in all fields—in politics, economics, education, training and more. Ideas win men's minds and influence their political and economic behavior. Conversely, political and economic behavior impacts on the world of ideas and often controls their destiny.

What survives in the history of ideas, whether in the field of politics or psychology, does not inherently embody "the truth," nor do newness and originality automatically capture that ephemeral prize. Rather, ideas, the product of human minds, exist in human contexts and can serve or battle within those contexts. The broader social, economic, political, spiritual contexts and processes existing at any particular time harbor and give life to, or shun and let die, many ideas. Some last long after their true usefulness, as a form of symbolic ritual. Others die too young, before they are fully formed.

Many an innovative and promising educational idea shaped into programs has died for a lack of continued funding when political views or economic priorities have shifted. Anyone who worked with many of the innovative programs in the 1960s and early 1970s in this country knows the experiences of half-done experiments, halted for lack of a continued sense of priority and, therefore, funds.

We can conceptualize an open "figure 8" feedforward/feedthrough/feedback impact loop—a kind of continuing mobius strip of ideas and events (Figure 1). They co-evolve and shape each other. This impact loop, however, is not closed, linear, nor even unidirectional. Contextual forces create the nutrient in which ideas congeal and grow, in which they stabilize, mill and

Figure 1

mold each other into new possibilities, evolving, ebbing, if for no other reason than that people who have ideas eventually die and those who follow do not value them so highly. Or conversely, new ideas, as well as music and painting styles, ignored during the lifetime of their creators, capture the imagination of the next generation, who work with and develop them, creating forms and derivative processes of which the originators scarcely dreamed. Ideas thus do not exist in a vacuum. They are intimately connected to people.

However, the more information that is available, and the greater the difference in the variety of information available, the more there is challenge to ongoing ideas and ways of believing. Old traditional ideas are shaken as new and different information begins to generate new questions which the old ideas did not answer. And new questions, once raised, create a search for answers. Countries (like families) that do not want to unsettle the status quo, such as China and South Africa, do not let new or "outside" information in. Other cultures (and families in them) that have been isolated from the ongoing information and technology of the rest of the world have continued their organic way of life unchanged for centuries. "Underdeveloped country" means less technological information, know-how, and productivity. Yet the introduction of such information changes the way of living, thinking, believing.

The idea behind this impact loop or continuing mobius strip is a key idea in the concept of open systems which are interconnected and evolving. It underlies the belief in, not progress, but coherence, fit, and change over time, with new information exchanged across system boundaries. It is a key concept, then, that ways of looking at the world, as well as epistemologies for training, teaching, or therapy, are man-made, change over time with new information, rarely embody the "truth," and are chosen. Epistemologies are useful metaphors for grasping whole images of the universe—for "explaining one's world"—and, as such, are value-laden.

THE INFORMATION IMPLOSION

Perhaps, without the enormous technological expansion over the centuries, we might never have thought this way. However, particularly since World War II, there has been an information implosion* (information bursting into our midst). The multiple inventions and technologies of television, space shots, recordings, and computers, with which we live, are as much the results of expanded information as they in turn are expanders of the amount of information and ideas available at any moment, all part of many impact loops. Each invention in any field, and particularly microtechnological inventions, increases the amount of data generated in the field. Those data become part of interlocking information impact loops.

So intimately are we each a part of these impact loops that today we watch in our living room and perhaps cry for a suffering child in Asia unknown to us, while ignoring our own child beside us. Through television we can experience multiple realities simultaneously (Duhl, B. S. 1976a). We can walk around the moon with the astronauts and look at earth through their eyes, while we wonder what's burning in the kitchen! We can watch a television tape of ourselves interviewing a family at the very same moment and in the same room that we are interviewing them. We have more information about ourselves and each other than ever before in history. It can and does confuse, and what's more, it boggles the mind.

With such an information implosion, and a context so large that it can include the entire universe, at least two paradoxical conditions evolve: 1) We begin to understand the interconnectedness of information, and we create new conceptual models, new metaphors, like systems within systems, or information theory and therapies to make coherent order of our new understandings, and 2) each individual gets smaller and smaller, and less in touch with, less in charge of, *experiencing his information directly,* and less in charge of interpreting it within any self-secure framework of conceptualization.

Each individual, becoming both more informed by the information available and less able to interpret it, then seeks out those who say they can. The greater the variety of information and the greater the areas of specialization, the greater the loss of wholeness, of unified views, and the more dependent individuals become on "experts." Or else, as media proliferates and dispenses more and more information on all conceivable topics, people become self-styled experts (Duhl, B. S., 1976a).

One option or route taken by individuals, families, nations when the

---

*Bruner, in speaking of this implosion, points to the necessity of generic theories, which can organize categories of facts and details (Bruner, 1973b).

amount of information is experienced as overwhelming is to close off, shut down, and refuse to let any more penetrate. While this procedure may be of survival value, it may leave those who have chosen it vulnerable to a lack of other information in the contexts around them, which can and does affect their lives in many ways. In family therapy these shut-down family systems are the ones that are often labeled "closed" systems, into which new information or ideas cannot come. They are, in my view, on a survival course, trying to keep the world familiar and trying to cope with change. Yet, without certain new information or frameworks, there are no new options for more successful coping and living. Patterns stay the same.

TRAINING AND THERAPY AS INFORMATION TRANSMISSION

In the less-than-entire-world context of training programs, therapy, and teaching, one deals in information, framework and idea transmission and interpretation, no matter what the name of the theory of human behavior. All try to make sense, in some way, of the information in people's lives and to interpret it so that it is coherent, so that it fits together.

Some human behavior theories "sell" the interpretation of particular experts. Others offer them and leave interpretations to be picked up or rejected, at will; still others seek to integrate the range of human phenomena under a large and suitable umbrella. All theories, however, were created by human beings, and tend to come out of the total multigenerational context, as well as the life experiences, exposure to ideas, and the personal creativity of their creators.

For example, Freud's theories of female sexuality were quite influenced by the Victorian context in which he lived, and certainly did not derive from information from women themselves, as did Masters and Johnson's later work. Freud's and others' concepts concerning human behavior are heavily value-laden, creating categories into which human experience is then placed by the theory-holder.

When such ideas and theories are engulfed whole, the context from and in which they originated and grew is often forgotten. Yet such values underlying the image-of-human* are carried with all human behavior theories, long after the original context has evolved into one in which those values no longer apply.

---

*Although somewhat awkward, I have deliberately used this phrase, image-of-human, rather than image-of-man, since the latter tends to reinforce the concept of viewing human beings as full-grown and male. In image-of-human, I thus hope to widen our horizon to include all ages, sizes and sexes of people as they develop, grow and change over time, in varying contexts. In that meaning, I am taking the liberty of using human to replace the generic term man, meaning all humankind and capacities of human beings.

Values which are embedded in the prevailing society and image-of-human at the time a particular theory is created get carried forward in time with the theory, while the society and image-of-human meanwhile have changed. Those values impact on the theory carriers themselves and influence how they then interpret others. Freudian theories, as "expert" opinion, still influence the way women and men in America perceive of themselves sexually. Indeed, Freud's larger framework of psychosexual development influences many other derivative theories. Yet the general American attitudes about sex in the 1980s are hardly those of Victorian Europe.

All theories and training programs which teach them evolve in context, exchanging information and ideas, and have a value base. Like children co-evolving with parents, those teaching and those being taught each help shape the contexts which contain them. Trainers and trainees are each shaped by each other, as well as by the prevailing forces in the larger context around them.

Sometimes the prevailing social, political, economic, and spiritual forces in the professional or larger context exert influence towards an orthodoxy, towards "one way" of seeing people, as in modern China. Once a framework is established, newer or diverse ideas are rejected as the contextual forces move towards pigeonholing human beings into a particular current (or not-so-current) view of human being.

Freud's theories did not sweep all of Europe off its feet when first presented. Rather, they took root in American soil before, during, and after World War II. Freud's theories were nurtured here by those Europeans who had studied, worked and argued with Freud in Europe and who, out of the historical events of the thirties, fled to America. Here in America, the land of individualism, the psychoanalytic view of individual man became *the* psychological metaphor. (It is still a, if not the, predominant psychological framework in psychiatry.*)

However, in times when new information travels freely, the larger contextual climate promotes open conflict in the marketplace of ideas, as newer or different images and metaphors of being human push forth. The community mental health movement began to change the image of human in psychiatry, by placing responsibility for individual mental health in the context of the community.** Further ideas challenged the image-of-human during the 1960s

---

*At one point, every university hospital Department of Psychiatry in Boston was headed by a psychoanalyst (see Levin and Michaels, 1961). That framework, that epistemology of psychoanalysis, then affected every patient who came in for any type of psychiatric issue.

**When Erich Lindemann (1944) was a Professor at Massachusetts General Hospital, although an analyst, his prime interest was in community psychiatry. The psychiatric training program and services reflected his interests in the impact of the social context and matrix on individuals and families. Lindemann's famous work with victims of the Coconut Grove fire led to his dis-

when humanistic psychology sought to enhance the individual's power to fulfill, to actualize his/her potentials in the world. Each framework represents different beliefs.

Yet each such framework is man-made. Each way of interpreting data and information becomes, when pushed to its final place, a matter of human belief, reasoning, and values, and therefore a matter of human preferences, choices, and aesthetics.

Even in the natural sciences is this the case:

> There must be a basis, though it need be neither rational or ultimately correct, for faith in the particular candidate (paradigm) chosen. Something must make at least a few scientists feel that the new proposal is on the right track, and sometimes it is only personal and inarticulate aesthetic consideration that can do that (Kuhn, 1962, p. 158).

VALUES AND TRAINING

If beliefs and values are so prevalent in training and teaching, in psychology and the social sciences, why are they so rarely identified, acknowledged, and discussed?

When people are in a social climate or culture in which there is consensual agreement as to beliefs and values, they are never discussed. Indeed, they are not even acknowledged as beliefs and values; rather, "that's the way life is." As with the air we breathe, we notice only unfamiliar and strange odors. The human mind notices only differences (Bruner, 1973, Bateson, 1979). And noticing differences requires, by definition, more than one experience or situation—a comparison, at least an N of 2.

With the information implosion, we have been exposed to myriad experiences and comparisons about values, lifestyles, and therapies, though less about training. Newspapers, magazines, radio, movies, and particularly television broadcasting nationwide 16–20 hours a day have created millions of experts who unfortunately have no cohesive, connecting overview:

> This televised information, however, is random in time and place, without individualized contexts that fit each viewer, and the processes for debriefing, or social sorting, leading to integration, are absent. . . .

---

covery of the importance of contextual events in connection with personal, intrapsychic existential guilt, in the non-healing of burns. When people were "heard" for their grief and guilt over loss of others in the fire, their burns healed. Lindemann thus began to connect the physical and the contextual as psychologically and experientially interrelated. These views influenced the framework for treatment of the population coming to Massachusetts General Hospital's Psychiatric Clinic at that time.

Today's bombardment of disparate bits of information supposedly makes "great thinkers" of us all. But alas, many lack a perspective, especially historical and developmental, in which to fit the information. For most children born since the mid-fifties, anything that is seen is considered possible (Duhl, B. S., 1976a).

In the fields of social service, psychology, and education, value bases about goals have often been taken for granted as being honorable and consensually agreed upon. With the information surge, coupled with the other active forces of equivalent democracy of the 1960s, many formerly untouchable ideological sacred cows were carefully inspected, questioned, and put on tethers rather than allowed to roam free as in the past. Means used towards achieving ends in therapy came under surveillance as the humanistic psychology and humanistic education movements made their impact felt. Underlying values and beliefs were being exposed to daylight.

The specialists to whom people go had shifted markedly from the clergy and physicians to all sorts of mental health and other professionals, as well as paraprofessionals. Since 1949, with the creation of the National Institute of Mental Health, the field of mental health, or rather the field of mental illness, has burgeoned. We have seen the continued development of mind-state changing drugs, such as tranquilizers, and the continuing recognition of the internal world of human beings as relational and governed by a different logic and ordering than mathematical logic.

Psychiatry, coming out of medicine, traditionally took care of crazy people, attempting to "cure" them. Psychology traditionally looked at human phenomena and strove to find relatedness between variables and factors, focusing on wider ranges of human behavior. Both began to come together in this country in the last 40 or so years. However, the values prevalent in Freudian theory were translated into social policy, for instance, in the labeling of actions as sick, neurotic, and criminally insane. The idea of mental rehabilitation prevailed in the world of law and criminal justice, as well as in the world of health.

On an international level, the theory of individual guilt joined that of the Christian-Judaic legal value system in the Nuremberg trials, following World War II. For the first time in recorded history, *individuals* were held accountable after a war as *guilty* of crimes against mankind. Paradoxically, the individual victors who held and presided at the trials were of the very same nation as those who developed and dropped the first atomic and hydrogen bombs on Japan!

The incongruity of our values-in-action and values-as-espoused began to hit closer to home as our technology made this type of information immediately available to all.

Assassinations of national leaders in the 1960s and the Vietnam war and riots of the 1960s and '70s brought challenges also of the ideal standards against which people were being measured. IQ tests as well as psychiatric labels were accused of being used to manipulate and control people (Szasz, 1960). Labels are value-laden. The bunching of people into various types of labeled categories based on minimal testing information led (and is still leading) to questioning these types of procedures. As Kuhn (1962) says, an instrument can only measure what it sets out to measure.

And the idea began to creep in that the national leaders, specialists, and professional label-makers were subject to the same general forces as the rest of society—and just as fallible. It became harder and harder to tell the good guys from the bad. A vice-president and a president resigned when discovered to have committed acts of questionable integrity. The whole of human beings in their human and environmental contexts began to be evaluated. Either everybody has to be considered neurotic or sick, or, as many felt, the full range of variation (Fox, 1967) of ways in which human beings live, develop, cope, love, solve problems, connect, think, disconnect, and die had not been looked at.

Today, people are demanding more and more control of their lives. Paradoxically, in the context of more information and greater specialization, which brings with it greater stress and fragmentation, more and more people are also turning to some sort of psychological aid, to another group of specialists, to help them *gain control* of their lives.

People seek relief from the problems that arise from living in a world in which they are more and more removed from the source of their information and from the results of their endeavors. They seek guidance in finding their way when there are fewer and fewer intergenerational and traditional patterned paths to follow, and where there are multiple expectations of how and who they are supposed to be. In such a situation, more and more people are seeking from specialists and from lay people some sort of interpretation, some coherent framework for understanding, some relief from psychological pain, some form of grounding, guidance, direction, and/or some sort of empowerment in handling their lives, or a mixture thereof in a chaotic world they never made.

The increases in self-help groups and in cults are also ways people have chosen to deal with fragmentation, psychological anomie, the lack of predictable patterns and the complexity of information.

The values underpinning training programs may seem inconsequential in the light of assassinations, wars, bombings and presidential and vice-presidential resignations. However, those previously mentioned events highlight even more pointedly the issues of values, of trust and non-trust in leadership. Trainers, therapists, and educators are a particular kind of leadership, whose "permission" to be effective professionally is based on an assumed trustworthiness and/or ethical behavior. The amount of information available about human life is enormous. Teachers and trainers *choose*, both in and out of awareness, selected types of information and frameworks to pass on.

In describing this situation in training, Michael Rossman wrote in 1975 of the 1960s:

> With the sorts of training now available comes also a subtler cost, which reinforces the same effects. However new their subjects, most involve equally a retraining in the old lessons of relation between teacher and learner, therapist and client. These lessons define again the authority of expertise . . . and ensure that the new knowledge will continue to be created, transmitted and used in contexts of dependency (Rossman, 1979).

An indication that the public, feeling disenfranchised by the expertise of specialists, no longer accepts "expert" opinion or behavior as unquestionable is found in the great rise in number and percentage of malpractice suits in the past decade.* Real specialization has brought with it distance between the expert and the consumer, between the practitioner and the client, where the client is not fully known by the practitioner and feels "acted upon" and "done to" rather than "acted and done with." The struggle for the rights of individuals as patients to have some say in their own behalf continues. Legal suits brought by mental hospital patients against the institution and its psychiatrists *for dispensing drugs or treatment without patients' consent* grow in number. In such cases, the patient/client does not feel known, heard, or cared about by the specialists who administer to him/her.

Therapy, training, counseling programs and education in general are the contexts where future "people interpreters" are offered theories, which help shape how they are to perceive, connect, interpret, and use personal information. Such programs vary in whether there is congruence between values espoused and values in action. Private epistemic world views and the values that go with them, already held by the recipients, are often ignored while a new epistemology, a new way of seeing and interpreting, and the new technology that goes with it are taught. It is as if the new framework and technology are to be welded somehow onto the existing substructure. Yet personal epistemic theories differ widely, as do more formal theories, and have a tendency to shape the particular epistemology with one's personal values, images of life, and human beings.

---

*For the past six to seven years, the American Psychiatric Association's biweekly *Psychiatric News* has reported consistently of the increase in such suits and the prohibitive costs of malpractice insurance.

Certainly, the value bases and processes of Carl Rogers's client-centered (1961) approach to people, psychology and therapy are as different from Freud's psychoanalytic approach as they are from B. F. Skinner's (1953, 1963) behaviorist stimulus-response model. Each theory or approach projects a different image of human being. Each purports to be a model for helping people in psychological distress and each has advocates.

The same can be said for approaches to treatment of people using a "systems" model, the most recent paradigm for viewing mental illness and health. As there are different variations on types of systems (as discussed in Chapter IV), so are there concomitant different variations in images of human beings in each of these systems models and theories. These images, in some cases deduced from the treatment modality, constitute the ballast values and beliefs in each ship of systems theory.

Both the theory as taught, with its view of human beings, and the technology that accompanies it are products of human beings. However, we live our private views. Those private world views of trainers and learners are individually enacted. Each advocate of a theory really takes from it, makes it his/her own, and then enacts his/her own version of it. The only true Freudian was Freud.

Hence there is no training program, no educational program, nor any form of therapy or system intervention in any context without a value base. Each person's or program's theories and practices are replete with implicit and explicit beliefs and values, core images, and ideas of who one is, who others are, could and should be; core images of man/woman/boy/girl and his/her potential or lack thereof, of his/her equivalency or his/her superiority/inferiority.

Beliefs and values imply goals and solutions, often dictating rules for *how* these shall be achieved. Any value base, any philosophical, theoretical or ethical stance of training, teaching, or therapy, is basically a political and economic stance defining relationships. Once enacted, it structures roles, relationships, information flow and control, creating hierarchies or equivalencies, and delineating standards for roles and processes.

Training programs, then, have beliefs and values which are interwoven with and welded to the subject matter itself. They frame images, color information, and shape ideas and people's lives.

With the people-helping industry as large as it is today,* it is difficult for the public as well as trainees to know the differences in modalities. All psy-

---

*A recent publication, entitled *Guide to Psychotherapies,* by Richard Herink (1980) listed some 250 different named varieties of "help" the consumer could explore and/or seek. Again, a consumer would be hard put to know what he/she was "buying."

chotherapies in this country have the eventual goal of helping people to feel better, to function better. Many therapies have the goal of helping people to become more "whole," more integrated and more responsible for self. How each *patient* views him/herself and/or others represents each *patient's* image of man/woman. Some therapists administer drugs to all psychologically distressed patients, which presupposes an image of causality and solutions. Other therapists, however, offer alternative images of human behaviors, of self, of what is possible, and the processes or contacts necessary to help clients achieve alternative images. Yet, whether the client is party to this process in any inclusive and valued manner is an ethical issue basic to all forms of therapy.

At base, then, every training program in psychological counseling or therapy is "selling" some image-of-human kit, complete with instructions on how to help oneself and/or others achieve this image. The kit hopefully also contains the tools needed in the construction process. Sometimes the image-of-human is more covert and ignored than overt, more implicit than explicit, and harder to pin down and acknowledge. If, however, each training program, including ours at BFI, is indeed "selling" an image-of-human kit, descriptions and advertisements are in order!

Exercise: Image-of-Human Kit

> In your role as a giver of help, write an advertisement with a description of the "image-of-human" kit that you are selling.

When we are concentrating on or comprehending others' ideas, our own can easily get pushed so far into the background that they are difficult to retrieve. Rather than seeing this work as that of another expert, to be "bought" wholly, you are invited to actively engage in sorting out some of the same issues for yourself concerning your values, your image-of-human. We have struggled with these issues over the years and continue to struggle with them.

At this moment, let me invite you to write out your own image-of-human kit, playfully, as an advertisement, as a useful way to begin to tease out and make explicit one's implicit assumptions about human nature. And so, before considering the image-of-human derived over these many years at BFI, I heartily suggest that you take a few moments to play with the image-of-human kit that you advocate or feel you sell in your work. As you then read, you may find yourself dialoguing with what is written here, sharpening and developing your own images further.

Exercise: Experiencing Your Information

What thoughts come to mind about the values underlying your current setting and program? About any training program or therapy you experienced? What is the image-of-human kit each sells? Are they congruent and the same for trainers and trainees, therapists and patients?

THE IMAGE-OF-HUMAN AT THE BOSTON FAMILY INSTITUTE

The image-of-human derived from the reflections and dialogues of dozens of people over the years at BFI is a major foundation for the kind of training developed and for what is presented in the rest of this work. This image and the processes congruent with it have been forged out of exchanging ideas, doing, and more exchanging. What is offered here is essentially a formulation, in one place, and at this moment in time, of what has evolved over 14 years, and will continue to evolve. The values in action will perhaps be more fully recognizable in later chapters descriptive of actual seminar processes.

First, as they cojoin our personal world views, there are a number of beliefs and values inherent in general systems theory that emerge as having been important to us and highlighted over the years at the Boston Family Institute. The beliefs and values that relate to our image of human are those that speak to:

- the symbolic capacities of each human being, who brings symbolic and conceptual ordering to the universe;
- the idea that the conceptual ordering humans bring also creates the concept of systems, as well as any other concepts by which we live;
- the idea that the human capacity for symbol formation and use renders humans different from animals, and from robots;
- the idea that each human being is simultaneously affected, involved, and influenced by all levels of living systems—from cell to supranational systems—and by the ecosystem as well;
- the idea that people are not things or concepts;
- the idea that human beings are more than a sum of their different parts;
- the idea that each human is both proactive and reactive, and can be more one than another at different times, in different contexts and conditions;
- the idea that living organisms, humans, are open systems with constant exchange of matter, energy and information, across boundaries, with the physical and living world;

- the idea that living systems at each level from cell to supranational entities, of which individual human beings "compose" one level, have the qualities of developmental growth, differentiation, and increasing organization, in a natural and evolutionary life-cycle;
- the idea that an "organism matures gradually, or in sudden critical periods, makes jump-steps, by means of differentiation of primary and undifferentiated structure-functions" (Grinker, 1967, p. x);
- the idea of equifinality, that there are many ways of getting to the same place, that many different forces and processes will achieve the same results;
- the idea that "organisms search out their goals in a purposeful manner to maintain and regulate life. They are also goal-changing, reaching out beyond need gratification, utility or preservation and thereby become creative and evolving" (Grinker, 1967, p. xi).

There are other personal world views and beliefs that shape our image-of-human that perhaps have nothing to do with general systems theory, but which certainly influence the way in which we train.

We believe that life is sacred, that it is a limited resource for each of us of about 75 years, and that it is to be treated with respect. In addition, individuals are more than the sum of experience, environment and genes. There is something else that defines life, call it spirit or soul or divine spark. We respect its presence and the uniqueness with which it appears in each of us (Duhl, B. S., and Duhl, F. J., 1981).

Individuals come into this world with different types of uniqueness, including different types of "wiring"—that is, with inborn tendencies towards particular styles of information processing. We believe these styles of information processing are shaped, molded, supported and thwarted in their dynamic interaction with human and nonhuman environments. These information processing styles are not the same as stages in cognitive development, yet are basic to how people interpret and make sense of the world (Duhl, B. S., and Duhl, F. J., 1975).

We believe that people look for a match between what is imagined or expected and what exists among members of a human system. Out of that image matching arises the *sense of the type of fit of members with each other*. Conflict comes out of the sense of the difficult fit of differences.

We believe that information important to younger developing individuals and the availability of differentiated, caring, and/or empathic persons with whom to sort one's thoughts and images are key issues in the growing of competent individuals whose self-esteem will be in their own hands. We believe that when there is a *deprivation of information,* as well as a lack of an adequately differentiated or empathic other, momentary issues of vulnerability become patterned as core images of context, of self in context and what to expect in the world (Duhl, B. S., 1976b).

VALUES-IN-ACTION IN TRAINING

We are interested, then, in trainees' closing their gaps of information and in offering them as full access to our thinking as we can. We believe that people have the right to the information which can shape their lives, to question and be in dialogue with others about it. We believe in making the covert overt, the implicit explicit, and in openly examining that which is subsidiary to focal moves and beliefs.

We believe that each trainee needs to be grounded in, centered in, his/her own life story first, as the core of integrity and identity which forms each person's sense of reality and coherence, and from which one's view of the world emanates. Each one needs to experience his/her own information in such a way that each can feel into it and know it for oneself, as well as extrapolate or approximate similar feelings empathically with others.

We believe each one needs to become observer to one's own experience and information in such a way that each can become bystander to it, weaving conceptualizations of a multicentric nature—a key to generic human systems thinking. Multicentricity evolves from the simultaneous acknowledgment of competing realities, which are explored in our training groups. We further believe in trainees' experiencing their paradigm shifts with as much awareness as possible.

As we have inquired into theory-building of pioneers in this field over the years, we have found that constructs about human behavior begin as individual "solutions" to personal questions, issues and puzzles, and then get tested more scientifically.* Yet history, anthropological and sociological studies, as well as ethnic legends and myths, illuminate that human beings have uncountable combinations of ways of being with each other in different cultures and contexts, over historical time. Thus, we believe in each person first tapping into, exploring, and discovering his/her own beginning constructs and theories, derived from his/her own life experience and personal world views. We have found that each person first takes from another's theory of human behavior those aspects that are "safe," that fit one's own epistemic world views. Familiar constructs require no shift in one's own premises. We feel that internal explication of one's epistemic world views and values, as well as

---

*See Anonymous, 1972; Duhl, F. J., *Dialogues: The Person in the Therapist,* Videotape series; MacLean, 1975; Gray, 1981.

explication of one's vulnerabilities and defenses, makes possible more paradigm shifts that are congruent with individual values and life goals.

We believe and aid in the integration of the person, in providing frameworks for a metamap of self-in-context, systems-in-context, and intergenerational systems over time.

We believe in teaching human systems thinking from the inside out, from the person-in-context, out to the eventual task of problem-solving with those in need. In most mental health training, people in and with problem situations define and become the matrix for training and thinking about all human systems. We feel from our experience at Boston State Hospital and elsewhere that the latter not only limits the range and type of systems thinking possible or probable, but also allows competency and self-esteem needs of the trainee to supersede curiosity and creativity too early. In addition, a hierarchical split is often created between images-of-human, and at least two images emerge: us therapists up, you patients down.

We want our trainees to risk with each other and with ourselves, to discover new answers and ways to combine curiosity and search, to mix the new and untried with the proven, yet not to accept the proven automatically. We want them to derive the formulas for themselves, and find the mode, path, and style that best fits each one's talents and style, after exposure to a range of ways of being and seeing.

We support "I wonder if . . . " and "the having of wonderful ideas" (Duckworth, 1972). We train for it. We believe that the symbolic capacity of human beings to generate new sentences is spurred by "I wonder if . . . ," by carrying thoughts to some creative juxtaposition of unlikely bits which transcend past and present experience. Those who carry that question carry within them a way of thinking that is open to unusual combinations, to new information, options, images, and symbol generation. "I wonder if . . . " allows us to spin imaged futures, and then perhaps to move toward those images in a pattern of "feedforward" (Richards, 1968).

"I wonder if . . . " is the key concept in problem-solving and is what many people in trouble do not, for whatever reasons of the moment or longer, have access to. We believe that the support of this process helps to integrate each person and to bring his/her whole person into the room in the body of the therapist/facilitator.

We value a horizontal/equivalency model of relationship, based upon respect for and awareness of differentiations of skills and capabilities among people, in place of a vertical/power model of status positions, externally derived. Over the years, we have learned as much and have been as influenced by our trainees as they have by us, for out of the "I wonder if . . . " of training have come many ideas spurred by trainees' new explorations and input.

We believe, then, in a collaborative, cooperative model, that the manner in which trainees are taught and what they are taught should be immediately relevant to and congruent with who they are and what they will be doing and how they will be expected to do it. Teaching and applications, means and ends, need to be reflexively coherent (Wideman, 1970).

We aim for the congruence of theory-as-espoused with theory-in-action on conceptual metalevels, as well as with specific modalities of intervention. We believe in collaboration with trainees in training, as well as with patients in therapy. Trainees as well as patients need to become empowered in becoming their own problem solvers, with tools to do the job. There will never be enough therapists to go around mopping up after the event in this fractured and fragmented world. If, as Watzlawick, Weakland, and Fisch (1974) state, *the attempted solution is the problem,* then we as a society should put energy not into training more therapists, but into developing each person's personal and family competence with problem-solving skills each chance we get (Duhl, B. S., and Duhl, F. J., 1981).

We believe that therapy is not life, nor is it separate from life. We believe that training in human systems thinking goes far beyond technique, into ways of being, thinking, imaging, relating to oneself, and one's world.

We believe that our approach to training allows each trainee to invent human systems thinking for him/herself, to experience his/her own paradigm shift, and to own and enjoy the process.

We value our trainees and know that we can only directly have influence or impact on those in front of us. We trust that there is a roll-over effect, an impact loop, a relationship between our image-of-human, the ways in which we train, and the ways in which our trainees will work with other people. Since each life is a first-time experience, and since we only find out "after the fact" which ideas, moves, or comments were the "right" ones, and since we can never know our full impact upon another living person or group of persons, we should at least move with caring curiosity, respecting those we train. For who knows, someday we might find ourselves in their hands, needing help. And would we then trust them to help us in a manner congruent with our personal values?

Exercise: The Trainer/Trainee, Helper/Helpee

As a seeker of help, what are the qualities in the persons you go to, or would go to? What image-of-human do they project? In what ways do these qualities match the image-of-human you were "selling" before, as a helper, giver of help? In what ways are they different? In what ways does each set of images inform the others?

SUMMATION

We are aware that the values underlying and intertwined in our approach to training are products of the particular people we are and the particular period in historical and conceptual times in which we live. Some of them seem congruent to a cultural ambience expressed during the 1960s and out of phase with the tighter political, economic, and social context of the 1980s, both in the world-at-large and in the sub-worlds of human systems training, therapy, and education.

Nonetheless, it seems increasingly crucial to us to stress internal integration and innovation in those we train in human systems thinking, lest we not push for the generation of those new sentences and ways of surviving creatively in a world system grown dangerously small, increasingly mechanistic, armed, and constantly changing. Our information implosion, technology, and political structures threaten to eradicate individual voices. We believe we must help each person we work with to find and express his/her differentiated voice, while working and living with others.

Thus, while we will discuss human systems training and its impact on, in, and for arenas far smaller than the entire world, there is present an underlying question: "I wonder if . . . training human systems thinkers in this manner can make a difference over time, in more arenas than therapy?"

> The man who embraces a new paradigm at an early stage must often do so in defiance of the evidence provided by problem-solving. He must, that is, have faith that the new paradigm will succeed with the many large problems that confront it, knowing only that the older paradigm has failed with a few. A decision of that kind can only be made on faith (Kuhn, 1962, p. 158).

At a BFI-sponsored conference in September 1979, Murray Bowen, M.D., was asked by a participant if, after all these years, he still thought his theory of family systems "was worthwhile." Bowen replied, "Well, it's been interesting enough for me to devote *my* life to."

While we will probably never know the answers to our query—"I wonder if this approach can/will make a difference?"—the question itself is interesting and challenging enough to devote our lives to.

The BFI Paradigm: A Framework for Training, Puzzles, and Problem-solving | VI

Exercise

Imagine yourself in front of a new group of trainees or students. You are looking at them. You have your image-of-human kit with you. What will you do with your kit? How will you apply it? To what? By what behaviors or statements will trainees know what is in your kit? By what process? Will you advertise it loudly? Will you leave it hiding in a drawer, with no clue that it is there? Will you display it casually and wait for its discovery? Will you set up a discussion about kits? Will you tack it up on the wall? What do you rely on to get the contents of your kit across? What is your way of knowing your images have been transmitted? Received? Accepted? Rejected? Modified? Incorporated? Integrated? Have you ever discussed this with anyone inside or outside of your own training program? Do you have anyone with whom to discuss it now?

How does any training program know that it is achieving what it sets out to achieve? How does any trainer know he/she is getting across? What are the clues and what are the cues? Do we teach content? Or do we teach people? Or both? If our messages don't get across, what sense do we make of that? Is it their fault? Ours? Both?

I am reminded of speaking some years ago with one of my children's sixth grade math teachers about my child's difficulty with math, asking if there were some ways that he or we might help her understand. He replied, "Madam! I have a curriculum to teach!" Whereupon I countered with, "Oh, I thought you had children to teach." Of course, it is both. Content and the mind of the child have to meet and interact. Education is derived from the Latin word *educare*, to draw forth. The understanding of math needs to be drawn forth from the child.

In training programs, we have adults for whom we have curriculum, or content, to present. And in the human services and educational fields, we usually have some image of an amalgam of content-person-processes we wish to

89

transfer. We usually have an image in which the people we train will emerge from our programs knowing certain ideas and processes and behaving in certain ways which incorporate and demonstrate that knowing.

However, as previously stated, the map is not the territory, and whatever particular content any trainer or program might want people to learn is not the learning process itself. The process must draw forth the learning.

In our program, a human systems epistemology encompasses an exceedingly wide arena of study, into which all human processes can fit. However, it is so large an arena that it cannot be "taught" all at once. Even if we desired to teach only abstract conceptual material relating to human systems, we would still have to make choices about what to teach, to whom, in what manner and when.

A problem-solving framework is needed for how to think about teaching, which is compatible with the values and image of human inherent in the larger epistemology.

Given the value base and image of human which those at BFI found themselves implicitly evolving and increasingly conscious of over the years, there was a search for such a goal-directed problem-solving framework. Early planning and conceptualizations seemed to jump around, from content, to varieties of message transmitting processes, to people, to desired behavioral outcomes. We were looking for a framework which would help us with the organic process we felt ourselves in—and *wanting* to be in.

Training programs are often reified as if they were concrete things. Like relationships, training programs are ephemeral essences, holograms. Training programs are not things or events, but a series of complicated interactions, processes, and events between and among people over time, and between people and things, like books, audio- and videotape. Some training programs are more organic or organismic than others. They seem to flow like rivers, without sharply defined edges, while others are like iceblocks, perhaps composed of the same river water, but carefully stacked with definite shape and form.

Some new training programs get built; others "just happen." Some get planned to death, flowing like yesterday's cement, while others are flung like kites into the airstream, where strong gusts take over and pull towards undefined destinations. And some come out of a mixture of all of the above and more. The key for each seems to be found in how trainers and teachers think about training and teaching and how they implement that thinking in action.

THE NEED FOR A PARADIGM: UNMUDDLING MUDDLES

When the Boston Family Institute program and its parent, the family therapy training program at Boston State Hospital, began with some basic generic questions concerning learning, families, systems, therapy, and change, the basic ways of approaching those questions were through trial and error. There was no map. Since all questions were opened to the trainees as well, many more answers emerged than might have if we had looked for them among faculty and colleagues alone. New findings and inputs continually reshape our thinking about training and human systems, and reshape our program as well as our therapy.

As trainers, we have played with sequential and overlapping arrangements of events, with hunches, hypotheses, and premises about coordinating our foci on the "end" content to be taught, on processes of exploring that content, on the people issues of trainees, in combination with central questions and conceptualizations about how learning and change take place at all levels of living systems.

However, in actuality, when as trainers we started to discuss these multi-level and multi-category questions, some rather peculiar, often humorous, though frustrating discussions tended to ensue! All sorts of good and not so good ideas got jumbled together, as well as levels of endeavor. When one is trying to juggle the multiple and simultaneous realities of content-people-behavior in any message sending/receiving training situation, some framework to unboggle the discussion, if not the mind, is needed. We can perhaps create an image, with our metaphoric and holographic right brain (Ornstein, 1972; Samples, 1976), of those simultaneous processes, yet we need our analytic left brain to linearly tease them apart to be talked about, planned for, acted upon, and written about.

With the exception of the fall semester of 1969, when Sandra Watanabe, together with Fred Duhl, organized notes of curricula planned, there was no *systematic* planning and review procedure until 1973. Although we had been categorizing and reworking our broad ideas and our training process findings in a loosely organized way, and although the author kept notes tracking training procedures since 1971 when she was invited to join the faculty, it was not until 1973 that we eagerly embraced a particular guiding framework for thinking about and planning curriculum and training. This basic paradigm for puzzle/problem, exploration/solving, had been brought into our discussions by faculty member and psychologist, Jeremy Cobb, M.A., from his organizational development work. Like a series of potential designs waiting for a kaleidoscope to organize them, we immediately gravitated toward this framework and adopted it as the organizer around and within which to cluster our information and our planning.

When we began playing with this framework for thinking, we found that we could apply it to organize the different questions we were asking, concerning different levels and arenas of systems in sequential and/or overlapping fashion. Thus, the use of the paradigm facilitated our becoming clearer and more differentiated about our own thinking. It facilitated our teasing apart the multiple levels and aspects of what seemed to be happening at any one time in our training program, as well as any other living system. It allowed us to delineate focal and subsidiary processes (Polanyi, 1958).

This paradigm, outlined below, becomes a more formal goal-directed framework for thoughts stirred by "I wonder if . . . " and "What if?" It becomes the organizer, the strict thinking framework for the loose hunches (Bateson, 1972). We have found it universally applicable to any level of puzzle or problem, from overview to minute details, with a structure for prediction, feedback, and assessment. We use it not only to think through and plan for total programs, and long-range overviews, but to plan for specific exercises, weekly seminar sessions, and workshops. We also use it as a framework for thinking about therapy overviews and specific therapy sessions (Duhl, B. S. and Duhl, F. J., 1981).

THE PARADIGM/FRAMEWORK FOR PUZZLE EXPLORATION AND PROBLEM-SOLVING

Goals: For the entire program, any seminar, or a specific project, therapy session, or intervention. One can include here outcome goals, process goals, and/or content goals.

Propositions, Premises or Implications: The knowledge or educated guesses on which we base our expectation that goals can be achieved. These premises can be systematic and predictive in nature, i.e., if we set x in motion, y can probably be explored. This category allows for the examination of the bases and the bias in our thinking about training procedures.

Faculty Assumptions (i.e., the assumptions of the person[s] using the paradigm at the moment): The attitudes, feelings, and issues that are evoked about selves and/or others, trainees or clients; where we are, where we think they are. Since this is always an element in our planning, we then make it overt. Differing opinions of co-leaders can be openly expressed here. New interpersonal information is revealed and can be checked out.

Exercises: The specific activities and processes by which to achieve goals stated above. Each exercise is meant to provoke and/or evoke information. Each exercise is spelled out with conscious inclusion or omission of step-by-step processes and structures, since each aspect of an exercise will relate to an aspect of goals. Exercises can be didactic, metaphoric, experiential, supervisory, analogic, solo, group, and/or in the form of interpersonal scenarios, written papers, diagrams, tapes, books, projects, etc.

Debriefing and Conceptualizations: That participatory process during which each person moves from being "in" the experience to being "outside" it —where each *reflects on* the activity or process and becomes bystander to it, by talking with others about self-in-the-experience and the information gained. It is both during exercises themselves and during the debriefing process that dialogue between trainees or between trainees and trainers takes place.

These new data from each trainee are then sifted and challenged for generalizations and metaconcepts. At that time new ideas or new additions to known constructs are drawn from individual and combined material and woven into conceptual systems by and in the group.

Evaluation: On various levels, from trainees and trainers, evaluation takes place of the context, of the fit between the goals and the processes in the exercises meant to evoke or highlight content relating to those goals, of the processes enacted themselves, of the way in which the exercise(s) was structured, of the manner in which each exercise was presented and/or carried out. Suggestions for the future often emerge here—how to do something "better" or in a different way.

In addition, in both Debriefing and Evaluation we look for *What else was happening?* In this unpredictable category, where innovation and discovery take place, what else occurred or was discovered that was not anticipated? This question is often the most important one, leading to "gold," by switching the focus to new discoveries, new information, beyond our expectation or awareness, and always "beyond the information given" (Bruner, 1973a).

Assignment: Tasks to be taken on, varying in time frame and type.

Feetnotes. Thoughts to take or not to take seriously, mostly from the trainers.

Back to New Goals: What we learned from all the above translated into the next step.

As one can see, such a framework can be used to plan a family picnic or a presidential election. The categories remain the same; their flexibility is in their ready application at any level of puzzle or problem.

Each week, we plan anew, with curriculum hand-embroidered for each group. The sheet is written up, typed and copied ahead of time, and given to trainees at the end of each seminar.

In actual planning processes, the framework does not delimit discussion. One or one's group can wander and explore quite a bit on and off the topic. However, the framework is always there and available, as a ready, neutral map to focus, locate, organize, and pull together each person's thoughts and discussions during planning, as it then organizes activities later. We found and find it useful for solo thinking as well as for co-leader or group planning.

Using this paradigm then for us was and is not an idle exercise. *It became and still is our tool for reflexive coherence—the measure by which we can check any part of a plan or process against the larger map.* Like a living system, this conceptual system or framework is applicable at any level of activity or planning, including therapy. And like an open living system, the debriefing and evaluation of processes and ideas create a feedforward/feedback/feedthrough/feedforward impact loop, informing us and helping to shape each next event.

The works of Malcolm Knowles, the exponent and titular head of the field of adult education, postdated the inception of the BFI model. He refers to such models, which he supports, as "process models" (1972), which are "andragogical" in nature (1973, 1975).

The growing edge is always folded back into the body of knowledge as a new edge reaches out, like dough being kneaded. Trainers and trainees alike are the kneaders, those who make it happen, those who create and shape the form, and they are the kneaded, the "it," those who have been formed and changed by the process itself.

In that respect, although the overview is basically firm regarding what we want to explore and in what order in our training program, the actual program has never been identical any two years in a row. No two training groups have ever been the same, the trainers themselves keep growing and changing in this process, and new ways of connecting myriad human processes keep evolving. Such a model supports the trainers' aversion to being bored, as they continue to co-evolve as the field at large changes and grows.

Perhaps the greatest prize hidden in this paradigm is that it sets up a framework for thinking about how to create new ways to explore the same "old" timeworn, familiar ideas with new people who do not yet know them. It sets up a framework by which to avoid dullness and *keeps the possibility of learning something new for oneself as trainer continuously open.* In that way, this paradigm, in addition to serving as a tool for reflexive coherence, also acts as an anti-tedium tool. Using it in training keeps one's own education going. And it costs nothing!

Any free tool that can help us generate new sentences, ideas, exercises, so that *we* continue our education and are not bored while helping *them* in their learning process is a very appealing tool. It is worth playing around with for a while. We did play around with it and we got hooked by it. We still are.

Exercise: Trying the Anti-tedium Tools

Think of some idea, some concept you are tired of, or bored with, yet have been trying to get across to trainees, students, your mother, a friend. Using the above paradigm as your anti-tedium tool, think of a novel way to approach this idea.

How you would do it becomes your Exercise. If you should want to try it out, you can ask for comments. In that case, you could experiment with debriefing it, conceptualizing what happened and evaluating its effects, which can lead to, of course, new goals.

AN IN-DEPTH EXPLORATION OF THE PARADIGM

In the remainder of this chapter, in which we will sequentially enlarge, elaborate, and inspect the different categories of the paradigm, we will skip over exercises, since much of the remainder of this book explores and discusses many different types of exercises. Indeed, there has been a sprinkling thus far, intended to stimulate the reader's imagination. Chapters VII–X are specifically devoted to thinking about exercise designs, analogues and metaphor.

There are a couple of phrases I picked up years ago, I believe from Dick Auerswald, which go, "You can't think what you can't think," and "You can't know what you don't yet know." These were heard with great relief by one who had struggled to "find out." I had come from a world in which "You're supposed to know before you know." This last phrase had always meant "You're supposed to know that which somebody else already knows, or has already found out, without your having had the experience, the communications about it, or the context in which to learn it."

Auerswald's phrases also apply to how we think and feel about planning for training, teaching, or living itself. Both sets of phrases deal with predictability. "You can't know what you don't yet know" gives one the chance to find out and leaves room for mastery and hope. "You're supposed to know before you know" is impossible. It is a paradoxical put-down, usually implying one-upsmanship of information control. The amazing phenomenon is that more people seem to be brought up and taught by the second phrase than by the first.

At BFI we support as base what one already thinks and knows, as the platform from which to find out everything else. The question "What if . . . " opens the door.

GOALS

Goals for Direction

Some of the "everything else" we have found out is that when you start to think of the *goals* for any training process, multitudinous criteria, topics, skills, trainee developmental issues, flood one's idea and image generator, as well as those beginning thoughts about specific goals for *how to* train. Goals in the beginning of any new program are probably more correctly called images, for any group of goals stated can be further branched, like arteries into capillaries. No one starts out with a clear sense of how a *new process* will be, in all its magnitude. No one can know before he knows. Our experience, like that of others, has been that in initiating a new program or course, some original goals are needed for starters, but the real delineation of goals evolves from the trying-out process, the teasing apart of what happened, afterwards, as precursors to planning the next event. Over time, with attention to the process, one discovers that many types of goals are being "serviced" simultaneously.

Types of Goals

As I tease apart our goals over the years, from my position now of integrative reflection, it seems to me that goals in our BFI training program can be gathered around three main headings: *outcome goals, process goals, and content goals.* It is important to define here what I mean by these three groupings and to state how these could be further divided into subgroups. It also seems necessary to mention those aspects we seem to have chosen over the years upon which to concentrate.

Objectives or Outcome Goals: These goals are those relating to what you want to see happen. Right away, the questions can be asked: On what level? For whom? For the people doing the training, for the trainees, or for the institution? For the therapist? The patients?

These are questions asked early in the game of starting a program and certainly must be addressed primarily, and then periodically. They are the goals that usually deal with the economic aspects of a plan, some of the organizational structures or functional positions, as well as long-range aspirations and hopes. In systems thinking, they are at a different level of organization than what happens in training itself.

For instance, when the Boston Family Institute was being formed in the minds of Fred Duhl and David Kantor while at Boston State Hospital, one set of this category of outcome goals was:

- to further develop a training program in family therapy, spreading the excitement they felt;
- to form a group of faculty from BSH who had been learning together for two years;
- to do so privately, as an independent, nonprofit educational organization; and
- to earn some income teaching.

These are certainly goals that have to be spelled out. However, they are not the type of objective or outcome goals on which we are concentrating here. Ours are addressed primarily to the microcosm of training itself, which becomes its own macrocosm.

Outcome goals for us have come to mean: *What results, what outcomes do we want to see in our trainees; what ways of thinking and what skills and capacities do we wish to see catalyzed in them?*

For instance, "for trainees to become integrated human systems thinkers, who are competent, creative and responsible therapists," is an outcome goal. This can further break down into goals for various skills and capacities. We will be more concerned, then, with such subgroupings as specific outcome targets, as you will see in a moment.

Process goals, for us, also relate to training itself, and mean: *What is the manner in which we want to implement our outcome and skill goals?* What are our goals for our method of training? These goals relate to the manner in which we wish to have learning take place. Such process goals are inclusive of and relate to creating the context, ambience, and atmosphere, the set in which that learning happens and where values become manifest in the image-of-human in action.

A process goal of ours might be: "To create a climate of excitement in and for learning." Such a goal sets in motion a series of questions about ways of being and ways of teaching, about exercises, with which we will need to experiment in order to see if our feedforward image (Richards, 1968) has indeed been brought from intrapsychic image to personal interactions, reflecting back "excitement in learning."

All outcome and process goals of this nature in our training program set up the requirements and conditions for a type of fit or match between images and expectations and their fulfillment in the dynamic interaction of trainees, trainers, and plans. We will be spelling out many such process goals.

Content goals in training programs and academic settings usually refer to the topic headings and list of books and articles that trainees are expected to read, as well as various projects each is expected to do. While we indeed have topic headings and such a list of books and activities, that is *not* what we have in mind to review here. Rather, when integration in human systems thinking is the outcome goal encompassing all others, the content goals take on another meaning in addition to topic headings and lists of materials.

Content goals also mean imparting information, experience, and theory concerning human processes. Human systems are not static entities, but are in dynamic interaction. *The content, then, called "a way of thinking," involves processes as subject matter.* The content of the course includes each trainee's discoveries and connections, elaborated in dialogue and discussion, which result from his/her readings, projects, and exercises with other trainees in their joint explorations of human systems.

For instance, under "family process," as a topic heading, a content goal might be: "To explore roles, rules, routines, and rituals in family systems." This might well include reading various authors on these topics. However, written works are seen not only as another theorist's and/or practitioner's views, but also as vehicles for eliciting one's own views as content. "Rules, roles, routines, and rituals" are causes/results of interactive processes. They comprise reflexive and/or circular impact loops. Any seminar on rules and roles, then, would include, in addition to readings, interactive processes in the form of a variety of types of exercises around rules, roles, rituals, and routines in human systems.

Thus, we make the interactive processes themselves the subject, the content to be studied. Another way of saying it is *we make the processes by which transactions in human systems occur the content of both receptive and proactive learning.* Human processes are content. We enact content as well as read about it.

I believe this will become clearer now, as we review these three sets of goals *as they have evolved over time* at the BFI. I am also inclined to believe that the reflexively coherent aspect of our holographic process will become more self-evident as we elaborate and spell out our assumptions about learning and adults in the following section.

Refining and Differentiating Goals

In 1967, the basic goals of the new family therapy training program at Boston State Hospital involved training staff to be able to work with family units as a way of solving the problems and symptoms of patients both in the hospital and coming to the Mental Health Center outpatient department.

At that time, all state hospitals in Massachusetts had become mental health centers, serving wide catchment areas for all sorts of situations. The catchment area of Boston State Hospital included mixed populations of varying economic, social and ethnic backgrounds, and the trainees in the program cut across services and hierarchical lines.

The trainers originally had felt their goal was to impart content about families and about systems. However, they found no one listening or really attending in any satisfactory way, leading them to switch the focus from directly imparting content to raising questions about information transmission itself. Thus, by the time they began with the first BFI seminar in the spring of 1969, their generic questions had switched to:

- How do you train for caring curiosity and competence?
- How do family systems "work"?
- How do people learn, change, grow, separate, connect?

Their goals then became searches for answers to these questions. Their two years of BSH experience already pointed the way towards some of the answers. The overt and stated goals of BFI in 1969 were:

- to actively involve the trainees in their learning;
- to discover what care-seeking and "normal" families were about in all dimensions;
- to attend to how trainees hear and learn, and make sense of their information;
- to learn from each other and to conceptualize from those data;
- to learn from the trainees and from the process.

Over the years, as we continually learned from our teaching, we became clearer and more articulate about goals—those still in need of being attained and those that seemed to be well taken care of. It is our current "crop" that I will elaborate here.

Can Our Goal-deriving Process Work for You?

Let us assume that you, the reader, will be asked to design a new course or program exploring human systems. How would you go about it? I will be writing the remainder of this chapter as if that is indeed so.

Exercise

Think of any course you have ever been to in relating to human beings. What were the outcome goals of the course? The processes for achieving them? The content of the course? Did the processes employed allow the goals to be met? And what other goals, planned or unplanned, were being met at the same time?

A word of caution before reading the following sets of goals: *Culling such lists of goals that appear to be serviced by the BFI approach to training some 14 years after the inception of the program is a very different process from prethinking a viable set of goals with which to start a program.* Ours have been surfacing over the years, as we have been satisfied or frustrated that planned-for images were met or not met.

Let me be clearer. All programs begin somehow in the middle, following some decision to do a certain something and then doing it. If goals and a program are to keep pace and remain in congruent touch with each other in an organic fashion, certain processes are necessary. It is by attending to what is happening, asking a few simple questions, and treating with dignity and creativity the answers one receives that goals and program can keep pace and evolve congruently in touch with each other.

More specifically, one can set up a few goals for one's outcome wishes, a few goals for the processes by which one will achieve the outcome, and a few goals concerning the content one wants to transmit. One chooses a way to try to get one's message across. Whatever one decides to do to meet these goals is then done.

Afterwards, one can ask a simple set of questions:

• What happened that we expected?
• What is being learned?
• What else happened, and what else is being learned, that we didn't expect?

Here, one uncovers the subsidiary processes, content, and outcomes that are contained in the total situation. They now can become focal (Polanyi, 1958; Polanyi and Prosch, 1975).

When we then ask:

• Where do these new findings fit in our map?
• And what else would we like to see happen, either inclusive of our new findings or in their stead?

we are then in a position for new decision-making, new goal information. The question then becomes one of hunch again—"What if . . . ?"—as the beginning of a process towards achieving the next set of goals.

As you read these compilations, please know that these have been drawn from an ongoing and organic 14-year process which, by now, gives us the substructure for calling our program an integrative approach, rather than an eclectic one. We start with the trainee as the center of our concern, as the one who will have to do the integrating.

Our subject: ways of conceptualizing human beings in their interconnectedness and their functionally autonomous separateness, and ways of helping people be connected while functionally autonomous. Simply put, our goals are to understand and help each person to be an "I" in fit with others in ways that can also be a respectful, flexible, and comfortable "we."

As we have stated earlier, this particular book is primarily concerned with aspects of the *first* part of these twin goals and the metaprocesses involved: the ways of exploring, understanding and deriving the map for the issues of fit in human systems and system patterns. Actions and processes for helping people in need readjust their sense and patterns of fit with each other, derived from this particular map, are the subjects of counseling and therapy and could be the subject of another whole volume.

Thus, as you the reader use these compilations to stimulate your thinking about your own settings and programs, please know also that the remainder of this volume is concerned with examining and illuminating some of the ways in which we go about meeting these goals in our program.*

If you have been thinking about your own program, the chances are, especially if it is a new program, that you have far fewer goals than those about to be listed here. If any program ever *started* with all the goals mentioned here, it would be top heavy and probably never get off the ground! However, once you focus on a few target goals in each category and get a program going, many other goals will appear as being serviced at the same time. Subsidiary goals shift and become focal (Polanyi, 1958).

Goals Under the Microscope, Magnified

Outcome Goals: (The following summarizes our outcome goals, in addition to those outlined in Chapter IV).

At BFI, we wish to train for integrated, multicentric and analogic human systems thinking, in adult persons who can also be competent, creative, empathic, responsible, and effective human systems actors. We want our trainees to be:

- capable of assessing self as/in/with all levels of systems;
- capable of assessing developmental processes and life-cycle stages in different human systems levels;
- capable of recognizing systemic interactive processes of all human systems, in direct and analogic form;

---

*A projected second volume elaborating special themes of system interface explored in our program will more fully describe how a number of goals are met: i.e., vulnerabilities and defenses, learning styles, core images and boundary behavior, among others.

- capable of analyzing human systems criteria and component parts as inclusive of and separate from self;
- capable of recognizing and assessing different types of information processing styles and stages at any level of human system;
- capable of recognizing and tuning into the sense of vulnerability and the concomitant defensiveness at any level of system;
- capable of capturing the contextual and idiosyncratic core images which seem to direct all human behavior;
- capable of engaging in "short-term empathy"—that ability to sit in another person's skin and then return to one's own;
- capable of "going into" an experience, and "pulling away" to become bystander to self and others;
- capable of suggesting which types of actions will catalyze change in each system level, towards the goal of the interconnected/functional autonomy of all component parts of a human system;
- capable of demystifying these processes and empowering others with similar tools for their own problem-solving.

We want ourselves and other trainers to continue to integrate and become more competent, creative, empathic, responsible, and effective human systems thinkers and trainers. Most of all, we want trainers and trainees to enjoy the process!

Process Goals: Above all, we attempt

- to train in a "reflexively coherent" and analogic fashion wherein the manner by which people are trained is analogic and congruent with what they are learning to do and how they will be expected to think about it and to do it;
- to ground each person in his/her own information, in his/her own life story, in his/her own ongoing experience and assessment of it;
- to promote the process by which learning takes place from the inside out, starting with one's own information, one's own life experience and metaphors as the coherent, integrating base for analogic thinking;
- to provide sanction for adult trainees to explore how they think, feel, sense, image, act; to explore what systems and contexts influenced that thinking, feeling, imaging, sensing and acting, without trainees having to justify why;
- to provide sanction for adult trainees to take the time (one full year of our two-year program, part-time) to integrate parts of self as/in/with systems, before acting as therapists and attempting to change others;
- to provide a "safe" place for risk-taking, in which nondefensive, inclusive integration is possible, in which the place, the processes and a metamap for that integration are provided for all life experiences of the trainee;

- to catalyze the integration of the person in the therapist role and to continually recognize the functional autonomy of individuals in larger systems, while recognizing the influence of larger systems for each individual person and the systemic interconnectedness of any transactions by system members;
- to catalyze the processes of analogic thinking, making full use of any and all of one's own experiences, life roles, and positions;
- to aid trainees in using and eliciting from others verbal, spatial, kinesthetic, aural, imagistic metaphors;
- to create awareness of the multifacets of self and others, expanding each trainee's range of roles, ways of thinking, for use of and with self and with others;
- to demonstrate and catalyze in trainees the facility to track and evolve inner images and awarenesses into externalized, interpersonal behaviors and transactions;
- to employ "both sides of the brain" (Buzan, 1976);
- to promote, expand and elaborate the full use of digital left brain linear thinking in cooperation with analogic, systemic, right brain thinking (Ornstein, 1972);
- to act with and teach responsibility and responsible creativity—which means self-trust, self-awareness, long- and short-term empathy, and daring to own, trust and try out one's hunches, and thinking originally for oneself (since no one else can do it for you anyway);
- to catalyze natural warmth and spontaneity, curiosity and empathy in trainees towards themselves and others;
- to teach the necessity of play;
- to help trainees discover that continuous, responsible exploration and play keep each human systems thinker and/or actor a generative open system.

As stated before, each of these process goals suggests that the exercises we design, that is, the way in which they are implemented, can be scanned to track their meeting of these goals, as well as of the content goals they are supposed to meet. As we then outline our goals, our image-of-human-as-trainee expands to include the capacities and attributes outlined in all categories of goals.

Content Goals: For us, perhaps like or unlike some other programs, the content we wish our trainees to engage in learning includes generic categories of human processes. Thus, we wish:

- to teach the basic concepts of general systems theory (as outlined in Chapter IV) from the inside out;
- to explore learning styles and stages of each trainee-in-context(s);
- to explore vulnerabilities and defenses of each trainee-in-context(s);

- to explore boundary phenomena of each trainee-in-context(s);
- to explore roles, rules, routines, and rituals of each trainee-in-context(s);
- to derive the rules of order and the rules of access of all arenas and levels of systems;
- to explore the range of phenomena that make up human lives and the "patterns which connect" (Bateson, 1979) in others and in self;
- to explore the issues of the wider context and culture, the core images, the grounds of learning-to-learn (Bateson, 1972, pp. 159–176) and the "incidental learning" (Bruner, 1973a) that helps organize how we think;
- to expose, explore, and experience a variety of developmental models; to demonstrate that differentiation and integration are processes congruent with various developmental stages;
- to explore the metamaps that the findings of those in the field lead to;
- to share "the continuum for assessment" (Duhl, B. S., 1978; Duhl, B. S. and Duhl, F. J., 1981; Duhl, F. J. and Duhl, B. S., 1979), in which many aspects of human systems levels can be integrated;
- to explore the personal aesthetics that make every human system different;
- to explore change processes and raise questions about influence, change, and impact, and the premises and implications of actions, based on each, in self and others, as well as to explore resources in context;
- to explore others' theories of human systems and theories of therapy, and fit them within the metamap;
- to elicit external pattern recognition of and in families and other human systems and subsystems; to explore those punctuations in the repeated circular or cyclical patterns or sequences of some human systems that allow for or do not allow for the introduction of new information;
- to demonstrate and elicit interventions: the "differences that make a difference" (Bateson, 1979).

As we look at this overview of content goals, we see how content is indeed hard to separate out from processes; in fact, in many cases, process—the "How does it happen, how does it work?"—becomes the content focus.

It will perhaps come as a surprise to learn that by no means are any of these goal lists full or complete! However, they pull together the general ideas of the various types of overview goals for the entire program (here with emphasis on integration in human systems thinking) with which the BFI has been concerned in the last decade.

If we now scan these three sets of goals, we find that our extended image-of-human includes that each trainee feel him/herself an authentic, organic, and evolving human being:

- capable of living, breathing and thinking a human systems metaphor;
- capable of impacting and influencing human systems, including the ones he/she is currently in, inclusive of the training program.

We seem to be assuming that our extended image-of-human is possible. We must then have some assumptions or constructs about how adults learn. Indeed, we do.

ISSUES IN LEARNING AND KNOWING

"If you can't know what you don't yet know, how're you gonna find out?"
If you think about it, we all carry an enormous amalgamation of assumptions—of bits and pieces of information and images, woven into a many-textured tapestry—on which we base our simplest moves, to say nothing of assumptions underlying complex procedures. These are assumptions about the way things/phenomena are, how they work. They underlie the sense of predictability we have in and of our world, based on all we have yet experienced and lived through. Parkes calls this our "assumptive world view" (1971). Bruner calls this past history, or "incidental learning" (1973a). Bateson speaks of "learning-to-learn" (1972) and I refer to this aspect of knowing and predicting as our "core images," which include the widest base of incidental learning derived from our culture-at-large.

All education, therapy and training programs attempt to transmit and transfer information, images, ideas, and processes from one set of people to another. Each of these persons, programs, and contexts operates on some either well or ill defined image-of-human learner.

Exercise: Your Image-of-Human-as-Learner

This might be a good time to pause for a moment and think about, write down, imagine, explore, or discuss: How do adults learn? How do you know that? How do you learn? How does your father or your best friend learn? How do you know that?

How Contexts Shape Processes and Traditions

Two brief historical notes seem to me to be warranted here, since they pertain to some assumptions about learning.

The first is that this style of teaching began and continued in a State Hospital in 1967, where attendants, nurses, psychologists, social workers, psychiatric residents and pastoral counselors and some spouses were all trained together in the same seminar. There were no "entrance requirements" for the hospital training program in family process and therapy.

When BFI was incorporated as a private nonprofit educational institution in 1969, separate from Boston State Hospital, it initially also had no requirements for admission to the *first semester* of training. The late 1960s and 1970s were also a time of multiple drug centers, storefront clinics, hotlines, the beginning of the radical movement in psychiatry, with concomitant attacks on vertical status hierarchies and value bases. At BFI people learned from each other. Each was a consultant on the process of what human systems called families were like. In this brand new field, the lack of set rules for content or processes in training allowed for the freedom to explore, create, and find out. The rewards of this discovery trip were so great that certain aspects of that freedom and flexibility became a core part of the BFI process and tradition in training. Indeed, we still train people from wide varieties of backgrounds—lawyers, college deans and presidents, teachers, policemen, businesspeople, and others not connected to the world of therapy—in multicentric systems thinking. Often they are in nodal positions to make a difference in *their* human systems.

The second historical note is a personal one. The author's active interest in learning styles had started in 1960, with the arrival of her first child. By 1961, as a newborn, child number two made it perfectly clear that he was a very different brand of being than child number one. That didn't change. As mother, the author learned to change *her* style of message-giving to fit each one in order for her to be "selfishly altruistic"—to get her messages across in a way that each could "take them in" and respond. And she had to change yet again for child number three. Thus, her interest and involvement in, and observation and data collection about, "hearing" and "learning styles" began years before she entered the BFI program in 1969. (It is quite possible that these same children's different styles also influenced Fred Duhl!)

These notes are mentioned to remind and inform readers how aspects of the external and internal contexts of our lives affect what later becomes theory or institutionalized processes. In addition, they are mentioned to remind readers that important findings, probably the most important findings, about learning and people can come from non-classroom settings. Piaget's basic work involved careful observation of and experiments with his three children, which he then researched and checked out in relation to other children.

Assumptions About Learning

Meanwhile, while many other programs have become quite rule and procedure-oriented and by 1979 two national organizations* were jockeying for

---

*American Association of Marriage and Family Therapists; American Family Therapy Association.

the power and prestige that will go with being THE organization chosen to set or impose national standards and regulations, we at BFI continue to invent new processes for exploring and mapping the experience and the territory of being human in human systems.

We have tried to remain clear and constant in our major overall modality of teaching systems thinking and acting through planned analogic exercises or common metaphors, which encompass wide ranges of systems issues, tasks, behaviors and processes, and goals, so that experiential *and* conceptual integration takes place in the trainee, connecting his/her life with people with his/her work with people.

This firm commitment to teaching by planned metaphors and exercises, which create the structures for spontaneity, is based on our assumptions about how all people learn and integrate their learning. These assumptions are being drawn here from those present at the beginning and from the ever-growing body of data we keep culling from our ongoing "learning laboratory." Obviously, not all of these assumptions were spelled out at the beginning. I write them now as fitting with our own and others' theories of learning. Some of these assumptions are applicable to children as well as adults. Assumptions about learning applicable primarily to adults will follow general assumptions about learning.

Over the last 12 to 14 years, then, we have paid as much attention to the *processes* of teaching and learning human systems thinking as we have to processes of intervening in and with systems. Certain already existing theoretical formulations seem to shed light on and describe what we have been doing, and I will refer to them. In true paradigmatic fashion, these conceptualizations followed from the inside out, from our experiences, as the author sought explanations of why this way of training seemed to lead to integration and multicentricity. The juxtaposition or connections of our way of training, from the inside out, with these theories of others are the author's.

Our Updated List of Assumptions

As we refer now to our paradigm for training, these assumptions are those held by the trainers, and underpin our way of training.

We assume that people learn best:

1) When taught in an atmosphere of respect, with a base of safety or equivalency from which one can take risks (Duhl, B. S., 1976b, 1978; Duhl, F. J. and Duhl, B. S., 1979). This means that people are free to learn from each other as well as from life experience, books, tapes, teachers, other schooling, and with regard and respect for each one's areas of expertise and vulnerabil-

ity. It means respecting, with tender nurturance, budding new ideas and images. It means the support and protection for "I wonder if . . . " and "What if . . . ?", so that beginning ideas are not judged against complete and long-finished theories. It includes room for new ideas and recognition that all the answers about human beings and human systems are not yet in.

2) When learning takes place from the inside out, in gradual increments, when new learning is based on previous learnings (Bruner, 1973b), "in a mastering of techniques that are embodied in the culture, and that are passed on in a contingent dialogue by agents of the culture" (Bruner, 1973a, p. x). In Piaget's terms, this is an assimilation process wherein "the environment is subordinated to the organism as it is" (Piaget, 1977b, p. 274). According to Gordon and Poze, (1973), when we make the strange familiar, that is learning. "External reality is changed so that the organism may remain the same" (Jimenez, 1976).*

3) Or when learning takes place from the inside out in abrupt bursts. Gordon states that learning is connection-making (1977) between strange and familiar. Making the familiar strange is innovation. According to Piaget, making the familiar strange is the process of accommodation, when "the organism changes itself to adapt to the environment" (1977b, p. 274).

Successful interventions, and teaching processes, make the familiar strange and the strange familiar. (Some leave the familiar familiar, and the strange strange!)

Our assumption is that people learn when the new activity, new information is not too far removed from that which was last known, when it is "novel" (Kagen, 1971). Piaget, Bruner, Kagen and others have found that the mind tends not to take in but to reject and/or ignore information which is too discrepant from that which is already integrated into one's schema or assumptive world view (Duhl, F. J., 1969; Parkes, 1971). (We shall discuss these concepts more fully in Chapter VII on metaphor.)

In learning both from the inside out and outside in we assume that each person learns best when he/she can locate him/herself in connection to the information.

4) When each person's learning style, that optimum idiosyncratic mode of processing information is respected and honored (Bandler and Grinder, 1975; Bruner, 1973a; Duhl, B. S. and Duhl, F. J., 1975; Duhl, F. J., 1969; Grinder

---

*For a fuller discussion of these concepts, consult Chapter VII.

and Bandler, 1976; and myriad others). If water does not find the crack in the wall, it will flow over, rather than seep in. People are not necessarily fully in touch with their own information processing modes, except on the grossest levels (Duhl, B. S. and Duhl, F. J., 1975). However, we believe that people do not learn, grow, and change unless the information is available to them in their own mode of representation, their own input channels (Bandler and Grinder, 1975; Bruner, 1973a; Grinder and Bandler, 1976).

5) When the modes of teaching incorporate multiple ways of learning (Bruner, 1973a, 1973b; Duhl, B. S., 1978; Piaget, 1952). We believe that people learn by immersion and reflection, by analogy and metaphor, by detailed analysis, by imagery, by doing, seeing, looking, hearing, feeling, writing, drawing, reading, describing, modeling, imitating, exploring, by challenge, by making the strange familiar, the familiar strange, using right and left brain functions (Bogen, 1968; Buzan, 1976; Gazzaniga, 1968; Ornstein, 1972; Samples, 1976), and probably other ways as well.

6) When there is invitation, room for and appreciation of the "having of wonderful ideas" (Duckworth, 1972) that keeps the spark in life and the sparkle in living.

7) When the body is involved in physical activity (Duhl, Kantor, and Duhl, 1973; Piaget, 1952), in which the integration of meanings and concepts recapitulates each stage of cognitive development, from sensorimotor through formal operational functions. Piaget's (1952) conception that in children all learning is based in sensorimotor activity seems to extend to a great many adults (Duhl, B. S., 1978). It certainly seems to apply to catalyzing integration in systems thinkers with more than an intellectual understanding. In addition, the body has memories and associations the verbal mind knows not of (Duhl, Kantor, and Duhl, 1973), which we uncover in sculpture and spatialization, as well as other action metaphors (see Chapters IX and X).

8) When any aspect of processes, persons, or content is grist for the learning mill of human systems. Thus aspects of trainees' or trainers' lives, institutions, families, cultures, as well as the thinking behind any exercise, intervention or idea is open for discussion, questioning, experimentation, challenge, and change.

9) When all can be safe enough to take risks of new integrated learning and innovation, and have fun and enjoy the process (Duhl, B. S., 1976b; Duhl, F. J., 1976). Humor is a needed item in every teaching/learning setting, if not in

all settings. Not only is humor a great teacher in and of itself, but we assume it is an absolute requirement for balance and sanity.

10) We assume that people learn best (and learn systems thinking too) when they are aware that their style of learning has an impact and helps influence the style of teaching, that the interactional fit of learning/teaching styles is key between themselves and trainers, educators, or therapists. The same interactional fit is key between people in families, and between therapists and clients.

11) And finally, we believe each person learns best when information is transmitted in "the language of impact" (Duhl, F. J., 1969). Sometimes that language has no words.

All of the above assumptions hold for trainers, as well as trainees, and other real people.

Assumptions about Adults and Needs for Adult Learning

As we begin to conjure up the associations to and assumptions of our image-of-human-as-learner, we find there are many. We will be continuing to discuss these throughout the book. Since our trainees are adults, let us look for a moment at some of our assumptions about adults and learning. All our teaching, in all contexts, has been from college age level and up. Our oldest trainee was 69. Thus we have gathered many impressions and assumptions about what adults bring to a context that perhaps differentiates them from children in their learning.
We assume:

- That each trainee has been brought up within a family or social context of one form or another and therefore each adult trainee has core images of and expertise in at least one model of family system;
- That adults bring with them core images, their epistemics (MacLean, 1975) and assumptive world views (Parkes, 1971) which color their lenses; that these core images, like the air one breathes, are taken for granted and guide one's thinking and active behavior until challenged and differentiated (Bruner, 1973a); that each adult trainee needs the opportunity to explore the constructs, hypotheses, and concepts, the epistemic theory of family and image of human that each brings with him/her into the program (Duhl, B. S. and Duhl, F. J., 1974b);
- That each adult already has a theory-as-espoused (what I say) and a theory-in-use (what I do) (Argyris and Schon, 1974) which may or

may not have anything to do with each other. Certainly, each adult has a theory-in-use relating to his/her personal image of family systems and has perhaps no theory-as-espoused as yet;

- That each adult's personal theories are idiosyncratic and can be drastically different from those of others, often depending upon the interaction of each person with all aspects of the culture, the family and social contexts, and one's individual learning style;
- That adult trainees bring with them, in addition to their knowledge and skills, many developed aspects of self, in their learning styles, in patterns of vulnerability and styles of defensiveness, which are connected to the phenomena of core images and actual interactions at the boundary with all people;
- That adults reflect in themselves and in their interactions, like a fragment of a holographic plate, aspects of all the systems of which each has been a part;
- That thinking, feeling, sensing, imaging, and acting are all aspects of threads weaving the fabric of self; adult trainees can be aided in each sensory process, noting their similarities while distinguishing the differences;
- That each adult is equivalent and different from each other trainee and trainer; that each is singularly expert in knowing most about one's own world view and how to best be oneself;
- That in this utilitarian, technological, and cost-effective culture, *adults need permission, heavily reinforced, to take time to be curious about and focus on the integration of self* and how one experiences, senses, thinks, images, and acts, in a setting other than therapy, that is, *when there is absolutely nothing wrong with oneself.* (In this culture, the only excuse for concentrating on self, towards integration of one's life and one's theories, has been a therapeutic context, even for those training to be therapists.) We believe that some adults need to see this permission as a requirement. We insist that the exploration of each trainee's active and reactive self-in-context and of the impact of various contexts on oneself be the focus of concern—the process goal and product of trainees' endeavors—for a given period of time;
- That adults need permission to see, feel, and experience in new ways, in non-routinized roles and contexts;
- That adults need to analyze how self-in-systems and other humans-in-systems are analogous to one another;
- That adults like to play, once given permission and a structure;
- That adult trainees need to know they can influence others and systems, including the one in which they are trainees. Over the years, we have relied upon trainees' feedback, discoveries and evaluations of curricula as well as upon observed and personal reactions of faculty to shape curriculum content as well as processes;
- That adults, when in an atmosphere of safety from ridicule, delight in

being stretched as persons, theorists, and therapists, and welcome the challenge to increase their range, to add on, to innovate and make the familiar strange (Gordon and Poze, 1973), and to dare to have wonderful ideas;

- That trainers, teachers, and therapists are adults who get bored with repetition, and "tune out" just like trainees, parents, and others when the same things are said over and over again. Repeated dialogues, like recorded announcements, give no new information, scan for none, and wear us down. We assume that exciting training and teaching, as well as therapy and parenting, mean arriving at novel ways to encounter similar material, with curiosity and search, humor and play;
- That adults, trainees and trainers alike learn best when stimulated to participate in a concrete experience, to reflect on their doing, to draw some generalizations and hypotheses about what happened, to plan a new event and try it, repeating the process cycle (Kolb, 1974), though not the content;
- That although "grownup," adults can be at different cognitive stages (Piaget, 1952) and different self-knowledge stages (Alschuler, Evans, Tamashiro, and Weinstein, 1975), as well as demonstrating different learning styles; that because in our experience this is so, not all adults can evolve into systems thinkers at the same rate or during the same period of time;
- That no training program in human systems thinking is a total substitute for wide ranges of life experiences, although such a program can expand, catalyze, and help integrate those life experiences and other suggestions for the patterns which connect them (Bateson, 1979). Experiencing, having "been there," is a different kind of knowing than knowing through analogic exercises, or knowing about; analogic exercises and simulations are far better than no exposure at all.

Lastly, "integrational" and multicentric thinking may well be the next stage after the formal operational stage of Piaget's theory. I believe such a stage to be the result of extensive exercise in uniting right and left brain functions through metaphor, in all forms. Perhaps the further subsequent stage is holographic. As the studies of Piagetian principles and cognitive development show, cultures in which there is no support or process by which to develop to the next stage will not develop to that stage; *development does not happen without context and exercise of the function* (Bart, 1977; Luria, 1976). *Adults need a context,* and *time* for that next stage to gel, *in which to experience their own major paradigm shift.*

Thus, we assume that integration in adults is an organic developmental process which takes time, which cannot be instant and cannot be rushed. One can help catalyze it and shape its direction, beginning with acknowledging and providing structures for the spontaneous connection of ingredients already rooted in the person. Such connections we believe are best made through exercising the analogic functions of mind.

The ways in which these assumptions guide our thinking about and planning for training will become evident as we explore specific themes later in the book. At this point, it seems important to explore what impact such a set of assumptions about learning holds for trainers. Let us now take a look at some of these implications.

PREMISES AND IMPLICATIONS FOR THE FACULTY OF A BFI-TYPE OF TRAINING PROGRAM

Exercise

> Imagine again an old and timeworn idea you are somewhat bored with. Imagine yourself having successfully presented it in a novel way to your group. They have "caught" your idea, and you are very pleased with yourself and with them. Imagine now, you wish to teach them to be able to do the same thing with another group. How will you go about it? *Can you think up a novel way to teach them to be novel?*

If we think about this exercise for a moment, we begin to realize that the price of such pleasure in teaching implies a fair expenditure of energy and effort, creating, implementing and monitoring the teaching/learning process on the part of the faculty. Like a good relationship, you have to want to be in it. Otherwise, it can seem burdensome.

That is, perhaps, the first premise or implication of following our goals and assumptions for a training program. As we follow the framework of our paradigm, we become aware that if we want our goals to be achieved, and if we acknowledge our values and our assumptions, *we have to want to be there*, working at the interactive process of shaping procedures to meet goals.

What else must we do to make our goals happen? What will it take to catalyze processes in and between people? And, how can we evaluate the process?

It is difficult at this time to recapture the innocence and the electric excitement of enthusiastic, surefooted naiveté that pervaded this program at the beginning! As we become knowing and educated by the findings of our and others' virginal endeavors, we struggle to keep alive a certain quality of enthusiastic curiosity. "I wonder if . . . " and "What if . . . ?" free us by keeping our conceptual map an open one, constantly expecting new information and ideas to emerge, to be incorporated and integrated into the whole.

Excitement at the beginning of a program is one thing. However, if training is to *continue* in an exciting way, with a growing edge for trainers, faculty members will need to meet regularly to discuss teaching goals, processes and outcomes. Over the years we had meetings devoted to new ideas and experiments, meetings devoted to administrative scheduling, meetings discussing trainees. After a while, we realized that when and if our meetings were fully devoted to administrative detail and/or trainees, we ourselves began to be irritable and less enthusiastic. At that time, we realized that *faculty members need to have some input for themselves,* some growing edge discussions, on a regular and close basis. The faculty needed some sort of process analogous to the one set up for the trainees. As trainers, we found we needed to create an environment that was boundaried, open to experimentation, and safe from put-down and ridicule, so that the trainers themselves could take risks for a new kind of learning, without the need for justification or defending loyalties to old learning.

This is not an easy process for trainers, who even more than trainees feel they are "supposed to know" when maybe they, too, are not always quite fully sure. Especially in the field of psychology and psychiatry is this prevalent. In this newest arena of science, skill, and art, professionals seem to feel the need to insist that their own map is complete.

All the usual group and system issues can and do take place among faculty members unless there is a conscious and cooperative process to change the faculty environment into one open for new learnings about self as trainers and training processes. This is easier said than done, and requires constant attention and monitoring, as well as specific processes respectful of all input.

While BFI trainers had developed new ideas for new ways of exploring concepts, it was not until 1974 with the author's invention of the "vulnerability contract" (Duhl, B.S., 1976b) in a theory lab seminar, that we had a tool for the emotional safety of risking new ideas and behaviors among ourselves.*

As trainers, our best times have come when planning a new curriculum becomes a dyadic (if co-leaders) or group process (if several section leaders are planning together) and we are openly able to challenge, explore, and formulate new constructs or integrations in our planning. This is priority time.

The paradigm forces us to be clear, by the time we are finished. However, during the process of planning, new, rather than tried and true, methods of imparting ideas are sought. New and expanded integrations are striven for. Brainstorming of new "what if . . . " exercises takes place, and as faculty, we "try on" any appealing exercise or idea briefly before using or incorporating it. In this process, we must refine our thinking. We are free to ques-

---

*This special process, as well as others uncovered along the way, will be the subject of another volume, dedicated to exploring the integrating themes of systems interfaces.

tion whether values are being respected with any design. We can examine which processes of mind are being called into play, whether the exercise under discussion is also analogic to issues in therapy, and so on. Such discussions constantly keep faculty creative and aware. We have found that when we have not made time for our own dialogic sharing in this manner, the way in which training takes place suffers.

This process over time has increased the reflexively coherent sense of integration of concepts, processes, and practices in faculty members, enabling them to further aid trainees in the weaving processes of connection-making and innovation. More importantly, this process energizes and rewards the faculty, keeping them involved with attention to their current thinking.

Implications for Trainers Concerning Trainees

Trainers will need to pay attention to what is already known by trainees about themselves, about families, about all levels of human systems and the ecosystem, about people in particular and in general and in all types of contexts, as well as about their epistemic assumptive world views (Parkes, 1971) and formal epistemologies.

In such a program trainers will need to invite discovery and new connections among themselves and trainees. They will need to design procedures in which they and all others can experience making the Familiar Strange and the Strange Familiar (Gordon and Poze, 1973; Gordon, 1977), and linking the resultant findings together in metaframeworks. Trainers will need to invite each trainee's "set molecules" to rearrange themselves in new, evolving patterns.

In designing, trainers will need to create a great variety of learning situations to explore what is already operating, present new content, and promote new processes. They will need to invent new designs to explore all the arenas of interest listed in their goals, taking into consideration their values and assumptions.

Trainers will need then to design both real and analogic experiences and simulations, to provide the widest arena of exposure, experience, rehearsal, feedback, and evaluation, all of which lead to organismic integration.

The seminars themselves will then also be seen as analogic in that the training process is to the trainees as the intervention process is to families and other human systems. Trainers are to the trainees as interveners are to families; processes in training are analogues for processes in therapy. The way one thinks is the way one thinks.

Trainers will have to then design direct and analogic situations in which many levels of human systems can be explored (direct) or evoked (analogic) (see Chapters II, VII–X).

If trainers can indeed create such analogic exercises, they will find that such exercises carry within them the metaphors touching all levels of living systems: cell, organ, individual, family (group), institution, community, national, international. One as trainer will never be exactly sure how many levels are being touched by what, whom, and when; so again, we will have to ask for and gather that information each time.

As the systems represented in the seminar itself are explored, through each trainee as a "bit" of a holographic plate, each person can be both valued for his/her uniqueness and connected to others by shared similarities. Thus trainers will be able to highlight the unity in diversity, the part/whole constructs, and the generalizations which can be made from concrete data.

In the best of all systems worlds a key implication of this form of training is a dynamic systems one, which emerged at BFI rather early: If the trainers were indeed interested in message reception and interpretation, in how people hear and learn, they then needed to include both self-report and feedback from trainees, as well as their behavioral observations as trainers on the results of their hypotheses, tested by whatever teaching plan they had constructed and tried.

Thus the trainers' curiosity about message reception, internally as well as behaviorally, in combination with the trainees' evaluations and self-reports, created a cooperative and continually shaping feedforward/feedback/feedforward loop. This implication was not conceptualized and highlighted first as a theoretical systems concept to follow. Rather, it was a systems concept, consciously being enacted as a practical matter and conceptualized later.

The early goals and assumptions began to lead to implications for a model which would allow input from trainees as well as trainers. Such a model as began to take shape was a collaborative model of equivalency, where power began to be shared by teachers and learners.

As a trainer using this model in a new program, one will need to solicit and receive feedback from trainees in such a way as to demonstrate that one has been influenced. As trainers do so, the training group's sense of competency and confidence is affirmed. Not only will the model with them be analogous to therapy, but the affirmation (validation) of trainees' imagination and risk-taking will reinforce their becoming more authentic and imaginative as human systems thinkers and change agents.

As the BFI model emerged, the fuller implications for a training program not only in family therapy but also for integration in multicentric human systems thinking became much more clearly delineated.

We became aware of the ultimate implication of our training program: *When each trainee derives theoretical formulas anew, as generalizations from experiences and observations of him/herself and others, each trainee experiences his/her own paradigm shift and in that process each trainee re-invents human systems thinking.* The entire map is available from the inside out, and one is free to choose which route to take when, depending upon the assessment of context, components, boundaries and situations. One can enter and work at any level of human system and know that all are interconnected.

The trainee who then owns the process of invention within the wide map of human systems thinking is never at a loss in any human system for a way to think how it works at any level of system, find out more, and arrive at goals to influence it in ways congruent with and in conjunction with the participants in that grouping. One then designs interventions, implements and assesses them, with the empathic competency that remains in touch with the human experience of each person involved.

Trainees thus learn the basic processes needed in any human systems intervention, whether it be one in organizational development, school systems, or any type of therapy.

Thus, another key implication of this type of training is that in creating various kinds of setting, context and exercises drawing on different levels of human systems, each trainee learns to learn the process of following hunches, thinking about and designing goal-oriented inventions.

A Hole in the Hologram

In elaborating the full paradigm by which we train, one could discuss or set up a series of exercises at this point. Indeed, we have been sprinkling some throughout the book thus far, to enlist the reader's imagination and participation.

To list exercises by some name or even offer a cookbook full of recipes would be completely inappropriate. Rather, the remainder of the book will investigate designing metaphoric, analogic and other exercises, how we think and go about designing and planning.

DEBRIEFING AND CONCEPTUALIZING

In summarizing here the framework outlined in our paradigm, the subject of debriefing needs some general comments.

On one level, papers written or given about the program (Duhl, B. S., 1978; Duhl, B. S. and Duhl, F. J. 1974b, 1975; Duhl, F. J. and Duhl B. S., 1979; Duhl, Kantor, and Duhl, 1973) become the conceptualizations that emerge from our plans and debriefings. For us, debriefing and conceptualizing of *any* event are guided by questions which can lead to the integration in human systems thinking:

1) What did you find out—or what did you learn?
2) About yourself and others? At what level of systems about interactions of self and others?
3) What does that new information do? How and with what does it connect? What generalizations can you make about self and others? About interactions of self and others? About the whole system?
4) What is new that was not expected?

Much of the debriefing and conceptualizing from our 14 years of training is being evidenced in what has already appeared in this book and what remains to be read. Debriefing and integrating are ongoing and never-ending processes.

Exercise: Debriefing and Conceptualizing Your Experience

Perhaps it might be interesting now for you to get in touch with what you have been experiencing while reading this book thus far. What have you thought about? What have you felt? How have you acted? Have you tried the exercises? If not, why not? If so, why?

a) What got stirred up in you and what did you find out just now in answering the above questions? About your own experience? About yourself and about any other people? In which level of systems? About interactions between yourself and this book and/or any other people involved?

b) What does any of this new information connect to? That is, does it remind you of any other reading, learning situations you have been in? Or any other contexts or situations? How does it tie in? What themes are there in your life which connect this experience to any other?

c) What generalizations can you make about yourself? Or others? About interactions of yourself with learning materials, other situations or people? What patterns do you see? Make a generalization about them.

Basically, that is a basic debriefing framework, and, as you perhaps can surmise, can be used at any level, and for any type of endeavor, with lesser or greater scope and detail.

We are also aware that time is an important component: how and when one answers questions like those above will depend upon each one's *learning style.* Some people need to put new information and ideas on the back burner, to simmer, while others make new conceptual sandwiches immediately.

EVALUATION

When we evaluate a training or therapy session, or any procedure, a different set of questions is required. Basically, it is here that we look for "reflexive coherence" (Wideman, 1970) on a variety of levels relating to the design itself, the carrying out of the design and feedback about the design.

The long-range, overview questions are basically the same ones we ask after each seminar. In a general and more informal way, the questions were asked irregularly from the inception of the BFI program on. However, once we included evaluation in our paradigm thinking, this key to reflexive coherence became more regularly used. The questions are important for both trainers and trainees:

1) Did the exercises we designed evoke or allow for exploration of the desired content? Utilize the imaged processes? To what extent were the exercises successful compared against the backdrop of our image when we designed them?
2) Should anything be changed? What? To improve what? To reach what goal? (Outcome, process, content?)
3) What new information or ideas or connections emerged that we did not expect or imagine? What have we (trainers) learned from that about our thinking and training? What new constructs does that new information lead to?

Realistically, these evaluation questions are not asked in all that detail consciously each week. Periodically, they are asked at the end of seminar sessions and at specific feedback, evaluation, and planning sessions on the program which involve trainee participation. However, at some level the faculty discusses these evaluation issues constantly.

As faculty trainers we discovered early in the game that if we repeated curriculum exactly we got bored. So we began to devise new ways of evoking or exploring the same content or processes. Still, we found that certain processes and exercises seemed to work beautifully to achieve desired results with one group, but not as well with another. Our evaluation sessions allowed us to compare different groups and to arrive at the perhaps slightly different versions that would allow for the wished for "messages"—processes and content—to be explored with specific groups. We could ascertain the "difference that made a difference" (Bateson, 1979).

The key questions in evaluation seem common to many arenas of experience. However, it is important to underscore that the questions we ask are inherently self-reflexive. The answers often lead us to new information. For instance, when we ask, "Did we achieve the results we expected?" a negative answer does not presume fault or blame for a failure. A negative result wherein we evaluate that "no, this plan did not achieve our imagined outcome," invites our curiosity about design, about sequence, about where trainees are at, about the fit of plan with people, and about the processes involved.

With such a paradigm and such an approach to human systems issues, there is no right or wrong—there is only new information. Subsidiary information or processes then become examined and focal (Polanyi, 1958). The new information derived corrects assumptions that were way off target and realigns the fit of plans with people.

It is precisely through the process of investigating what happened that we did not expect that our new learnings and integrations have occurred. We do not have to cut down or cut out any territory. We simply enlarge the map to include the new findings. We promote the application of the same principle to therapy and other settings where learning or change is expected.

ASSIGNMENTS

This is no new category for anyone! In our program, it can relate to a wide range of tasks: from reading articles and books to writing papers, to interviewing a three-year-old, to tracking intergenerational themes in one's family, to drawing a flow diagram of one's learning style, to interviewing members of one's own family, nuclear, enucleated, extended or overextended. Any task creates new living experiences and that basic way of knowing. The report of the project or assignment describes knowing about and helps to integrate in another way.

FEETNOTES

This whole book could be called a "feetnote-on-a-14-year project." Like the house-that-jack-built, in feetnotes are the theory-spinnings that faculty share with trainees, coming out of the seminars themselves, and the metamap connections that have been made from the ideas evoked from exercises, faculty meetings, papers, readings, and our own thoughts. All feetnotes are meant to be sharings, dialogic in nature, and not dogma.

The use of the word "feetnotes," albeit corny, was deliberately chosen to be both within the form of this more formal paradigm, yet not of it in the usual type of footnote meaning and content. "Feetnotes" was/is meant to free up trainers as well as trainees to risk writing up new "I wonder if's . . . ," explorations and weavings. The word has acted as a nonthreatening invitation to take one's budding ideas seriously enough to share in written form with others, yet not seriously enough to believe or feel that such ideas need to be stuffy, formal, complete or perfect. Here we include the learnings, the generalizations, the new weaving of conceptual material, in a brief, new thought form; the interrelatedness of this material with group processes and human beings; new ideas that the faculty or trainees have spun; comments on the process; and humorous bits.

More recently we have instituted trainees' writing short feetnote summaries of each seminar, which are distributed the following week to all, along with each seminar's planned curriculum sheet, in which the entire paradigm is spelled out.

SUMMARY

This paradigm then has been found to be remarkably useful as a meta-paradigm for any reflexively coherent and/or goal-directed activity or program, including therapy.

In terms of planning at any level, one can start at any step in the paradigm, and work forwards and backwards from there. Let us suppose one starts with an idea for an exercise. We can then ask what goals would be achieved, what material would be evoked by this exercise? Does the exercise have anything to do with where we think the trainees are at? And so on. If one should start with this last question, relating to faculty assumptions or the assessment of where the trainees are at, we can then ask: Given how we see them, what do we think will reach them in a connecting way, in order to get an idea across? When such a model is followed for each seminar, the synchrony between people, content and processes is more readily maintained. Trainees are and feel included in the designs. They know that how they learn will shape how we teach.

By this time, it would be possible to do a microanalysis of the development since 1973 of curriculum planning, of the development of our expanded goals, assumptions, propositions, implications, and exercises developed, as well as the evolving theories on training and therapy, from all the seminar teaching plans designed over the years.

Each week, the paradigm guides the planning for each seminar. As mentioned previously, a sheet following the paradigm form is written out ahead of time and given to students at the end of each session. Thus, each group of trainees has a written record of plans, of where they have been, and can reflect later on an evening's design—or a whole semester's plan.

Thus, paradigms such as this one are operational models for *how to think about* wide varieties of situations, settings and issues. Once values are clarified, this framework is available to serve as the structure in which and by which spontaneity can take place. In addition, the paradigm serves as a yardstick against which all the events within the program can be judged, readjusted and measured for their:

1) Predictability
2) Congruency
3) Reflexive coherence
4) Impact and effectiveness
5) Generation of new sentences

As such, this particular conceptual system, this paradigm, fits with an open systems model of human systems. Built in is the analogue that each set of processes creates an impact loop, helping to shape the next event. With the conscious evaluation process contained within it, all involved in the program can, and indeed do, influence that evolving shape.

System as Metaphor: Metaphor, Analogy, and Organismic Learning | VII

In Chapter IV, we defined "systems" by a formal and verbal linear abstract map of living systems, in the framework of general systems theory. But if we ask ourselves again, "What is a living system?" we must rely not on an abstract concept of linear and logical thinking, but on our own *images*. . . living system, dynamic interaction of component parts, within a boundary, in/over time-space. There are so many phenomena occurring at once, each suggesting an image, that we cannot comprehend them by any manner of simultaneous focus.

As Polanyi states (Polanyi and Prosch, 1975), when we visit a house or building and see several rooms, *only the mind can connect their simultaneous existence by some sort of inner imagery.* So it is with living systems in dynamic interaction. Only by some inner imagery, some image of the senses, like the hearing of an orchestra, or the imaging of a dance, can we capture the *idea* of living systems!

Living system, then, *is a metaphor* for a whole, whose simultaneity we cannot comprehend. It is a metaphor for a sense of the summative quality, the greater than the parts, whose essence we cannot see, touch or kiss. It is a metaphor for the betweenness, for the sets of relationships, which we must sense, imagine, connect, create. Thus, living human systems are like a moving hologram again, constantly shifting planes and fields, there but not there. The only comprehension we can have of living, human systems is metaphoric, analogic, organismic, synesthetic. "Living, human systems" is not even a way of thinking; it is an invention, a way of imaging the world of people and oneself in it.

How, then, does one train in ways that others may invent an image/conception of the world of human beings, with oneself in it? How does one unite abstract theories about living systems to the trainees, who are, by these definitions, concrete living systems, and also parts of larger living systems? How does one connect external conceptions called living systems theory to each person's invention processes, to internal thoughts, images, feelings, sensations, ideas, actions? How does one train others to unite that which we call experience, personal knowledge (Polanyi, 1958, 1969; Polanyi and Prosch, 1975) or one's epistemic view (MacLean, 1975), the map from the inside out, to consensual or public knowledge, to epistemology, the formal views, the maps from the outside in?

The answer for us at BFI seems to be through involvement in metaphor, analogue, and action.

The discussions of training at the family therapy meeting in 1979,* where the question came up about ways of getting trainees to think metaphorically, analogically and systemically, struck me with a sense of surprise and delight. I realized that while finding solutions to other puzzles in training, we had indirectly developed and evolved answers to quite a few of those questions being raised. Since the first "how do you hear?" exercise, trainers at BFI had been involved in experiential learning. We had been very aware, since 1973 particularly, of our intent to assist trainees in integrating all aspects of their experience, akin to the tuning of an instrument, so that all notes could be called upon to play in whatever combination necessary. Our basic vehicles in that experiential learning which resulted in integrated and multicentric thinking had been and is metaphor and analogue in many forms—spatial, imagistic, verbal, kinesthetic, aural.

We had been providing exercises, or common metaphors, as analogic isomorphs. As psychologist Larry Allman, BFI graduate and founder of the Los Angeles Family Institute, puts it, we had been teaching "non-linear material, non-linearly."**

In this chapter and the next three, I will be exploring some of the ways of approaching and thinking about such experiential learning or action techniques.

CONNECTING THINKING IN CHILDREN TO THINKING IN ADULTS

The questions at the 1979 meetings had brought to mind for me ones that I had had a year and a half earlier, when, as a doctoral candidate at the University of Massachusetts, I took two courses on Piaget with Klaus Schulz and with George Forman. Although I had read Piaget years earlier, I was in a different place in my life, and so read with completely different focusing and associative tracking. The more I read about children, the more I thought about adults and specifically about our methodology of training at BFI. Both Fred

---

*International Forum of Trainers and AFTA meetings, 1979—see Prologue.
**Personal communication.

Duhl and I had been interested in the issues of fit (Duhl, F. J., Kantor, and Duhl, B. S., 1973), how people learn, and in different learning styles (Duhl, B. S. and Duhl, F. J., 1975) since the birth of our children, if not before.

In these Piaget courses, I kept trying to find some links between learning styles and learning stages. The more I read and discussed Piaget, the more I kept puzzling as to why and how our way of training seemed to result in train-ees' becoming capable of decentering, while staying in touch with their own point of view. I kept wondering where our way of training fit. I kept seeing in our training the integration of right and left brain functions (Bogen, 1968; Buzan, 1976; de Bono, 1970; Gazzaniga, 1968; Ornstein, 1972; Samples, 1976).

During the spring of 1978, I was in the fortunate position of having in George Forman a professor who, although an authority on Piaget and *children*, listened to my concerns and curiosities about the *extension of Piagetian stages into adult life* and the integration I felt we were achieving with trainees, primarily through action, metaphor and analogue. But Piaget does not talk about such events, particularly not in adults. Through Forman's suggestion, I began to find the conceptual underpinnings which explained why what we did worked. This book is an extension of that process, another "knot in the handkerchief" (Bateson, 1972).

George Forman had suggested that I look into an article written by Jacques Jimenez (also a University of Massachusetts School of Education graduate some years before) in *Piagetian Abstracts,* entitled "Piaget and Synectics" (1976). I read the article and felt like those who cracked the code on the Rosetta Stone must have felt! For here was the missing link I had been looking for. Like the house that reportedly sits straddling the four corners of Utah, Ari-zona, Nevada, and New Mexico, this article straddled and linked the arenas of concern to me.

Jimenez had put together the basic processes of intelligence, of assimila-tion and accommodation, as elaborated by Piaget (1952), with W. J. J. Gor-don's *Synectics* (which "taken from the Greek, means the joining together of different and apparently irrelevant elements" [Gordon, 1961]). Synectics is concerned with creative problem-solving through the use of verbal analogy and metaphor.

A paper I wrote at that time, entitled "Piaget, BFI and Metaphor," was my first exploration of the linkage between our way of training, Piaget, Bruner and other learning theorists, and the metaphor-making processes of the mind (Duhl, B. S., 1978). Fuller explorations of some of my newer dis-coveries relating to integration and multicentricity appear throughout this book.

PIAGET, SYNECTICS AND BFI

According to Jimenez, Gordon states that "the mind has two basic jobs to perform. One is to 'Make the Strange Familiar,'* that is, to incorporate new facts, events, experiences, etc., into the frameworks already established by previously appropriated facts, events, experiences, etc." Gordon calls this "learning." This is Piaget's assimilation process, occurring in play, in which the child uses the world as an extension of himself, and celebrates himself as the paradigm of the world. "Symbolic play is merely egocentric thought in its pure state" (Jimenez, 1976, p. 104).

According to Jimenez's account of Gordon, "The other process of intelligence is the opposite. It is to 'Make the Familiar Strange' that is, to free something already known from the stereotypes we have put into it . . . to alter one's angle of vision to meet new realities" (Jimenez, 1976, p. 104). Gordon calls this "innovation." This is Piaget's accommodation process, accomplished by imitation. "Here, the child adapts himself to what he sees, and tries to understand it by imitating it, getting the feel of it from inside . . ." (Jimenez, 1976, p. 104).

"Children's play is a form of 'Making the Strange Familiar,' or of simply keeping everything as familiar as possible. Children's imitation is a form of 'Making the Familiar Strange,' of exploring the unknown." (Jimenez, 1976, p. 105)

At BFI, we design exercises which involve both play and imitation, making the Strange Familiar and the Familiar Strange.

Jimenez quotes Piaget's description of when J. opened and closed her mouth after watching Piaget opening and closing his eyes: " . . . The model is assimilated to an analogous schema susceptible of translating the visual into the kinesthetic." He goes on to say:

> What Piaget has done in this passage is to give a description of metaphor at work. In assimilation/play the work of metaphor is to reduce the world to the child, to "Make the Strange Familiar." In accommodation/imitation, the work of metaphor is to expand the child to the world—to "Make the Familiar Strange." It is precisely Gordon's discovery that metaphor is the simple device by which the human mind, both child and adult, accomplishes its twin prodigies. The difference between the child and adult is not that the child thinks by metaphor, and the adult without it, but that the child does not know he is thinking

---

*In this chapter, in presenting Gordon's concepts, I will capitalize Strange and Familiar when they appear together, for emphasis, as Gordon does.

metaphorically, while the adult does know, and the child cannot control or balance the metaphor while the adult can. Piaget's circular system of assimilation and accommodation is therefore, explicitly: a description of the workings of metaphor . . . (Jimenez, 1976, p. 105).

And so, putting Piaget and Synetics together, we may well have a three-word definition of intelligence: the complementary processes of *assimilation* and *accommodation,* both accomplished by means of *metaphor* (Jimenez, 1976, p. 108).

THE APPLICATION OF PIAGET, GORDON, AND OTHERS TO TRAINING THERAPISTS

One may reasonably ask: How does all of the above have anything to do with a training program for adults in family therapy?

At BFI, through a series of exercises done in a group interview, we choose people for training who have some observable sense of systems and empathy, who seem to be able to report and make sense for themselves out of what they have just experienced. We are most concerned with how they look at interface issues—the happenings *between* people, between aspects of self, for these are the issues in family and other human systems.

Yet a system is also not a "thing" but a metaphor for patterns of actions and relationships, which interact simultaneously as well as over time, eluding linear description. *Systems are "wholes" of relationships; metaphors grasp "wholes."*

We see every trainee as a representative of at least one family system. The way we teach family systems is by analogy and metaphor, in action as well as words, using the "raw data" of trainees' lives and families as analogues, as well as data and concepts about families "out there."

DISCOVERING THE "SET"

To train people to be change agents, on line, with live families, in a setting where the only tool is oneself and one's ability to conceptualize what the relationships are out there in families, means to also train people to draw forth and to know what representations of systems they already carry in their mind. Such representations, such core images, are already "coding systems" (Bruner, 1973a). If people do not know what their own "set" is, they will impose it on whatever situation is in front of them. As Bruner (1973a, p. 226) says,

Obviously, the principal giver of instruction is our own past history. For, by virtue of living in a certain kind of professional or social setting, our approach to new experience becomes constrained—we develop, if

you will, a professional deformation with respect to coding events. . . .
One's attitude toward learning, whether a transient or an enduring
thing, will then determine the degree to which one is equipped with coding systems that can be brought to bear on new situations and permit
one to go beyond them.

Trainers cannot approach the "data" coded by trainees directly. Such information can only be approximated, through metaphor. Certain already coded data are equivalent to closed systems, in that they are out of awareness and
not available. At BFI we have felt it is necessary to make that which is taken
for granted overt. In this sense, we are "Making the Familiar Strange," in
Gordon's terms. *Metaphor "evokes the preconscious, and watches it work"*
(Jimenez, 1976).

When the Familiar is made Strange over and over again, trainees learn to
learn options—options in ways of thinking, being, seeing, doing. Learning is
connection-making (Gordon and Poze, 1977). Trainees learn to learn that
how you look and intervene and label depends on where you stand, your
"set" or "professional deformation." "The more freely and frequently one
makes such analogies, the more freely and frequently will he be *thinking*.
Thus, in his teaching strategy, one will teach not only the subject matter itself, but also how to think *about* the subject matter" (Jimenez, 1975, italics in
the original).

From this other Jimenez paper, I had found a key to our way of training:
*Through our use of metaphor, analogue and action, we were teaching not only
the subject matter itself, but also how to think about the subject matter.* We
were using the metaphor-making processes of mind to discover the metaphors by which we live and work.

WHAT IS A METAPHOR?

David MacDermott (1974) states that the word metaphor translates literally from the Greek as "a carrying from one place to another." That is the
sense in which we will use it here: *A metaphor is the transposing of an image
or association from one state or arena of meaning to another, highlighting
similarities, differences and/or ambiguities.*

We all automatically carry many associations and meanings from one
place to another. Thus, *metaphor is the linkage of meaning—that which connects any two events, ideas, characteristics, modes.* And metaphor is hardly
only linear and verbal. Paintings are linkages between what an artist perceives, or imagines, and what is transposed, transported, and transformed by
the artist with brush and paint. Choreographed dance is metaphor, as is

music. Verbal metaphors can carry the past into the present, as well as the totality of images of one person onto another, as in, "You're your father, all over again!" Metaphors in any form—spatial, imagistic, verbal, kinesthetic, aural—are symbolic linkages and transformations of meaning, generated by a human mind.

Metaphor, then, seems to be *the* key in that integration or equilibration process of mind (Jimenez, 1976) in which the individual transforms experience from one mode to another, from "outside" self to "inside" self. If we restate the main process here, Piaget describes J. opening and closing her mouth as a *translation* of his opening and closing his eyes. J. has translated (I would say transformed) the visual into the kinesthetic. Jimenez (1976) comments on this process as *"metaphor at work."*

We have no related action verb form of this word for this process. Mac-Dermott uses the word *"metaphoring,"* which seems an appropriate one to use when speaking of the activity itself, and is the one that I will use. The child is then "metaphoring"—in the process of mentally carrying a perception, awareness, or image from one place to another, from one mode to another, from one realm to another. Metaphoring is the process of making relationship, of connecting. Mind *is* metaphoring process.

Human beings seem to be born with the capacity for metaphoring and for creating metaphors. These processes of mind are found operating at each and every level of development and at every stage in life. When we play or imitate we are metaphoring—carrying experience from one realm to another. We each seem to have basic stances towards the world, basic styles. We tend to make the Strange Familiar, make the Familiar Strange, and try to keep the Familiar Familiar.

The intentional creation and spontaneous process of metaphoring seem to me to be key phenomena in the developmental processes of decentration (Piaget, 1977b, pp. 277, 434–444). What we translate and transform during decentration processes are not externally perceived behaviors or events as Piaget's J. perceived, but another's internal attitudes and constructs of mind.

AN ASIDE ON DECENTRATION

Decentration in Piaget's terms is intrinsically and originally related to perceptual activity—and focusing or centrating—and is key in systems thinking. "The passage from one centration to another (or *decentration*) thus tends to the correction or regulation of centrations by each other, and the more numerous the decentrations, the more accurate becomes the resulting perception" (Piaget in Piaget and Inhelder, 1956, italics in original).

From those beginnings to adult objectivity, however, is a long and continuing pilgrimage.

Essentially, the process (of objectivity) which at any one of the developmental stages moves from egocentrism toward decentering, constantly subjects increases in knowledge to a *refocusing of perspective*. . . . Actually, it means that learning is not a purely additive process and that to pile one (newly) learned piece of behavior or information on top of another is not in itself adequate to structure an objective attitude. Objectivity presupposes a decentering, i.e., a continual refocusing of perspective. Egocentrism, on the other hand, is the undifferentiated state prior to multiple perspectives, whereas objectivity implies both differentiation and coordination of the points of view which have been differentiated (Piaget and Inhelder, 1958, italics added).

In decentration, or achieving integrated multicentricity, in the process of trying to understand another's world, we need modes of translating or transforming another's words and behaviors from "outside self" to "inside self." We need modes of metaphoring, of trying on and experiencing another's micro and macro world views and carrying them from another to oneself, as a way of both differentiating and integrating them. We need ways of perceiving relationship between events *as if* through another's eyes.

In decentration, we expand our experience to include a view of ourselves and the world by *mentally inhabiting* a space outside our own skin. For a moment or more, we *image* the world, our own behavior, or another's experience, that which is Strange, *as if* we were seeing with someone else's eyes, experiencing another's sensations, and make them ours, Familiar. In this internal metaphoring, we carry ourselves mentally from one place to another. Momentarily, we leave our own sense of self on the shelf, as it were, *as if* we did not at that moment possess an epistemic view of the world, and we attempt to approximate another's, thereby making that which is Strange Familiar.

Approximation is the closest we can ever get to knowing another person's internal world or to communicating the essence of an idea, feeling, or image to one another. Empathy derives from such approximating. Various forms of metaphor serve well as vehicles for this process. I call the type of metaphors by which we do this "metaphors of approximation."

Metaphor does not exist in nature or naturally. Metaphors are inventions of the human mind, whose use of them seems to function in the service of integration, connecting disparately experienced realities and multiple phenomena. "Metaphors are made by a brain perceiving a relation between two or more clusters of characteristics" (MacDermott, 1974).

Our minds work to create order, integration, and coherence. Metaphoring then seems to be the mental process of inclusion and connection, implicitly, in preverbal or paraverbal awareness and connection making. Metaphors are the explicit expression of that connection of unity in some symbolic, humanly created form: spoken or written words, created objects, expressions or patterns. *"Patterns are clusters of metaphors. . . . Realities are clusters of patterns"* (MacDermott, 1974). Theories, epistemologies and paradigms are also metaphors.

The human mind, then, is an interactive event. It seems to be a set of processes requiring contexts and other human beings to metaphor into relationship. Without belaboring the point, in order to develop, each new human being requires at base other persons, as well as both nonvocal and linguistic interactions with those persons. Each child, however, begins to give meaning, long before there is language. He/she metaphors into relationship vast amounts of data. MacDermott, an artist, speaks of "clusters" of metaphors. Piaget stated this in another way: that each infant very early begins to create schemas and weaves clusters of schemas into schemata—to create the sense of reality, of how things are. The human mind creates relationships, which are neither one thing or the other, but are something else instead. These relationships, these metaphors for betweenness, are created in the mind of each human being.

Intelligence thus begins neither with knowledge of the self nor of things as such but with knowledge of their interaction, and it is by orienting itself simultaneously toward the two poles of that interaction that intelligence organizes the world by organizing itself (Piaget, 1977b, p. 275).

MYTHS, METAPHORS, AND METAPHORING—
THINKING ABOUT THINKING

If we extend these concepts out from the individual to the sense of a totality of individuals, to a society, we can look at culture and the processes practiced in a culture as illuminating the concepts of both metaphor and metaphoring. Anthropological and sociological studies aid us in this direction.

If we look at pre-technological and isolated cultures, such as the Netsilik Eskimo culture or the Tlingit Indians of British Columbia before the invasion of Westerners (and Western metaphors for how to live), we can say that the people in them lived a holistic, organic metaphor or reality, wherein all aspects of their lives were connected to all other aspects. The clusters of patterns and processes were interlinking clusters of relationships. Within such cultures, there was no bit that did not reflect the whole, no abstract, rational thinking that did not loop back into organismic integration. The artifacts of the culture were organically related to living. They were often both utilitarian *and* symbolically related to the belief systems. The traditions of dress, the practices, were the metaphors of the culture, the linkages of meaning, carried in time. Each new member born to the culture soon learned and connected, or metaphored, the same meanings.

Such an organismic culture then carries its ideas from one place to another within the culture and over time in a congruent and interconnected fashion, so that the images of life in that culture are shared ones. The roles, rules, routines, and rituals *fit* together in an interwoven, interlinking fashion with beliefs. There are common metaphors that have the same meaning to everyone. Each person's core images of meaning, ways of coding events, are essentially the same.

When such a culture is isolated, little or no new and strange information from outside crosses its boundaries. New information always forces members to think and connect new relationships or to exclude and reject the new information. When there is no comparison with other ways or other cultures, there is no diversity; there is nothing Strange to make Familiar; there are no mixed metaphors. The macrometaphor remains essentially the same, and the inhabitants have a surety of their sense of reality. It is shared and stable.

In such a culture, the clusters of patterns and practices continue unperturbed, generation after generation. Such a macrometaphor of clusters contains and defines the whole story of life, all the events within life, "explaining" the patterns that people have learned to learn in that context. With such a pattern of meanings, the Familiar is kept Familiar (equilibration) and the "patterns connect" (Bateson, 1979).

Within such a culture, the *metaphors of identity*—the ways by which people know who they are, over time—*are shared as consensually accepted metaphors of identity*. These metaphors are usually related to sex, role, task and status, carrying meaning from the outside in. These meanings progress and evolve for each person according to the culture's set rules of order and succession for each stage of life. What is expected is clear. The image of self from within matches the images of persons from without, and each person is an integral part of the macrometaphor of the culture. It is a reflexively coherent culture (Wideman, 1970). Everyone has a place and knows relationships. All are inside, within a "boundary."

These rules of order and succession also prescribe the rules of access to each person, and one is regarded and approached according to one's position by consensual rules.

The experiences "under the skin" are not acknowledged, differentiated phenomena. They are expressed in metaphoric stories, and are not dealt with in direct and personal terms as aspects of self, subdifferentiations of individual entities, where one is responsible for one's own actions, decisions. The myths and metaphors of the culture place one's actions in relationship to the context, to the whole. The myths of the culture, like Indian stories, symbolically express the unorderly, nonpredictable yet *expected nonrational* ways of being. The legends, tales, and myths wrap coherence around all experience and lace individual experiences with a sense of integrity, of fit, of relationship to the whole. One accepts oneself and the world as the way it is. One is consciously and unconsciously linked to and part of the macrometaphor.

Types of Metaphors

Thus, in such a culture, the *metaphors of identity* are also available to be utilized as *metaphors of approximation*—the ways in which each person can best imagine how another acts and experiences the world. Both such sets of metaphors are part of and connected to the *metaphors of organization*, expressing what we call the structures and hierarchies of the culture, the *ordering* of relationships expressed through rules concerning roles, defining who can do what with whom, and when, in prescribed relationships. All three such groups of metaphors are automatically and equivalently interwoven with the *metaphors of operation*, exemplifying processes and procedures which embody the patterns of *how* people enact relating and relationship. Such metaphors of operation capture the standardized practices, the routines and rituals, the movements and exchanges that happen *between and among* those in standardized roles. Such integrations of a sense of self, others, functions, structures, purpose and belief make for the reflexive coherence of such cultures. (Paradoxically, in a reflexively coherent culture, these terms are already metaphors subdividing that which has no subdivision).

MAJOR METAPHORS AND PARADIGMS IN AMERICA

The predominant myths and metaphors of our contemporary American world, however, are not integrated, holistic, and congruent, and do not loop back in a reflexively coherent fashion. Images from within do not match those from without. One can be many varieties of person. Many functions and structures within this society do not flow one with the other, in pursuit of common purposes and images.

Let us consider the macrometaphors—or ways of thinking—of our contemporary Western world which seem to be operating in contemporary America. We have those of the 18th century Age of Reason and the Idea of Progress, in which rational thought, abstract reasoning, logic, and order are championed. This way of thinking led to the development of the scientific approach, the ability to explore the physical universe and to postulate the predictable laws by which it seems to operate. And this development of abstract thought and the concomitant development of the ability to translate physical properties into concepts and again into numerical symbols expressing relationships led to our technological processes and creations. What is new has been considered "progress" and therefore good. This way of thinking also carries with it an ideal image of human alone and in relationship, as rational, mature, reasonable, objective. Such a way of thinking teases things apart in an orderly fashion, from the outside in, leading to differentiation, to a logical aesthetic sense of separateness of aspects of self, of things, events, understandings. This ability to analyze, to be objective, has also been captured in a more recent metaphor entitled "left brain thinking," expressing the human capacity for and need to create logical order, for making the Strange Familiar and understood.

In America, we also inherited the macrometaphor of the 19th century Age of Romanticism, in which emotional complexity, organicity, creativity, nature, intuition, and spontaneity are emphasized. The stressing of love, passion, and man's full and deep range of emotionality led to rich and expansive expressions of human capacity, human images, and dreams in metaphors of art, literature, music. This way of thinking tends to blend images together, from the inside out, leading to connection and to integration. There is a linking with an organic aesthetic sense, of people's actions being related to, or an expression of, internally held meanings. This way of thinking also carries with it images of people in relationship as governed not by reason but by the senses and the universal human need of belonging and bonding. Certain aspects of this subjective way of thinking are currently framed by the metaphor "right brain thinking," expressing also the human capacity for and need to create personal statements, to make the Familiar Strange, in new whole images.

And lastly we inherited in America the predominant macrometaphors of the Judeo-Christian religions and ethics, which comprise the moral base and belief system underlying our laws and our valuing of human life. America is the first place on earth that we know of to be voluntarily populated by peoples from many, many lands, and unified by egalitarian codes of law. Such codes are metaphors of operation and organization inclusive of basic human respect of and for each individual human life. From the Judeo-Christian macrometaphor we also inherited our belief in the work ethic, our ideas of sin and goodness, our beliefs in a righteous Being higher than man, who is both rational and expressive, and who, for some, determines our future if not our past and present. This way of thinking gives a particular expression to the sense of the human spirit or soul, and the human need for a sense of purpose in life. Multiple ideal images of relationships of kindness, respect, sharing, and righteous living among individual members are inherent in this way of thinking.

The values of the particular men who wrote the American Constitution reflected the Age of Reason and the Judeo-Christian ethic, preceding as they did Romanticism. Their values also reflected the bondedness people had to their ways of being and to their ways of being different *from* each other. These values found societal expression in the newly emerging concepts of equivalent democracy. The keeping of certain myths, images, and metaphors, the traditions they had brought to this new country, carried in time and geography, were ways of assimilating, of making the Strange Familiar. Ways of thinking and believing, like skin, come with people when they emigrate. *Meanings* of roles, rules, routines, of relationships in other places came as parts of patterns, of interactional dances and ways of being, to be kept or consciously avoided. At the same time in early America, the Familiar was Strange with the sense of new freedoms and new empowerment to make the rules by which to live.

"America" as macrometaphor has also carried a variety of images at different times to new immigrants and those already here: It has meant freedom, land of opportunity, the new frontier, space, the good life, the land of milk and honey, the melting pot, the home of the brave, the Horatio Alger story, the land of democracy, the country where a pauper can become president. It has meant equality, the land of plenty, the land of invincible technology, and goods for all. These image/ideals allowed people to put energy into their tasks with the idea of "getting ahead," of making "progress," of making life "better" for themselves and their children. While none of these metaphors could capture the actuality of life for all, they were (and still are) predominent metaphoric ideals against which experience was and is measured.

The Western emphasis on rational thought gave impetus to science and technology and to human control of the environment. As the level of technology increased, bringing us these imagined products of the good life, we began to use them. Some, like railroads, steamboats, automobiles and planes, took us new places. Others, like wireless, radio, telephone, television, and computers, bombarded us with new information, continuing to change how we lived. We had more and more part roles, part relationships, more and more part decisions about how to live and how to be a "full" human being.

In this century, space exploration, imagined in what used to be the Strange *Flash Gordon* fiction of my childhood, became reality, brought to us by our ability to both imagine, to make the Familiar Strange and to analyze, plan and produce, to make the Strange Familiar.

The "I wonder if . . . " feedforward metaphoring (Richards, 1968) of images of what does not yet exist fires the ideas of science, the creativity in art, in music, in technology, to explore and create—to metaphor the image from inside the mind to the creation of it outside. We then make manifest our image. We create it in real time and space. It then becomes part of our contextual world, part of "the way it is," with which we interact. Often, we begin to describe ourselves by the new metaphors we have created.

As creatures of context, we first understand the world by the act of transposing what is outside to a corresponding something inside, as J. did, with Piaget. We draw our metaphors for understanding ourselves from those already existing, as we begin to create new ones in "combinatory play" (Piaget and Inhelder, 1969). We make the Familiar Strange and the Strange Familiar when we use a metaphor or way of thinking in one arena that borrows from another one where it would normally not be used. As Gordon wrote (1961), Harvey could describe the heart, because man had already invented a pump. The principle operating to create an external metaphor, pump, could be used for a way of understanding the principle operating for a part of the human body, heart.

METAPHORS AND METAPHORING IN MENTAL HEALTH: BORROWINGS FROM OTHER FIELDS

Thus, the subdifferentiations of science have given us new metaphors. New ways of thinking in science have given us new ways of understanding human behavior. After all, the *ways of looking* at anthropological man, of looking at cultures, come to us not out of the myths of the people themselves, but out of our Western and scientific recognition of parts and wholes and interrelationships, first applied to total "foreign" cultures. Our *meanings* for the workings of a whole culture can be described from the outside by metaphors, carried from other places. Yet our descriptive map of that culture is not the same as the territory of that culture, i.e., the interactive patterns themselves, nor is it the same as the experience of living in that culture.

The human mind must metaphor into existence the rules underlying processes. The metaphoring processes of people involved in science and technology have created greater and greater subdifferentiations, uncoverings, and explanations that we must cope with once they are made overt, *for the processes of technology change our lives as much as the products*. We have information, images, and new processes by which we live, without the integrating and connecting processes to get us to "there" from "here," or congruent belief systems to guide us in coping (Duhl, B., 1976a).

As actions create ideas create actions (see Figure 1, Chapter V), so "macrometaphors generate micrometaphors generate macrometaphors," and so on. Fields of thought in a culture develop with the prevailing ideologies and macrometaphors, and human systems thinking is no different. Predominent metaphors and beliefs change slowly, while technology changes our concrete *existence* and actions quite rapidly.

As science uncovered smaller and smaller units, investigating that which was subsidiary in what heretofore was focal (Polanyi, 1958, Polanyi and Prosch, 1975), man looked deeper beneath the skin for subsets. In divorcing itself from philosophy and "romantic speculation" and in attempting to become a human "science," psychology has traditionally employed the metaphors of the physical sciences and of religion. Such metaphors allowed for the carrying of images and concepts from an observable outside to an unobservable inside.

In this century, Freud borrowed freely from prevalent macrometaphors. However mixed the metaphors may be, Freud's leap was to begin to define the subunits of the individual person as a total system (Rapaport, 1960). He began to explore individual processes and to theorize that they were universal. He operated within the language and metaphors of the time in which he lived and created new ones. Borrowing from religion, the superego replaced a deity and the human being was organized by good and evil forces (id). Borrowing from science, the rational, "reality oriented" human (ego) was seen as developing over time (a biological concept) from infancy on, and slowly winning internal battles to be in charge of the irrational (romantic) human. Freud, however, fully valued the power of this irrational element, which he labeled "the unconscious," to make creative, symbolic and analogic leaps. The divisiveness of science and religion was also inherent in Freud's theory, in which energy was then a concept metaphorically transposed from physics into human relationships, which were seen as operating according to certain innate mechanical "forces."

Freud's genius in putting such metaphors together is an adult version of "combinatory play" and the metaphoring process at work. For people to then reify the ideas of id, ego, superego, as concrete entities, as if they were realities of emotional and conscious human beings, was and is a huge error of map and territory. The metaphor is not the event itself. However, the overviewing conceptualization, in which man is envisioned as having subsets to his psychological self which interact and "fit" together, remained.

Psychodynamic theory was not inherently related to living and ongoing cultural and interpersonal contexts, nor to the cognitive, social and creative development of mind functions, nor to life as actually lived. Many other psychologists, sociologists, anthropologists, neurologists, and brain researchers have provided information and filled out the image of mind as an enormously complex, interacting, contextual entity.

The concept of internal interactions of aspects of self or of mind (again, dividing that which has no subdivision) is a systemic one, available to fit with concepts about observable external interactions of people with each other.

In America, more recently, new and different metaphors have entered our realm of thinking about how human beings act and relate. These holistic metaphors seem to come both as a result of increased communication in our postwar shrunken world and as an outcome of the unexplained wave/particle mass/no mass conundrums of subatomic physics. From the East come strange and unresearched forms of medicine and ideas about how mind and body work together. From physics come concepts of quarks, quasars, and unexplained "black holes," as well as the continual subdivisions of next smallest units, reaching the ultimate concept that *relationship between* intangibles creates something tangible! These ways of thinking, these carrying from one place to another of ideas, these metaphors, challenge our traditional Western concepts and our sense of reality.

In the several realms of psychology and mental health, the full range of metaphors of science, spirituality, economics, religion, and ethics finds representation. As the latest *Handbook of Family Therapy* (Gurman and Kniskern, 1981) makes evident, this is true of family systems thinking also. It is time to pull ideas together. The metaphor of general systems thinking may well provide us with the opportunity to do so.

The Metaphor of an Expanded General Systems Theory

Von Bertalanffy's general systems model of human systems, deriving primarily from the metaphors of the biological sciences, cybernetics and religion, allows us the greatest flexibility to fit our epistemics (the world view and beliefs we learned-to-learn, our subsets or aspects of self and our behaviors) together with epistemology (the formal, consensual way of looking from outside). With such a model, we can be as concerned with the metaphors of identity (individual isomorphs) and approximation (transfer) as we are with metaphors of organization (structure) and operations (function). General systems is inclusive of all of these. We can be concerned with how people experience their changing reality in developmental time, wherein the Familiar becomes Strange and the Strange becomes Familiar.

We can be concerned with how human beings bond in varying combinations and with the roles and processes people enact, by which they make the Strange Familiar. And we can be concerned with how information is transmitted and received in ways that confuse or clarify the bondings and the metaphors of relationship. We are free to consider the metaphors and macrometaphors of contextual life and social organization, by which people learn language, how to think and how to behave. With a full metaphor of an evolving ecosystemic universe, we can look at the whole of life as interconnected and related.

People carry with them their learnings, their metaphors, from one context to the next. A changing context can also make their metaphors obsolete and ineffective. We can only look at institutions and societies of which we are a part once they have broken down, to see what made them "work" and how they functioned and fit together. The absence of smooth operation allows us to investigate, compare, and explore what is missing.

When traditional institutions and processes facilitating life, connection, and growth in this society break down, therapies of varying sorts arise to "cure" people. Unfortunately, many of these therapeutic processes fail to look at the fabric of life as lived. Many look at human distress as if each person were solely and totally responsible for his/her condition. As we try to cope and to live the processes our technology forces upon us, *we live more and more part relationships*. The rules, roles, routines, and rituals for how to be and see oneself in relation to others in personal, work and other settings, as well as to a macrometaphor, have changed dramatically in the last 40 years particularly. We live by our images, many of them television fantasies, our metaphors clustered into "realities." Yet the concrete realities of our lives no longer facilitate those idealized realities in being reached (B. S. Duhl, 1976a). We do not know how to make the Strange Familiar, to image the many parts we each have to play into human wholes that fit the human needs for functional autonomy *and* bonded connection.

The "compressed conflict" (Gordon, 1971) of the presence of opposing aspects in the same event or situation arises when what is one of *the* relevant metaphors of our lives, *technology*, is then experienced as irrelevant and antithetical to our sense of *connectedness and sense of self as individuals in relationship* in this society. Yet this sense of self as separately functioning and meaningfully connected is necessary for effective emotional, rational, and spiritual, to say nothing of physical, survival in today's world.

LIVING WITH MIXED METAPHORS

However, while the macrometaphor of technology is here, in America, the full acceptance of it as the common metaphor of personal and cultural identity is not. Many people find that the technological, cybernetic, and consumer metaphors of the current world are too limited to carry their images fully from one place to another. These metaphors do not further the person in encompassing or grounding one's understanding of his/her own experience as and in human systems, nor in approximating the experience and metaphors of others around him/her.

The social rebellion of the 1960s in America highlighted the search for differentiated, self-actualizing personal and idiosyncratic metaphors of identity, while at the same time searching for new common unifying and coherent cultural metaphors of identity. This search continues today. The contexts and focus of the search may be different, but the overall search is current.

When people in the same neighborhoods can grow up with similar ethnic and religious backgrounds, but "incompatible" personalities, when every marriage is a "mixed" marriage, when family forms are practically matters of choice and include every possible variety, when women with women, and men with men, as well as women with men, differ on their roles, rules, and routines and rituals, then we can safely say there are few *common metaphors* of identity that many can feel are representative, consistent, and suitable for all. In this particular culture, we have so many diverse groups, ideologies, levels, psychologies, and views of the elephant that we have few common metaphors of personal identity. There are almost too many discrete aspects of the culture to draw upon, without any inherent reflexive coherence of parts to the whole.

This lack of common metaphors creates the need in each person to search out his/her own grouping or constellation of metaphors of identity in defining who he/she is. The only true commonality is diversity. When there are so many idiosyncratic metaphors of identity, there is more need to create opportunities for metaphors of approximation to be exercised, so that individuals may be in communion in their communication.

This participation in the activity of metaphor creation, communication, and transformation is essential in a culture in which the individual, family, and societies are all different. The covert ways in which people expect to be approached and connected with are personal, and the social rules of order and succession for what is supposed to happen when and how in life cycles of individuals and/or families are no longer stable.

Thus, people who would learn the totality of a full organic model of human systems thinking need ways of grasping their metaphors of identity so that these metaphors can become the route to approximation. They need to explore their personal metaphors of organization and operation in order to know others and connect themselves in new congruent metaphors and patterns. And they need to know how to connect experience, behavior, and beliefs with images, past, present, and future. If you don't have an image, you can't get there.

METAPHOR AND ANALOGUE IN TRAINING

Given the diversity in this culture in general, the rapidly changing technological metaphors and processes, and the relatively new metaphor of living systems theory, one could not necessarily expect those in the early stages of the family systems movement to have formed clearly defined and usable images of human systems. One could not necessarily expect that even the words "human system" themselves would or could conjure up similar images of "component parts in dynamic interaction."

System, being a metaphor already, can only be perceived through other metaphors and analogues which carry associations from one place or arena to another.

Over the years at the Boston Family Institute, we have been creating exercises or common metaphors that act as analogues to various aspects and levels of systems as they draw on and draw forth different aspects of people's lives. Each trainee dips into his/her well of images and experiences, retrieving and creating personal *metaphors of identity* for examination and comparison by self and others.

When you train or teach by setting up exercises, you are providing *common metaphoric experiences* which connect trainees in the here and now, which are real and stand for themselves, as they are also analogic. As analogic experiences, in which each trainee's idiosyncratic personal meanings, memories, and metaphors are evoked and elicited, previous, current or future contextual situations are also evoked in the mind's eye, as are images of the persons populating those associations. These characters in one's life, in context, and in dynamic interaction with oneself and each other, are then available to be looked at as system. System on one level with self as member is then available as analogue to other units or levels or metaphors of system with self as member or nonmember. From there, it is an easy step to abstractions, in this case, systems conceptualizations and general systems theory. When training occurs in this manner, there is much less ambiguity about which images, aspects, or concepts of system, such as those previously differentiated in Chapter IV, are being referred to. *When people share common metaphors of experience, they more easily accept each other's metaphors of identity as metaphors for approximation.*

Theories are complex metaphors, complex images of the world. When you train with analogic exercises, each single exercise can stand for the whole, as bits of the holographic plate can reflect the entire hologram. Conversely, as one can find the whole *in* the bit, one can design the bit *from* the whole. Analogue is a many-faceted phenomenon. (See Figure 1.)

The designed exercise, which creates the structure for spontaneity, thus becomes the common vehicle which allows trainees to carry personal imagery and ideas from one place to another. Exercises, as common metaphors, become the vehicles of transformation.

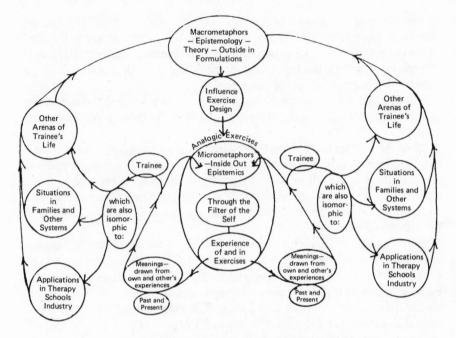

Figure 1. Analogic Exercise Through-put Loop

MATCHED AND MISMATCHED METAPHORS

I am reminded of being on two different panels of trainers at different times. The first took place in 1972, in Chicago*, in a room full of eager emergent family therapists, excited by the not-yet-defined metaphor of family therapy. They had all had some experience with working with families, in one way or another. This audience listened attentively to whatever the panel said of training and therapy, at a time when there were no sharply defined, delineated or defended modes. In that setting, each listener brought his/her idiosyncratic metaphoric image of working with a family and of training to the conference, and placed what panel members said into that image/vessel. Each took his/her filled-out image home, to translate and transform into action. In this case, each participant at the conference already had a metaphor of family system. Some may even have had an image of a way of training people to work within the metaphor of family as system.

---

*"Growing Family Therapists" sponsored by The Institute for Juvenile Research, Chicago, 1972.

Another panel concerning training on which I participated took place December 1976, at the convention of the American Academy of Psychoanalysis, whose topic was "The Family."* By this time, training programs in family therapy had proliferated and some had become quite well formed, and very different, though not well differentiated from each other in articulated conceptualizations. Panel members represented varying ways of looking at the elephant. However, the audience members came from a "distant land." In that setting, to begin with, three-quarters of the audience were hostile to the idea of therapists' seeing more than one person at a time. The prevailing metaphor for therapy of those in the audience was one-to-one, therapist-patient, with a boundary of confidentiality around that dyad, exclusive of other family members. Therapy as such was seen as a private and circumscribed experience.

When a therapist sees a whole family together, that boundary of one-to-one exclusionary privacy disappears, as do some of the secretive concepts of confidentiality of information between members. In addition, at this meeting, each panel member drew from his/her personal image or inner vision or training program for preparing people to do this very "public" form of therapy. The combination of unknown, unshared metaphors and language of family as the patient of therapy, plus training for such an event, created tremendous dissension, dissatisfaction, and annoyance in the audience. When given the opportunity to do so, most of the audience left. The remainder stayed, struggling to connect in a positive manner with this new idea of family as unit for systems therapy, while the panel talked about diverse ideas and methods in training and therapy. The result for me was like forming a container for liquid with loose sand.

I came away from that last experience, saying I'd never do that again. I was aware that while panel members might hold different views of the elephant or camel, some common experience or common metaphor had been needed for each person on the panel and in the audience to acknowledge that an elephant and/or a camel had indeed been in the room at all.

Each panel member in the room had an image, an idea of what he/she meant by certain words. And several panelists had different meanings for the same words, as did audience members. Yet words are like metaphors—they are symbols for things, for states of being and ways of seeing, and so on. The literal meaning of a word still conjures up one's idiosyncratic version of that word. When there was misunderstanding, there was no other metaphor to move to. One could not say, "Let me show you," in that context. There was no film clip or role-played family or videotape to refer to. An immediate

---

*Atlanta, Georgia.

event, witnessed by all, even if not actively participated in, was necessary to act as a common metaphor to analyze and discuss, in order for audience members as well as panelists to feel connected, to feel heard, to feel included. Without a common experience to act as organizing analogue, much of the audience walked out on what seemed to them a Tower of Babel. Similar events happen in families.

The panel members, like Japanese Noh players, were performing in concert and in Pidgin English roles from different plays, to English-speaking tourists who searched for meaning by watching and listening to what they presumed to be a performance of one play.

The wonderful irony here was the people who habitually train others in family *systems* did not catch the analogue that panel/audience is also a system, and panel/audience communication is a living systems issue, no matter how you boundary it, package it, or assign blame for the meeting's failure.

Yet the panel leader and members treated that setting and situation *as if* they were external to the communication problem and *as if* the audience indeed had common metaphors as vehicles of transformation. Analogically, the situation was akin to a different common metaphor—that which many parents and many teachers act on or presume with children, "You're supposed to know before you know."

I learned at that time that it is as easy for a group of supposed experts as for a group of beginners in human systems to assume system is what they're talking about rather than what they *are while* they are talking about it. They *are* the territory, while they are talking about the map. And each one's experience is idiosyncratic, depending upon strangeness or familiarity of images and meanings.

I learned it is as easy for experts as for beginners to forget and lose their analogic awareness when their usual context shifts. In each case, there is an assumption or presumption of shared and common images and metaphors when in actuality there are none. The lack of these common images or metaphors precludes any clear communication, as well as the very learning, exchange, evocation or change of perception that was intended. In these cases, there is no vehicle to successfully carry a message from one mind to another.

As Dick Auerswald used to say of such episodes in families and communities: "Both sides are playing cards—except one is playing poker while the other is playing bridge."*

In real life, there is no human setting or situation which cannot also be seen as analogous or isomorphic to another at the same or different levels of system. The individual level of system also encompasses many component "as-

---

*Personal communication.

pects" in dynamic interaction, other than physical "parts." What happens *between* individual subsystems, how one thinks, feels, senses, images, and acts *are* the component aspects of individuals, and create the larger system. There are those models in the family therapy movement which tend to ignore individual persons as non-systems and to make system synonymous with family only, as if looking at what happens between total persons (individuals) does not also include how each individual thinks, feels, makes meaning, acts. Yet the interventions are based on interpreting individual behavior *in context*. Individual minds, those subdifferentiated units of people, and behaviors, images, thoughts—individual systems—*change* when total systems change and vice versa. Each level of system, conceptually from intrapsychic through interpersonal to transactional, is analogous to another and can be evolved from the inner image to an active transactional interaction.

The key is to play with and train people to recognize the organismic and nonlinear connection of isomorphs, the leaps of metaphor and analogue from one level to another, from one realm to another, and to learn the languages of translation and transformation. Actual and mental escapades of this sort generate new definitions of experience—for oneself as well as for others. Skilled facilitators create many types of new metaphors of hope for people in need.

Learning the holography of human systems thinking involves inventing human systems thinking through metaphors and analogue so that each can own it for oneself. It evolves out of the invitation to trainees for exploration, for "what if?" discovery, and the "having of wonderful ideas." We invite trainees to make the Strange Familiar and the Familiar Strange, and to experience, heighten and illuminate the compressed conflict in all systems. During this aspect of training, there are no experts and no novices—there is only each one's inner challenge to oneself, to play with novelty and draw from oneself its connection to the already known.

In some programs, only one level (group) and one type (family) of system are being addressed, so that all that can be compared are analogues of the same level and type. The trainee as person, integrating self in, as, and with systems, is often left out.

We believe that when training programs include a focus on self as experiencer, organizer, conceptualizer, and actor in systems, self as a system, and/or self with systems, each trainee develops many analogic routes from the hub of self to family, society, out to the far-reaching rim of multinational systems. After all, *it is the analogue-forming mind of the trainee that will need to carry the concepts from one realm to another after training.* Many of these realms will differ, according to the differences of people's contexts and the issues with which they come in contact.

As multiple analogues are explored, trainees not only develop wide ranges of new metaphors of identity and approximation, but also learn to learn (Bateson, 1972, pp. 159–176, 279–308) the process of metaphor-making and analogue scanning. They see differently and originally. Any human experience can be represented in metaphor, can be carried from the intrapsychic realm to the transactional and back again, in various types of metaphor—verbal, spatial, or kinesic.

I say "back again," for the thoughts, feelings and ideas about systems, as well as the images of and the metaphors for systems are all experienced in a human mind—that which we label the intrapsychic realm. It is here that we make the Strange Familiar, the Familiar Strange and keep the Familiar Familiar.

Each trainee begins to develop an available reference gallery of analogic experiences and metaphoric associations. Contemporary contributions to the gallery are offered periodically, as products of practicing, rehearsing, and exercising the creative freedom to assume any role, to play with any image or role, and to *break through old rules* of behavior and concomitant labels of "bad," "silly" or "absurd." The freedom to play with "what if . . ." over time expands each trainee's sense of reality, allowing the same event to be seen in many different ways, a key to reframing in therapy, and to options in life.

A COMMON METAPHOR RIGHT NOW!

The metaphor of "labels" is as good a place as any to share an exercise which will illuminate our organic and analogic processes of training in which people begin to invent a systems image of the world. This first example is an exercise we originally developed for a workshop setting and brought home to the training program.

An Aside on Exercise Design

Our primary goals in this original situation were: to create a vehicle to transpose 50–60 people from outside the room to inside, to have them meet each other in a way which would be fun and feel safe, in which each person would be in self-control, and to create a vehicle which would *introduce participants to each other and to systems material* all at the same time!

The following exercise, designed to meet these requirements, was our answer to those wishes for goals. It introduces people to each other in a playful manner, one in which the Familiar is made Strange and the Strange Familiar. In addition, this particular common metaphor quickly locates one in and as member of systems, radiating out by analogic extension, to all levels of system.

Exercise: A Label by Any Other Name

Think of two labels—nicknames, adjectives or phrases repetitively applied to you as a child—one which felt positive to you at that time and another which felt negative. These labels could have been given to you by family members, playmates, kids at school, teachers, relatives, neighbors. They could have been nicknames, qualities or attributes. Take a moment to remember. Now, go around the room to each other person and introduce yourself by your labels only, as if they were names—first your positive one and then your negative one. Do not explain anything at this point. Just introduce yourself with your version of: "Hi, I'm Hardworking, and I'm Mule."

The Action

As people mill around the room introducing themselves in this new way, some are awkward, others do it with gusto. Usually, if it is a workshop, there is some self-consciousness. In all settings, there is laughter and the aha's of recognition. We have never met anyone, including people from other cultures and countries, for whom this particular exercise was not a valuable resource. We are asking participants to take that which is familiar and private, and use it in a strange and public way, for connection, with individualization.

When people have introduced themselves to each other, through the metaphors of their labels, we ask for samples of the pairs of labels, which we write on newsprint. We write them down, since some people "hear better by seeing." We ask for the meanings of those labels not obvious or those "usual" words which may have idiosyncratic meanings (images within metaphors within images!). We ask then for a very quick connection between the labels and the aspect of self labeled.

In between asking for pairs of labels and jotting them down on the newsprint, we also ask:

1) Whether individuals met others with labels that also could have applied to themselves.
2) Whether other memories and associations contextually related to labels were simulated internally as they introduced themselves and heard others' labels.
3) Whether each person could indeed have chosen several other labels for self which would have been accurate metaphors and still be within the requirements of the exercise.

The answers to these questions have always been "yes" with examples and samples of other monikers. Some people report how they changed their introductory labels during the exercise, as they became more aware of specifics about past contexts. Others hear and recognize appellations long blocked or forgotten as more appropriate to their own early life than the ones they originally chose in this exercise.

The Experiential Context Discussed

We then often ask participants to discuss the derivation of those labels—the where, when, who, how come and what about—with another person. Here we are asking for origins, for the characters in context. We want each person to have a little private air time to reexperience, in the telling, other aspects of the original, to carry it more fully into the present. And in listening to each other's label stories, we also want each person to have the opportunity to *approximate* another's original situation and content.

Person/Larger System Interface

In further debriefing this exercise in metaphor, the issue emerges that labels *are often boundary markers used by the label givers*, i.e., that labels often define and delineate whether one is inside or outside a system boundary set up by the label-maker him/herself or by a larger context or system in and of which the label-user is an agent. These label boundaries are not necessarily permanent and fixed. Indeed, they can be quite arbitrary.

Thus, someone positively labeled "Hardworking" and negatively labeled "Mule" finds himself labeled for the same quality either in different contexts or when fitting or not fitting the label-giver's image of and for him at particular times. "Hardworking" was so called, in a positive tone, when he was seriously doing what his father wanted him to do. "Mule," in a rejecting tone, was his father's name for this man as a boy when he was thoroughly involved in doing something he wanted to do for himself, of which his father disapproved.

We aid in the differentiation of types of labels, distinguishing those which refer to physical attributes from those which refer to attributes or characteristics of style or cultural origins, and so on. Being long-legged, short, blonde, or dark-haired, blue-eyed or club-footed are accidents of genealogy, as ethnic and cultural origins are accidents of history.

Sometimes the labels that go with these attributes are metaphors of affection and connectedness. Others are meant to be disconnecting and disapproving. There is not much one can do about the length and skinniness of one's legs, as in the taunting label "daddy-long-legs," nor is there much that anyone can do about being born of Italian, Irish, Jewish, or Black parents. Yet in these as in those other labels which refer to perhaps changeable attributes of self, *when the label is negative, the person labeled often feels burdened and defensive, as if he/she were responsible for and expected to change the attribute.*

Thus, an exercise such as this becomes, for many people, their first awareness that labels represent another's metaphors for oneself, another's world view and/or wishes, and as such are representative boundary markers of larger systems and contexts.

Steps Toward Multicentricity

This type of exercise sometimes represents a major step in the empathic decentration process of self-in-system: that ability to look at oneself in one's own dynamically interactive systems of past and present, from a variety of positions.

When the person called "Mule" begins to think of those situations in which he was so called by his father, and those in which he was called "Hardworking," he can begin to analogically inhabit his father's skin, and to see himself and his behavior from his father's eyes and wishes, *as if* he were his father. He can begin to look at and experience by approximation his father's images and methods of achieving those images, momentarily, even as he has been on the other side of them. In so doing, he can experience another side of the compressed conflict, in which opposite meanings can be attributed to the same behavior by the same person.

Adding "*Be* the label-giver, in voice, tone and gesture" to the exercise instructions adds a command role-reversal which moves each person even further analogically into the approximation and decentering modality. (This can be a loaded situation for some people. We would not add that command unless the setting were one in which a climate of trust and safety had already been established for the participants.)

Change Points and Updating

We will ask participants, "Are you still referred to today by those labels? If so, with whom and in what contexts? If not, what happened to those behaviors of yours that others hooked onto, if indeed they were behaviors? Did you change or did others change? Did your context change?"

We sometimes ask directly about self-imposed labels—those metaphors that people make up for themselves along their way through life. Have these changed? When and how and where?

With these types of questions, we are engaging participants in the process of rethinking their experiences and their change processes. We are asking, in contextual terms, whether past behaviors, attributes, and the metaphors for them have continued into the present, unchanged, based on others' labels or one's own labels. *We are asking about change points.* We are asking if externally observed change is linked with one's internal image or if one's self-image has remained the same while one's physique (from heavy to thin, short to tall) or behaviors have changed.

Many people hold onto old metaphors of identity and do not update them until given the opportunity, an invitation, and a process by which to do so. Until one asks, "Is the familiar still familiar and current?", people often have not caught up with themselves that the old familiar metaphor is no longer appropriate—it may even be strange indeed. *We all tend to describe ourselves as when we last stood still*, in some previous time or context. The metaphoring comparisons of past and present in this form can allow for updating the "information—the difference which makes a difference" (Bateson, 1979), into new metaphors of identity. Each participant is also learning, with cognizance (Piaget, 1976), a process by which change can take place in therapy and other settings.

As a tool for exploration, any such exercise is a rich well of metaphors and analogues for wherever one wants to take it. Once each trainee has plumbed the depth of the well, each brings to the surface the data from which generalizations and conceptualizations can then be made. Each is in an *equivalent* position to do so for *each has equivalent data to draw upon.* While the trainers may have played more with the total map, each trainee has explored his/her own territory and can now begin to create his/her own map, in context, through dialogue with others. In addition, as each listens to others' descriptions of their experiences (territory) and their generalizations (map), they are easily followed, for they derive from a common exercise and concept of labels as system metaphors. By extension, then, each trainee can recognize the differentiations—the range of diversity—in common themes, and include them within a meta-generalization. They do not get caught up here in differentiating details.

Generalizing from Concrete Experience

Generalizations from such an exercise can range from near to far space ideas.* "Near space generalizations" are those that are close to home, relating to aspects of self in system, to family, in a first level of abstraction from raw data.

---

*The "near and far space" concept has been adapted by the author from Jane Hart's conceptualization of how infants explore space. See *Where's Hannah?* (Hart and Jones, 1968).

Examples of near space generalizations would be:

1) Parents' labels for children reflect parental wishes and expectations.
2) A child's self-definition or self-image includes the labels others assign to him/her.
3) Parental labels demarcate boundaries for children. These parental labels can delineate overt or covert rules of behavior.

"Far space generalizations" are concepts that are extensions of these ideas either to systems further removed from the hub of self or conceptual systems further removed in levels of abstraction.

Examples here would be:

1) Labeling by parents of children is analogous to labeling by society of its citizens.
2) Those persons are said to be deviant whose behavior does not conform to the ideal of the enforcers of the cultural norms.
3) Boundaries are a metaphoric representation of the rules of inclusion/exclusion.
4) James Miller's (1978) entire book on *Living Systems*!

At each level, the trainee can feel him or herself connected to the generalization from the inside out. Each can follow through extension of the metaphor of labels the route from his/her own experience and data—his/her epistemics—to labels in general, the function of labels, and so on.

Labels of self are then transported by each person's metaphoric extension from singular incidents in one person's life to a class of incidents in the life of all human systems. This class of incidents, i.e., the labeling of members, is organized around the concept of the fit, the match or non-match of actual behavior with ideal images or standards of behavior at every level of human system. The metaphors of identity given to members *define the fit* within the label-givers' image, or within the label-givers' metaphors of organization and operation.

Larger System Labels

Prolonged discussion or quick mention of the subversive labels given many Americans (Hellman, 1976) during the McCarthy era, labels given anti-Vietnam War demonstrators, or even psychiatric labels of "neurotic" and "psychotic" is a natural extension of the label metaphor, with analogies on a national scale.

Trainees discuss *contextual* shifts in their own lives, as well as in the culture at large, which alter the importance or power of labels, thus transforming the impact of these metaphors of identity. Formerly subversive people are exonerated and/or reembraced. Amnesty forgives draft evaders. One's awareness and knowledge of regional customs, history, and politics become personally useful, locating people and their labels in context.

Children outgrow old labels. Conversely, formerly benign or descriptive labels become negative or pejorative. "Cute" at age five is very different from "cute" at age 25. "Asylum" meaning refuge becomes a euphemism for "crazy house." *Reframing in therapy gives new labels to old meanings and makes the Familiar Strange.* Trainees begin to look at words, labels, and concepts in a new way.

ANOTHER ANALOGIC EXERCISE

In the aforementioned example, we have stimulated the individual's world in microcosm through a few basic directions only: 1) to think of positive and negative labels of childhood, 2) to walk around, introducing oneself by those labels to others, and 3) perhaps to employ the voice of the labeler. We have suggested in this metaphor of labels that *a part (label about self) stand for the whole (all of self)*, and we explore it *as if* that were indeed so. In so doing we have made something old but Familiar (i.e., labels) Strange, allowing oneself to look at it.

In another type of exercise, we activate the opposite processes in which we suggest that *a whole stand for a part*, and in which we make the Strange Familiar.

Exercise

Think of an animal that best represents your learning style in academic settings. Go around the room being that animal.

This probably seems like an unusual request for adults with such a serious subject as learning. However, we find that when the climate for safety, fun, and exploration has been created, adults can be freed for incredible learnings of far-reaching impact for themselves and others. Trainees get into the mood and play out their imagined animal metaphors.

We ask, when the grunts, squeals and laughter have died down, "What were you? And what aspects of your learning style does this animal represent?"*

---

*We have been playing with such animal metaphors of identity since 1973 and wrote a fable employing them in a paper entitled, "Cognitive Styles and Marital Process" (Duhl, B. S. and Duhl, F. J., 1975).

People in the room begin to single out qualities or attributes of self through their animal metaphors of identity.

One man said, "I'm a boa constrictor. I take a subject and slowly wrap myself around it and squeeze it. Then I swallow it whole. Then, I take three months to digest it and discard waste and keep what is useful."

Another calls himself a lion, who waits for the lioness to kill the prey. His translation: He waits for someone else to search out and prepare the material and then he is very ready to engage in the process directly.

A third sees himself as an eagle—soaring above, slowly, deliberately, scanning the terrain below, with an overview. When ready, he becomes a predator. He swoops down, targeting his prey, grabs hold, and soars away.

Metaphors of identity such as these allow one to look at oneself in totality —i.e., as if one were an animal—to see which attributes fit a part of self— one's academic learning style. This externalized image is now available to be played with, explored, and questioned with curiosity. Trainees find themselves enjoying the process without defensiveness. The range of appropriateness of that animal's attributes to oneself can be sifted and sorted to increase cognizance and differentiation of one's style; i.e., "As an eagle, are you a loner in your academic learning style? Do you soar alone or with others?" It is important to keep the questions related to the original target, in this case academic learning styles, though one can go far afield in extending such metaphors, often with humor and wit.

While this last aspect can indeed be enjoyable and is useful when the purpose is different, one must not lose sight of the goals:

1) To use the animal metaphors as analogy in a more pointed search for differentiation of learning styles;
2) To explore one's optimal conditions and contexts for academic learning;
3) To offer new metaphors of approximation to others by one's own metaphors of identity.

Treating animal metaphors as unfocused imagery and fantasy, while enjoyable, can lose the value of specific analogic positions. Trainees learn to treat such exercises with a kind of spontaneous and expressive fun in the doing. They often joke a little, commenting on self and others as they move into the reflective space. Then, they debrief their metaphors starting with "What were you?" and "What attributes of self are represented?" While there may be wonderful double entendres in responses, the learning style metaphor comes through clearly. Trainees learn by the trainers' modeling to ask analogic questions with a *gentle and respectful dignity for the "as if" reality that accompanies the "what if you were"* (an animal) *supposition.*

When the original focus of such an exercise is lost or gets muddled, adult trainees feel foolish and embarrassed and one can see that they have switched from intellectual curiosity to self taunters, from a stance of explorer to one of social critic.

Breaking through the boundaries of one's sense of self requires that a new mode not just be something new and different for its own sake. *The novelty of and in the metaphor must contain a real and meaningful analogy to self and others and offer new information.* Then one can take oneself seriously while playing with absurdities like animal forms. The focus of the questions and goals provides boundaries for safety. The metaphor then furthers the image of the self and one's own sense of *acquaintanceship with oneself*—that meeting of a part of self in a new decentered position.

To make the acquaintance of a part of self means not to explain it away or absorb it or to be aware in the usual sense. It means to treat an aspect of self as if it were an independent and, for the moment, external entity. Via metaphor as analogue, one then interacts with the chosen aspect of self and uses the metaphor to discover and compare isomorphic qualities. It is another way of decentering, while integrating: "If I were looking at me, how would 'me' look to 'I,' and how would 'I' describe 'me'?" It is a way of making that which is subjective objective, momentarily, so that it can be reintegrated in an expanded base of self-knowledge.

Becoming acquainted is the opposite of taking for granted. Novelty, focused curiosity, and attention are keys to that process of becoming cognizant (Piaget, 1976). One makes the Familiar Strange (Gordon and Poze, 1973) so it can be seen freshly. Analogic metaphors provide the vehicle for people to become acquainted with aspects of themselves and others in new ways.

A SUMMARY OF OUR THINKING THUS FAR

When we design metaphors in action, we find that the body movements, for instance, of one's animal of choice seem to stimulate different thoughts and associations than *thinking about* an animal. The active process certainly enhances the precision of the image. More resources in oneself are called upon in "becoming" an animal than in thinking of oneself as animal. When we use our primary sensorimotor equipment (Piaget, 1952), we tap into other aspects of self.

In the earlier exercise, more resources and memories are stimulated when one becomes an active label-giver than when one remembers labels one was given. (There will be more discussion of the importance of action in Chapters VIII, IX, and X.)

A curious set of phenomena occurs in this type of externalization in a group setting. Each person:

- is in control of the original image;
- has complete freedom to accept or reject comparisons;
- has useful shared metaphors by which to achieve approximations of meanings of others. Through these approximations can come meaningful dialogue.

Each person:

- can play with the idea, since one knows one is *not* an animal, whereas the usual adjectives descriptive of attributes and qualities about oneself can be argued with by others and can thus prove threatening to exploration;
- has given novelty a chance to happen, has generated a new idea, has a new image to bounce off which helps clarify self and self in systems.

One can extend the metaphor in various directions, as we do, and ask what type of animals represent the learning styles of other family members? And how do these animals get along? Trainees can rethink difficult and often emotionally charged relationships in this way, extending metaphors of identity and approximation into metaphors of operation and organization; further, they are learning modalities for and analogues to working with real families. In addition, they are developing metaphors to keep tabs on themselves as they explore themselves in new ways. They are also developing new images by which to tune into others. Similarities and differences take on a new configuration, as they are seen as noncompetitive.

If you extend the metaphor in another direction, one can ask and enact, as we also do, how each one's animal metaphor for styles of learning is similar to or different from his/her style of teaching or doing therapy. And which animals could represent those styles? Which animals would symbolize the styles of teaching each person experienced others as employing in schools? In training? In therapy? Are one's own learning styles and teaching styles the same?

Again, the analogues to different aspects and levels of system are present, as are the *issues of fit* of styles of any two or more people. *For the essence of system type is the type of fit and pattern various parts make in their dynamic interaction. Different types of fit create different metaphors of organization, i.e., different types of systems.*

I am reminded of a formula I made up years ago, following the birth of our third child: "The first, an N of 1, is experience. The second, an N of 2, offers comparison. And the third, an N of 3, offers the opportunity to find patterns —patterns in children, patterns of parenting, and patterns of parent-child interactions." Multiple analogic experiences offer each trainee multiple N's of experience to scan for contrasts and patterns, in both the experiences and resulting conceptualizations.

Over time, trainees begin to ask themselves before trainers ask them: "For what is this exercise also an analogue?" When they do that, we know that they have learned to learn (Bateson, 1972) a metaview, that events can stand for themselves and stand symbolically for something else.

A not uncommon concept in the family therapy literature in general is that a symptom in a child represents a disturbance in the parental relationship. This concept is another level of metaphor and analogue. The child's symptom is seen as carrying disturbance from one place to another. However, that construct is already at a level of abstraction of metaphors of identity within metaphors of organization and operation that tends to remove people from their felt experience.

Our trainees begin to learn that any experience in a family, like any exercise in a seminar, will contain several levels and varieties of meaning. In so knowing, trainees are open to explore, from the family's epistemics, the family's inside-out metaphors and to use their own creativity in the process.

Trainees are empowered then to know that there are many possible descriptions and analogic meanings given to system processes and no one correct one. Many ways of intervening are then possible. Using the general systems term of equifinality, "There are many ways of getting to the same place." When people's metaphors of identity and epistemic metaphors of organization and operation are explored, they feel grounded in their lives and the coherence of their internal patterns. Change can then be connected to seeking relief from their own compressed conflicts, such as making their own worst fears happen.

A SUMMARY OF PROCESS

When training thus creates exercises which then become analogic backdrops for personal images, meanings, and metaphors, it is not difficult to lead each trainee:

1) Back to the original or other systems and settings wherein each one's idiosyncratic and personal world views are formed;
2) Into an exploration of all those systems, like neighborhood, family, school, church, and the factors and dynamics operating;
3) To capturing the metaphors of identity of self in system and in context that each trainee carries like hidden badges from the past into the present;
4) To trying metaphors of approximation—ways of understanding each other in the seminar;
5) To exploring the elements in the current systems one lives within, highlighted by the exercise, including the training setting and system, and developing beginning metaphors of organization and metaphors of operation;

6) To radiating to far space isomorphs;
7) To conceptualizing and generalizing one's learnings gleaned on such a journey, into ever expanding maps into wider metaphors of organization and operation;
8) To designing metaphors for intervention and change.

Thus, our image of "living systems in context" far exceeds the boundaries and limits of family systems as the only system of focus. We span and explore the range of systems and interfaces in such a way that graduates are as much at home thinking and acting in school systems with principals and teachers, with clinic personnel, with homes for delinquent adolescents, and with people in business and institutions, as they are with parents and children. With such use of analogic exercises, we can expose trainees to simulations of situations they could not necessarily encounter in a clinic setting.

Yet the learning from such analogues carries them from one place to another and prepares trainees to identify and choose appropriate and relevant interfaces of focus for interventions. As Jerry M. Lewis, M.D., stated at a workshop,* "If you are thinking and working on one level of systems only, you are missing something and you are making a mistake."

Analogic exercises, as structures for spontaneity, can:

• project into the future via an experimental "what if?"
• simulate and replay or explore very current material of the recent and timely now;
• evoke by reenactment memories, associations and meanings of long-past events;

Each analogic exercise can also draw on that which is Familiar or that which is Strange (Gordon, 1961; Gordon and Poze, 1973); on conceptual material in analogue form or concrete material to be conceptualized; on persons in the room as real in relationship and as actors in each other's lives, and so on.

No matter which arena and aspect are incorporated in an exercise, for trainees it is happening *now*, in the present. Each trainee then is in the process of information exchange, enacting and drawing upon both the planned tasks, themes, ideas, and constructs intended by the trainers and the novel, unknown ones brought by each person. Each is creating the *now* information in the present while also creating another metaphor from which to refer and from which to generalize ideas later.

You may remember that we spoke in Chapter IV of information as "now," with an urgency of current and immediate status. Ideas are *about* and are

---

*BFI sponsored workshop, Boston, March, 1980.

formed in moments of reflection and metaprocessing. *These exercises provide the structure in and by which each person creates the now information firsthand in a vital way, from which he or she will weave ideas.*

There is no doubt that these exercises are also meant to be important to trainees in their relationships with each other in a seminar. Each exercise is also a route to knowing each other in very full ways—to empathic approximation, to trust and the dialogic exchange of equivalents.

When exercises can become relevant to trainees by analogy to a variety of settings and/or relationships inclusive of the trainee's personal life, trainers find trainees excited, energized, and actively integrating their understandings in a wide variety of ways, both inside and outside the seminars. They keep bursting through the membrane which forms the boundary of their experience—and that process becomes a high that is habit-forming. It becomes one's own anti-tedium tool.

Thus our organismic, analogic presentation of simultaneously existing material allows for organismic learning, even though the paradigmatic teaching plan and process may follow a more predictable and even sequential process. With each exercise or created event, there may well be questions to be debriefed that would include some or all of the following:

- What memories or associations or ideas were stirred up by this exercise?
- Where were you? With whom? What happened?
- At and in what system level were you ? What contexts?
- What did you learn then that this memory association or image stands as metaphor for? or
- What is/are the rules or messages implicit in that image or memory metaphor?
- How are the present events, exercises or people connected to your associations; that is, what characteristics in this event are analogues or isomorphs of a previous event? In structure? Process? Content?
- How is/are the present event and persons unlike any evoked associations? What new metaphor can you evoke?
- What is the current message this new metaphor contains and in how many of your contexts is it applicable?

All of the above types of questions are intimately related to each trainee in his/her own contexts, past and present, in a very personal way. In addition, as each trainee exchanges information and reflections about personal experiences and ideas set in motion by the same exercise, a range of responses emerges that allows for the development of metaphoric themes of new constructs, with variations in varying systems and contexts.

Strange and Familiar images and ideas combine in new ways. From such themes come new concepts and beginning theories. Such themes become the jargon of insiders—those who share common metaphors. The jargon of insiders incorporates those communal verbal metaphors of identity into system metaphors of operation, or concepts, which create boundaries of exclusion for those who do not share the images and have had no approximation opportunity. Jargon is that which is familiar to those inside and strange to those outside. Trainees together invent or create a jargon which is comprised of the verbal metaphors for common core images. Out of such shared experiences comes each trainee's sense of bonding with others—emotionally, intellectually, actively, conceptually. They learn to connect and translate their epistemic jargon into epistemological theory and back again.

A MINI-META RAP

Each field has its jargon—its metaphors of identity. Not all have metaphors of approximation, organization and operation, which loop back in a "reflexively coherent" manner (Wideman, 1970).

We find that through creating the common metaphors of designed exercises and by raising to consciousness each trainee's theories-in-action and each exercise's inherent analogical potential, adults in training invent new connections between aspects of self and other systems within a common meta-framework. Connection at *some* level is assumed. The questions always ask: where, when, how, what and who. The "patterns which connect" (Bateson, 1979) are elicited and evoked.

There is no right way to make connections. We are concerned rather with the fundamental question: *Can trainees see, comprehend, make connections for themselves out of their own data that fit for them?* Can they weave their own life experiences via their metaphors of identity and approximation, into systems metaphors of organization and operation? Trusting themselves to find connection and to create or adapt theory that is experienced as coherent and appropriate gives trainees the base of trust in themselves as therapists, to work from the inside out. Trainees thus work from their epistemics to epistemology. Each one's epistemics run like fibers in the rope of epistemology.

In training for working with family systems, we are training people for both the known and the unknown, and we attempt to have them be open to both, to be competent (I know what I can do) and creative (I don't know yet, but I'll invent something) therapists and teachers of others.

Bruner sums up what we *attempt* to do when he says:

I would submit that it is only by imparting "casually fertile" propositions or generic codes that general education in the broad range of human knowledge is made possible. General education does best to aim at being generic education, training men to be good guessers, stimulating the ability to go beyond the information given to probable reconstructions of other events (1973a, p. 237).

These "probable reconstructions of other events" are metaphors, and as David MacDermott (1974) says, "Brains make metaphors. . . . All metaphors exist in brains and nowhere else. . . . All metaphors, at one time or another, have to be invented."

At the Boston Family Institute, the idea is to train people to recognize, invent, and intervene with moves and metaphors which facilitate competency and quality in living.

Each exercise then can be looked at also for its level of metaphor as well as system. Other exercises we will explore throughout the book are concerned with varying types of human systems and metaphors. Trainees translate, transform, transpose. They carry themselves from one place to another—yet never lose that essential and existential thread of connectedness of person to his/her own felt experience, with each exercise being run through the filter of the self.

And we find, like the Greek hero who mastered the Minotaur, that following the threads of connectedness leads one out of the maze of self *and* system to the freedom of integration.

Family-as-System; Family-as-Theater | VIII

Exercise: On Transferring Knowing

Consider if you will that you have experienced three very distinct types of families, and you wish to convey the sense of their differences to your trainees. What medium would be most effective for getting across your images of differences? For getting across the feel and ambience of those differences to family members themselves? How would you know that trainees understood both your view from the outside and the feel from the inside? How would you explore this problem?

ON GENERIC QUESTIONS AND GENERIC PROCESSES

When one begins a training program with a seemingly simple set of generic questions, and when they are periodically brought to the forefront of thinking of the trainers, then it is akin to sailing a boat in both calm and rough seas: The purpose is to stay afloat and to get to one's destination, with oneself and one's boat in good shape. Sometimes, one must tack into the wind and go in what seems like the wrong direction, in order to be able to utilize the wind and wave force to help one to get to the right place.

So it is in training. Generic questions can guide the overall direction of a training program, as stars and sextant guide the sailor. Yet often destinations cannot be reached by a straight line. Sometimes the best route is indirect and circuitous.

The first basic goal at Boston State Hospital—to train people to work with families as systems—had hit rough seas and bumped into a basic generic question, "How do people hear?" or "How do people learn?" Other generic questions, such as "How can one train therapists to be competent and creative systems thinkers and actors?" took the training ship into unknown and unusual seas. Inherent in the very words competent and creative are multiple subdifferentiated images of what those words mean to different trainers and trainees. The same is true in therapy.

161

Thus, strong winds while sailing are akin to subsidiary generic questions: Each relates to the actual processes to which we must attend in order to reach generic goals. Each time we have hit a forceful wind coming directly at us from the direction of our goal, we have had to pay attention and tack. Thus, it has been necessary to tack in many different directions during this voyage, in order to stay afloat, to go further towards the stated goals, while constantly charting the new discoveries along the way.

Perhaps unlike sailing, within a training program one has choices of many goals. Every moment we are free to alter direction, timing and processes, for training/learning is a human systems issue. Since the purpose of training programs such as ours includes that trainees grasp ways of thinking as well as ways of doing, what one does as trainer is only half the story. What trainees think/do is the other half. Fortunately, in a training program one has the resources always present in the persons of the trainees, the sailors, to be collaborators during the voyage. They can indeed help chart the waters just passed through and can contribute direct information concerning what gets in the way of us all in reaching desired goals.

As self-chosen captains of a new type of ship on a maiden voyage, the original new trainers had to find out how to sail while they were sailing in order to keep sailing! They had never been there before. They had never taught or taken such a course before. As captains of the ship, however, they could enlist the sailors to collaborate in the process of sailing, so that they all could succeed.

With hindsight I can say that whenever trainers at BFI did not pay attention to issues raised by trainees, and the trainees were seen as "resistant" or lacking in some other way, as trainers we found we had been ignoring an important generic issue or question. "Resistant," it should be remembered, is an outside-in label given when trainees do not fit our image of how and where they should be at that time.

Originally, when trainers began asking "How do you best learn?" somehow the trainees' "resistance" disappeared and was replaced by involvement, curiosity, and openness to risk new learning. Generically, when trainers *explore* what is occurring and ask new questions, new processes open up in trainees. The same is true in therapy.

Trainees, then, more and more over time actually were invited to help sail the ship. They were invited to attend to the learning process, to be curious about themselves. In a reverse process, they were invited to give trainers the "answers." The trainers could then incorporate these answers in their teaching frameworks. The issue of type and quality of fit could then be attended in ways congruent with those present.

When, during the early years, hassles between group members disrupted the learning context and rendered continuing with the planned material impossible (see Chapter X), we found, after trial and error, that we would do best to let the sail out and run on a broad reach. That is, we would do best to use the situation as a systems issue, making it an opportunity to explore the disruptive interface in a new way, which would bring us all new information about the people, the context, the expectations and processes which had created the environment we had labeled "disruptive."

Such switching of direction led to the discovery of yet other generic processes, each connecting with what happens between and among people, and new information. Each time we solved such a problem and uncovered a generic human process, we incorporated it into our systems map, our training program, and our therapy.

Through such explorations, I feel we have uncovered many of the interconnecting and overlapping routes of access at the interface between any two or more human beings, whether they be trainees, family members, trainers or co-workers on a job. The rules and routes of access, discovered while solving different questions for ourselves at the time, basically rely on *how people process information* in its widest sense, through sensing, imaging, feeling, thinking, and acting.

In exploring the phenomena at the boundaries of interface between people, we have uncovered generic systems processes pertaining to all people, relating to one's sense of self, aspects of self, and the fit, the interactive dance of physical and verbal behaviors with others.

Thus, whether in training, family therapy, or organizational consultation, *we can focus on the particles, the persons, or the wave, the transactional betweenness*—the component parts/dynamic interactions, at any level of system, in context.

What happens between people *is* the way they behave and process information, make meaning, metaphor connection and relatedness, and respond or generate new messages. *We each also are the entities between the flow of transactions.*

These then are the questions and issues that we have found interesting enough to spend years thinking about and playing with—exploring generic processes which relate to:

- how trainees learn, behave, change;
- how all people learn, behave, change;
- how any system, especially family systems, can be explored, experienced, looked at, explained, facilitated in changing;

- how inside felt meanings and dynamics can be externalized and how external interactions can be explored for their meanings to all, including theorists;
- how the intrapsychic, interactional, transactional and intergenerational aspects of any human event are all parts of the same and can be approached and explored and linked through analogue and metaphor;
- how ways in which we explored led to the realization that we had discovered a cluster of ways of approaching basic generic human processes, an interface where information takes place;
- how such ways of approaching the ways in which trainees think, feel, image, sense, and act are all contextually linked; how by looking at individuals in context, we look at systems, issues of fit, and types of fit —the being of people in relationship.

In the next two chapters we will look at those generic stances and the generic methodologies introduced at the beginning of BFI, which, by *involving different tasks and processes of mind, provide the structures, tools and language with which to explore and discover everything else.*

SYSTEM FORMERS

Specifically, we will look at two basic frameworks operating at the beginning of BFI, which I name family-as-system and family-as-theater. We will see the way in which these two very different thrusts provided the fullness of range which allowed us to explore families and all other levels of human systems holographically from the outside in as system, and then from the inside out as theater.

Two very different types of processes developed early which seemed to be linked. These two different stances of looking at people through the conceptual lens of "system" and the felt, experiential lens of "theater" promoted the development of two different methodologies for exploring people/system or people/theater: Analogic Design, as begun by Duhl and Kantor in the "How do you hear?" exercise, and Spatial Metaphoring, as begun by David Kantor in Family Sculpture (Duhl, Kantor, and Duhl, 1973).

Each of these methodologies draws on different mental processes for participants. *Family-as-system emphasizes the exploration of interactive processes, how people behave with each other. Family-as-theater emphasizes the exploration of the experience, the drama, the meanings of living in the midst of those behavioral processes.*

All of these ingredients were present in neonatal form in the training program during the very first semester of BFI in 1969, and contained within them, in the way in which we seem to have utilized them, the critical elements for developing our current way of thinking and training for integrated multi-centricity.

Let us turn our attention now to a closer look at these first two basic process-es, so that we can illuminate the subsidiary generic processes which formed the foundation for the focal ones (Polanyi, 1958).

As you may remember from the anecdotal story in Chapter I, the first group of BSH trainees were bored, not "learning"; they were not hearing the messages the trainers thought they were sending. They were not taking in the information.

Fortunately, this predicament created a need to do something different in order to dissolve the block. That problem fit right into the inquiries raised in the Educational Techniques Laboratory with which the trainers had been ex-perimenting. There, they had tried lighting and dramatic settings with props and platforms, as settings for learning, in which messages could be delivered and received in more meaningful ways than lectures.

The "How do you hear?" exercise was analogic to "How do you take in information?" or "How do you learn?" It was also analogous to how people in families hear, take in information, and learn.

In taking the problem and making it the issue to be explored, the trainers had *switched the focus* to the generic question underlying mutual message-sending/message-interpreting transactions.

EXPERIENTIAL LEARNING DEFINED

And in the process of so doing, the trainers plunged the trainees into what is termed "experiential learning." However, experiential learning is as gross a term as "classroom teaching." There is no type of learning that is not "ex-periential" in some manner, including the experience of being bored to tears, where that message is not quite the one the person teaching thought he/she was sending.

However, if by experiential learning we mean that we ask that trainees base their constructs on active personal experience, that is something else. We can then involve participants in any of a wide range of activities, designed to evoke personal experiential data. Such information can then be elucidated by each trainee into conceptualizations, which when drawn together and cate-gorized create generic maps of experience.

If we think of experiential learning in the above manner, there are exceed-ingly different types of activities we can draw upon. Certainly there are those that involve imitation (accommodation) and those that involve play (assimi-lation) (see Chapter VII). There are those based on part/whole constructs, those involving metaphors of identity and approximation, as discussed in

Chapter VII. There are those that make the Familiar Strange and the Strange Familiar. In addition, there are those experiences which focus on how people interact in patterned ways: metaphors of operation and metaphors of organization (people-as-system, people-as-theater). And last, for the moment, there are those which go from the inside out and others which go from the outside in. For purposes of clarity and definition of these terms particularly in this chapter, arbitrary as they indeed are, "outside in" here refers to exercises which are planned by drawing on a theoretical construct or formal metaphor of organization/operation, whereas "inside out" refers to an evocation of personal and idiosyncratic images, beliefs, metaphors and constructs as yet unlabeled and a-consensual.

To speak of outside in and inside out depends on who you are, where you stand, and what you are doing! As I am thinking of these terms here, the trainee is at the locus of concern. In an outside in design, trainees enter a construction preformulated by the trainers, into which participants bring their versions of roles and enact them. In an inside out design, trainees themselves create a construction in which either they or others participate.

Thus, in either outside in or inside out exercises, the trainees are involved in evoking the raw data, the material from which either the system aspects and/or the individual, personal, and dramatic aspects of a situation can be grasped.

IMPORTANCE OF TWIN FOCI: FAMILY-AS-SYSTEM/FAMILY-AS-THEATER

Within the first month of the inception of BFI, the underlying juxtaposition of these two different metaphors—family-as-system, originally through analogic designs, and family-as-theater, through sculpture—emerged in this new training program as the twin holographic laser beams and lenses by which we would be able to discover the full hologram later. At that time, the beams were not labeled or focused, nor did they necessarily work together. Nor was the light very pure.

For convenience, I am using the terms family-as-system and family-as-theater to refer both to families and to people at all levels of system in the model of general systems theory. Thus these terms are being utilized as generic terms in this discussion. When completely inappropriate to speak of "family," I will speak of people-as-system, people-as-theater. The emphasis for me here is on *system* and *theater*. People-as-system refers to conceptualizations *about* the *experiences* of being human, i.e., the map. Theater allows us to explore experience, and the territory. Words are *about*. Experience *is*. Both are necessary to grasp the whole. The multicentric glide from approximation to observation, from inside to outside, from territory to map, and vice versa, allows us to "know" aspects of the hologram in different ways.

Thus, both family-as-system and family-as-theater were explored experientially at BFI, from the outside in and the inside out, through analogic design and spatial metaphor. Soon they began to overlap. Role playing in analogic exercises became an important way of entering into the drama and theater of people's lives, in which people struggled with their issues of bonding and belonging. Sculpture and spatialization became a way also of expressing the metaphoric nature of a system, in ways that provided nonvocal and synesthetic (of the senses) definitions for cognitive constructs. We found that relationships between territory and map, through analogic design and spatialization, could be bridged.

Thus, as I consider the evolution of our current way of training, *I would suggest that the exploration of both family-as-system and family-as-theater are essential elements in the development of a sense of congruence, coherence, and integration between epistemics and a systems epistemology, and between theory-as-espoused and theory-in-action.* Additionally, such an exploration is essential in the development of the actor in the therapist, who is able to take many stances and roles in order to know all positions from the inside out and outside in. I would also suggest that the marriage of family-as-system and family-as-theater allows for and facilitates the integration in the trainee of his/her appreciation of his/her own family (life) as story, theater, and system, providing the analogic base for understanding others in the same manner. Such a marriage allows therapists not to lose touch with the people (the component parts) in the interconnectedness (dynamic interaction) of the members (system). As we stated in another paper, "You cannot kiss a system!" (Duhl, B. S. and Duhl, F. J., 1981)

The metaphor of *system* allows the *trainers* to plan from the conceptual systems epistemology, to then design an experiential example of the concepts, into which the person/trainee enters, bringing his/her personal world views or epistemics (such as the labels exercise). The metaphor of *theater* allows the *trainee* to move from his/her personal experience (sense, image, memory, feeling) to an externalization of it (such as in the be-an-animal exercise), and then to conceptualization (see Chapter VII).

The emphases in each are slightly different. In an analogic design, the trainee is a responder/role filler to another's suggestion; in spatial metaphor, the trainee is the initiator/creator of his/her own roles/images. Let us take a moment, with an example of each, to compare these two combinations of processes: 1) analogic designing, from the outside in, exploring family-as-system; and 2) metaphor designing, from the inside out, exploring family-as-theater, as through sculpture. Both of these are types of exercises we use in training.

ON OUTSIDE IN AND INSIDE OUT

Exercise #1: Family-as-System; Analogue to Metaphoring: Outside to Inside

I invite you to consider the following scene: A father and mother are arguing with each other about what their child should wear when they go out for a walk. If you can possibly do so with others, enact this situation through role playing. Debrief. What did you learn/find out?

Exercise #2: Family-as-Theater; Metaphoring to Spatial Metaphor; Inside to Outside

Imagine yourself with your family when you were a child. Where are you? What is happening? As you remember and image yourself with them, walk up to each person, in the theater-of-your-mind. Get in touch with how you experience yourself with these people. Whom do you like to be close to? To whom do you not go readily? Whom do you avoid? Who else connects with whom and in what ways? Are the members of your family touchers and huggers? Do they like distance between them? Who likes which?

In your training group, choose other people to represent your family members. Communicate your sense of yourself with your family members, they with each other and with you. In this instance, place them in appropriate positions with appropriate movements and gestures which capture the images on your inner screen of their relatedness to each other and to you.

What do you suppose is your mother's image of this same group of people? Your father's?

Now, what did you learn?

In each of these exercises, the processes of mind involved in doing them are different, and the persons exercising the mind processes are different. It is important to remember here that we are *focusing on the trainee,* on how he/she thinks, sees, images, conceptualizes, moves. We are concentrating on his/her processes of becoming an integrated and multicentric thinker, capable of analogic thinking and metaphor making, while working with others.

FAMILY-AS-SYSTEM

In the first type of structured exercise above, or structure for spontaneity, the trainers have some concept in mind, some specific sets of generalized systems principles that they may wish to get across. Or perhaps the trainers are thinking of the types of situations that are common for people to be in, from which human systems principles were originally derived, and they want trainees to explore what it feels like to be in such a situation, and/or what "original" systems principles are exemplified by such situations. The trainers could have been thinking either of systems principles relating to three-person systems, triangles, triangulation, or they could have been thinking of common types of family scenes to explore, in which there is dynamic tension.

As I write of "systems principles or concepts," I employ them as generic terms, and thus may refer to constructs drawn from general systems theory, or specific family systems theories, or family therapy systems theories. For each of these can be very different cups of tea.

In either case, the trainers want to design a situation, an exercise, whereby in the experience of that exercise trainees will find the data, the process from which each trainee can derive and invent systems principles and analogues. The trainees will discover, through their own interactive experience, the concepts indwelling (Polanyi and Prosch, 1975) or immanent (von Bertalanffy, 1968) in the processes they have enacted.

In this case, the *trainers have to be thinking analogically and isomorphically,* in an algebraic equation of: This is to this as that is to that. They must go from "outside," i.e., abstractions, to "inside," a concrete experience. The trainers have to design an interactive situation: a concrete experience, which contains in the doing the abstract systems principles. Only after the experience is completed and debriefed can the trainers know if the exercise fit their image and accomplished the desired goals.

The trainees, however, are into different, though reciprocal, processes of mind. Trainees enter and enact the roles set up by the instructions. They bring their own ways of being, memories, images, and metaphor these into roles in action, in relationship to others. They play out a situation. Who they are and how they enact it will again depend upon instruction and what each person brings.

In then being asked, "What did you learn?" and other questions, trainees will be able to metaphor from that concrete experience to abstractions. The discovery of particular generalizations is rooted in what has just happened. The trainees first participate in creating an experience, and then are asked to generalize from the experience. They must then think analogically from the concrete experience to an abstract generalization, image or idea, a reverse process to that of the trainers. They are going from inside the experience to outside—to the conceptualizations or theories.

FAMILY-AS-THEATER

The second exercise above derives from David Kantor's sense of family-as-theater, which he developed under the different metaphor of family sculpture (Duhl, Kantor, and Duhl, 1973). Kantor considered that the one who had the images was *sculpting* the figures of one's internal configurations in external space. Family sculpture, then, is a means of creating one's condensed and essential images of a family's context and patterns of transactions in external space, so that one can experience and/or observe the whole of one's image enacted outside of oneself. As such, Kantor's theatrical creation brought the dynamics of action and living to "living systems."

In this modality, Kantor introduced a way of starting with each person's ethereal and internal sense of relationship, with the request that each person recreate that sense externally. In so doing, the sculptor of such a physical representation is moving from the intangible internal image to a concrete external representation. The trainee checks the fit of the inside image with the outside constellation.

Only later, through analogue, can this particular constellation of people in patterns with each other be "seen" as representative of systems principles. The particular family group is first related to other family systems and then to generic family system principles. At that point we are free to ask what outside constructs seem to provide a framework for these particular patterns. Or we are free to metaphor once again, poetically, framing the whole with verbal, imagistic metaphor.

SYSTEM AND THEATER TOGETHER AND SEPARATE

As we can see, these contrapuntal themes of family-as-system and family-as-theater call upon different metaphor-making and analogue-scanning processes in the trainee and in different sequences. In the first, the trainee is an actor in someone else's play or skit, enacting one role at a time, through approximations. In the second, the trainee performs the roles of the author, producer, director, choreographer, costume designer, makeup artist, rehearsal coach, and, oh yes, often an actor, in his/her own full production.

Let us take a closer look now at how these alternating positions of responsibility and task allow for the possibility of integration and multicentricity in the trainee that I continually refer to. Trainees learn to enter into family systems and to know the individuals, and to translate ideas into the metaphors of the family, their "language of impact" (Duhl, F. J., 1969). Trainees also learn to view and comprehend the total system from the outside.

Through the experiential processes of walking through many territories and creating the data from which the maps will be drawn, trainees thus expand their metaphors of identity and approximation into aspects of transactional systems, themselves metaphors of organization and operation.

Now let us explore these contrapuntal themes of people-as-system, people-as-theater (metaphors of organization and operation) through the structures of analogic design and spatial metaphor.

For the purpose of this exploration, I will separate these themes as resonating with different ways of analyzing the symphony of human life. In the two subsequent chapters, IX and X, I will examine analogic designs concerning people-in/as-system, and spatial metaphor, concerning people-in/as-theater, sequentially.

We will be exploring analogic designing and spatial metaphoring as generic processes, as goal-oriented ways of exploring issues, people, systems, rather than as prescribed ways to use specific analogic designs or spatial metaphors. For in this discussion, I am not directing our focus at particular techniques, but rather towards generic processes.

Analogic Designing and Family-as-System | IX

PEOPLE-AS-SYSTEM(S) AND ANALOGIC DESIGNING

At this juncture, I will do something that is not usually done in books. I will repeat the first few pages of Chapter II, describing my first evening's experience at BFI, for I would like to examine that experience from several different levels.

I would like to continue the exploration of creating structures for spontaneity, from my experience as trainee first, from the inside out, before we discuss the development of design and designing from the outside in. For what is so often left out in discussions of training and teaching are explorations of the process called upon in the trainees' performing any particular activity or exercise.

When as author I make a claim that the way of training developed at BFI can facilitate integration in the trainee, and can lead to multicentricity, I feel it necessary to explore what it is I am calling integration. To do that also means to look at what is happening for the trainees. As trainers, we so often do not look below the surface at the manner in which we send our training messages and by what processes we expect those messages to be grasped. Yet as trainers we are working with people, training others about people in systems. We are doing, seeing, sending, receiving many complex messages at any one moment, as are trainees. Over time, how trainees think and act changes.

What are the processes of mind involved in such learning? How do we go from experiences to constructs? From constructs to experiences? In discussing these questions here, we are still involved with the generic question, "How do you best learn?"

Let us now look at one set of analogic designs in depth, and at the designing process. Let us furthermore look at the processes below the surface for those doing the exercises, and examine those mind processes for their role in action-oriented, experiential learning.

I invite you to come and walk through the exercise with me again, this time, from beginning to end, debriefing and metaprocessing the whole.

172

Scene One, Take Two

When I walked into the room, the chalkboard said, "SILENCE! DO NOT TALK." So the group of some 14 adults sat and looked around, uncomfortably, smiling awkwardly. Some stared at the floor, others examined the peeling pale green paint, the steel-meshed windows. Eyes searched out the inanimate, moving upwards to investigate the four-sided balcony with slatted railing in this mammoth two-story room in an old Boston State Hospital building. Stark bare light bulbs hung in the center of the room, casting soft shadows under the balcony. Eyes scanned each other fleetingly, and then shifted away. One woman rummaged in her pocketbook for something. Anything so as to pass the time in nervous silence, wondering what this was about and trying to look casual.

If we had been younger, the chances are we would have giggled and whispered and hidden behind our hands. I knew two of the 14 people. They were a couple—friends through children who were friends. He was a businessman, she a homemaker. They were each interested in family and human systems and had just joined the Boston Family Institute course, as I had, during its initial seminars. It was September 1969. The leaders had had a first spring semester. Now they were going to start with a new group of trainees, while the first group "waited." After three months, both groups would be joined together—to continue a two-year, part-time course.

So there we were—no names, no talking, no exchanges of the usual social and verbal information. We were left without our usual tools of establishing our places vis-à-vis each other. Without such tools, we were amorphous. We were left to deal with information and communication with our first and earliest preverbal skills, and we were uncomfortable using or interpreting this language, directly, in conscious awareness.

I was reminded of sitting in doctor's offices, waiting rooms, the subway, airports, and all those similar places where you are supposed to pretend that you are the only person in the room, or else that you and "they" are invisible. The chalkboard only said: "Silence, do not talk." It did not say, "Do not notice each other. Do not communicate." Yet we acted as if it did.

The leaders* of the seminar arrived. I knew them. One said something like: "We want you to meet each other without words. We are going to divide you into two groups and those halves into two smaller groups and give you each instructions as to what to do. After you receive your instructions, you will mill about—using no words—carrying out those instructions. When we say

---

*Sandra Watanabe, Fred Duhl.

'switch,' you are to switch to the second instruction we have given you. Then we'll talk about this. Remember—no talking.''

At this point, the leaders arbitrarily divided the group down the middle and then again, in quarters. Each leader spoke to each of two subgroups, telling them what to do and in what order. Each small group knew only its own two instructions. Mine was to first be a "positive responder," who, when the signal was given, was to become a "negative responder." These ways of being were to be carried out completely without words, solely with movement, facial expressions and gestures with each other. No matter what others did, one was to stick to one's instruction, one's role, and not speak.

We began to move: awkwardly, avoiding, then tentatively towards each other. Some people looked "pleasant." Others looked "mean." All of a sudden, someone pushed me hard, looking quite angry. Automatically, I felt like pushing back. My instructions, however, were to be a "positive responder." I smiled and tried to take the person's hand. She shook loose abruptly, turning quickly towards another person whom she purposely bumped into. There was so much going on. I smiled somewhat rigidly, and nodded nicely no matter who did what with me. I noticed a woman slumped down by a pole. I saw others smiling, bumping, moving abruptly. One felt the sense of awkward tension of restrained energy, in the room. My muscles were tight.

The command "switch" came from the leaders and I became just as fixed as a "negative responder." I must say, for the first few minutes it was a relief *not* to be nice, to shrug others off and to turn away, to give a push back when pushed. My own tension and held back energy felt released. This situation, however, was awkward. We didn't know each other. We didn't know who we were pushing or avoiding. We were just "roles." We were grown-ups and strangers, not children. We were enacting these behaviors in awareness, and we "knew better." It was both fun and freeing, and equally uncomfortable and tense.

The leaders said "stop" and asked us to come sit down and debrief what had happened. They asked each person to mention his/her first name only as each spoke. They began by asking us, "What did you learn? What did you find out?"

My mind was swirling with images, impressions, reactions, thoughts. My hands still felt the memories of others' warm grasps. My shoulder still tingled from someone's push. In my mind's eye, I still saw the woman slumped down behind a pole. I realized with a start that we had not as yet said one word to each other. Still we each had available huge amounts of data: kinesthetically, through our bodies in action; tactually, from all the touches, pushes and body contact; aurally, from all the movement noises we had heard, from nervous laughter and sounds that accompanied movements; olfactorily, from the different odors we had sensed; and visually, from all that we had each seen both during this exercise as well as while waiting in silence earlier. All of these data had been taken in, and many had been given meanings from memories, images of other contexts, and rules of behavior whose origins were long since forgotten. Particulars were competing inside me for mention with more general associations, all stimulated by these people and these exercises in this context.

What does one talk about? Which data does one choose to offer to this group of unknown people? We had no guidelines. Questions are organizers. Answering through speaking involves selection, choice, censorship, omission. What did I learn? As adults in this type of a setting, one searches for a sense of appropriateness, a sense of context. That in itself was problematic here. There were no clues.

The social rules for the politeness of first meetings had been altered radically, in a way that was both freeing and frightening. The situation was freeing because one could not assign meaning to others by any context or situation other than the one we were all in at the moment. Therefore, one was free to say anything one wanted, without assuming one should have "known better," politically. Each could respond authentically in and of the moment, calling forth one's reactions and impressions freely. The situation was also frightening, because it would be difficult not to be authentic, since we had no contextual labels, roles, or rules of relationship to guide or hide us. Being authentic, saying how and what one really felt or thought at the moment, felt frightening, like premature exposure/disclosure against an internal sense of rules of order for such a process. We were to be with each other not for a quick encounter, but for two years, in a training program. We each had now, this evening, and a long projected future together. It did not feel safe.

I felt full of varying kinds of information. The context markers for trust were missing and I had to assume them as either present or absent. We did not know how the information in the answers offered would be received or dealt with, by each other or by the trainers. The questions that the leader had asked—"What did you find out? What did you learn?"—were wide open. Questions like these put a little more weight in the trust department. With such questions, it was hardly likely there was only one set of right answers, or that anyone would be ridiculed or put down for their contribution. But then again. . . . Somewhere in the middle of me I was feeling both scared and exhilarated.

DEBRIEFING THE EXERCISES

People began to speak with caution, exchanging responses to the exercises which included the sitting in silence at the beginning. We talked about that only briefly—for the moving exercise had much more energy behind it. One short woman said she had felt awful sitting there—like she was a very, very little person in a group of giants. She later stated that she was the youngest of eight children with significant age gaps between each child. Another said his only pleasure was that others looked as nervous as he was. He figured they didn't know any more about what was going on than he did, so he relaxed a little. Someone else said he tried to guess what others did and where they worked. The leaders acknowledged comments. Everyone had looked at and observed other people, yet not one person made any direct, personal comments. It was as if, without words or interactions, we had had no vehicle of connection between us, even though we had each been subject to the same experience. Comments were awkward, with a floundering, searching quality reflecting the nature of the experience itself.

A little lightness entered the discussion as people shared some associations. One woman mentioned trying to count the slats of the huge square balcony railing, but the peculiar lighting on them had created the effect for her of the slats moving, making counting impossible. All had wondered about this room and for what purpose it had been built, and no one knew. While it turned out that no one had liked the exercise, no one had disobeyed the chalkboard sign and talked. All had taken "Silence. Do not talk!" to mean: "Do not make conscious contact and connections with each other."

As we began to discuss the second movement exercise, the energy changed. Again, we had been asked, "What did you find out? What did you learn?" Everyone had something to say, all wanted to talk at once. People were animated and interested. It became clear as we talked that instructions related to a cross-grid of behaviors:

	Positive	Negative
Initiator	Positive Initiator	Negative Initiator
Responder	Positive Responder	Negative Responder

One woman, whose version of negative responder had been to withdraw into a sunken down position, with hunched shoulders, head tucked down, stated she had experienced several people either pushing her, or trying nicely to get to her, to persuade her to come away from hiding behind a post. She said the more they tried to move her, the more she folded into herself. She said she felt as if she were a child, having a sulking tantrum. Another person said that she too had used withdrawal as her form of negative responding, except hers was an active withdrawal. She felt that she wanted no contact, of any type, but that she would just keep moving, to avoid it. That meant she had to keep looking over her shoulders to see if anyone looked as if he or she was approaching her. As we talked, someone said "paranoid patients act like that." One leader commented how paranoia, then, may be a way of responding negatively in some interactive dance.

The positive initiators had felt very rewarded by positive responders. They had been smiled at, received and accepted. And not everyone was aggravated by pushy negative responders. One man said he felt energized by the physical challenge with which some negative responders met his very physical positive initiating. Those who were negative initiators had all been physical and provocative with others.

The leaders asked about, and we discussed, contexts and situations in which we had experienced or witnessed such reactions and behaviors. One man stated that another man, a negative responder, had acted "disgusted and mopey" with him "just like my older brother used to".

The woman who had been sunken down like a sulking child said of two positive initiators who had cajoled her: "I got so mad at you. I wanted to scream at you to go away! I also didn't want to let either of you know you could reach me at all, that you could have any effect on me. It was like being a kid again with my goody-goody sister trying to cheer me up."

A second person talked of how hard it was for her to be rejecting. "It made me feel guilty," she said. Another person mentioned how welcomed he felt when smiled at by a particular positive responder, who reminded him of a good friend.

Considering that this was just a "game," without a script, considering that there was no prior history with or information about the people involved in the game, and considering there had been no verbal exchange between group members, there was a remarkable amount of energy and interest invested in what had occurred and in talking about those incidents. In addition, I was amazed in realizing how much information had been generated, gathered, processed, all stimulated by two exercises, without any exchange of words, that had taken about 30 minutes altogether!

Somehow, it seemed to be easier to reveal personal material and images and impressions about self in relation to others in debriefing the second exercise than the first one. The exercise itself had acted as the vehicle for direct interaction to take place. It was evident that this activity had stirred up a lot of "stuff" for people. For as we talked, it began to become apparent that by entering into actions which each one associated with certain generic processes (initiating, responding) and certain generic attitudes (positive, negative) trainees were tapping into whole universes of feelings, thoughts, meanings, and images about people in interaction that we each brought with us.

As we now were speaking, all our previous life experiences had begun to creep into the room with us, in words, as they had in action moments before. Our only experienced history together as a group was what had occurred that evening. We had no other shared memories. Yet people were giving a lot of meaning to what had been happening. The meanings we were giving to others' behaviors and/or our own reactions began to reveal what I began to call our core images of ourselves in the world which we each carry with us from context to context in our timeless minds.

Our assessment of behaviors gave clues, if not facts, reflecting previous contexts and the learning-to-learn about human behaviors we had already done in many settings. Our freedom or restriction in disclosing reactions hinted at our earlier family upbringing and cultural rules. During the second exercise, people had moved, smiled, reached out, pushed, jostled, withdrawn from one another, as each enacted his/her version of certain words: "positive initiator," "negative responder," and so on. The process first of choosing behaviors and then seeing those of others evoked internal asociations to people and places, family, schoolmates, friends, and other people in one's past contexts and current situations. These interactions were now bringing forth comments relating to social and ethnic rules, going far "beyond the information given" (Bruner, 1973a). The exercise had acted as an "assumptive world view" mind-set stimulator (Parkes, 1971).

In this second action exercise, yet still without words, one had to rely on one's body and sensorium to transpose, transport, and translate messages out and in. Such simultaneous translations were possible to check for definition *only* in one's personal dictionary of core images and meanings. Each trainee had "brought in" such a "dictionary." Whatever each said in debriefing began to reveal definitions previously coded and entered. Some definitions were familiar. Others were strange.

Thus these two simple exercises had tapped into our total life spaces!

By the end of the evening, all were catching the drift. We had created roles with distinct interactive and transactional processes, devoid of specific content or personal relationship. We had actively experienced that as initiators we were free to move; responders had to wait. It became sharply clear that these assigned roles were limited in scope, thus accompanying processes were also narrowed in the range of options for movements, gestures, posture, demeanor. A responder has no option to initiate. An initiator does not stand around waiting to be responsive. Yet as initiator one needs a responder to initiate something with. A responder needs an initiator to respond to. There are patterns of interaction between the two. None of these metaphors of identity, no matter how stereotyped, and none of these processes can exist in a vacuum, without the others. None could have come into being without previous contexts.

We each had learned from those earlier contexts about behaviors labeled positive and negative, and could enact them here. Not only that, but the feelings evoked by those roles were also familiar. The positive initiators reported themselves most distressed by negative responders, for they felt rejected, angry and annoyed that their good will had been met with so harshly. Those feelings in these roles were brought in from other contexts, since we did not know each other, and each group knew only its own pair of roles. The roles were then contextually interdependent process roles of relationship, comprising human systems.

However, while cognitively this was very exciting, we still hardly knew each other except through the exercises. Socially it was awkward, and as people identified only by our roles, it did not feel safe.

Indeed, we knew more about the system elements of new meetings, but we did not yet feel connected to each other as group members. While the exercise had drawn on each trainee's experience, the connection with one's total life situations seemed "out there" and ungrounded for trainees in the room. These issues became important for the author during training and, later, as trainer. Certain processes that developed during our explorations, especially sculpture, began to take care of some of these issues of safety for risk-taking and integrated learning (see Chapter X).*

At this point, we will move from the experiential level as trainee, to a look at the exercise from the vantage point of those who had invented it. In so doing, we will explore the thinking of the trainers as a way of exploring one way of thinking in designing analogic exercises—highlighting people-as-system, from situation to constructs to designing an experience embodying the constructs.

In this particular discussion, we will recognize that the way of thinking of the trainers drew upon their prior awareness of group and system processes.

The First Exercise: Analysis of the Thinking and Planning Behind it

What situation are trainees involved in? This was to be a first meeting of a new "collection" of trainees. They were a collection—individual people who basically did not know each other. They were not yet a group or a system. There were no ongoing self-organizing, self-regulating interchanges as yet. They would be system-forming (Gray, 1976).

New meetings involve getting to know one another—introduction. The new trainers wanted to short circuit the usual system-forming social pattern-

---

*Other processes, such as the Vulnerability Contract (Duhl, B. S., 1976b) developed by the author in the seminars, will hopefully appear in a subsequent volume.

ing process before trainees were well into the age-old cultural ways of getting to know each other. Those standard moves in new social situations usually ended up with stereotypic relationships that were hard to undo. Such ordinary social moves include checking each other's badges by asking, "What do you do? Where do you work?"

The trainers had already learned in the hospital setting the difficulties involved in training in new ways which cut across the usual hierarchies. Badges are labels, metaphors of identity, which always carry the images of social and professional roles into a new arena. These images and assumed role expectations become early definers of attitudes, behaviors, and relationships, thus defining aspects of the subgroup and group levels of system from the outside in.

The trainers wanted the new trainees to be open to see, hear, act, and think freshly, differently, with each other and with the trainers. They wanted trainees to be open to new learning, new thinking, and a new paradigm, that paid no attention to badges previously worn.

The introduction of novelty was felt to be important to capture attention in a new, open, and opening-up way.

To change a pattern of social interaction from the outside one must change the process and guidelines by which that interaction takes place. If people on meeting usually make small talk exchanging context markers, as revealed in "Where do you work? What do you do?" then one can block that process from getting started. One simple way to prevent such introductory small talk is to insist on "Silence. Do not talk."

Thus, if we were to write up a curriculum plan for the entire evening, as we began doing in 1973, it would look like this:

First Session Plan

Goals

1) To create an open climate for new learning to take place.
2) To interrupt the usual social group formation process.
3) To introduce systems experience from the beginning.
4) To evoke personal images and meanings.

Faculty Assumptions

1) New meetings allow for new beginnings.
2) People tend to scan for status, for a place, in new groups, sizing each other up by title, degree and job status.

3) Entry behavior of new meetings and greetings reinforces old roles and interactions.

Propositions

1) If we change the way in which people can enter and meet each other, we will be able to change the structuring of the group.
2) New types of group structures and new types of interactive exercises can allow for new learnings.

Exercises

1) Write "Silence! Do Not Talk!" on chalkboard before any new entrant arrives. Leaders leave the room as newcomers enter, return when all have arrived. Debrief later.
2) Divide group into four subgroups. Instruct members to be positive and negative responders and initiators. Switch positives/negatives halfway through. Do entire exercise actively, without using words. Debrief. What did trainees learn?

Before we make any comments about this first exercise as a design, let us explore the thinking concerning the second exercise. Then we will return to comment on each, in order.

The Second Exercise: Analysis of Thinking

What content/processes are trainees in need of learning about? When one begins a program there are at least a million choices as to how to do that. In this case, the trainers were wondering how they could use the real life situation, i.e., a new meeting, as the situation to be explored for generic and systemic principles. The trainers then began to think analogically, as they thought about and analyzed new meetings.

The trainers asked themselves what people do at a new meeting, and what behaviors encapsulated the essences of processes taking place in social or academic contexts called "new meetings." They arrived at the behavioral categories of initiating and responding. Of all the greeting patterns in new meetings of people in this culture, these two aspects are predominant. Some people in new situations reach out to greet and connect, while others simply wait to be approached.

When the trainers then raised questions about the feelings, the affect, connected with such new social contexts, and the interpersonal concerns or meanings people brought with them into those settings, the issues of acceptance/

rejection kept cropping up. The concepts, acceptance/rejection, are already metaphors, symbolic meanings, given to very complex series of contextually related systems interactions for which everyone has images. Yet images of acceptance/rejection and the meaning assignment given to those concepts differ in different cultures, subcultures, families, and individuals.

The twin categories of acceptance/rejection were then further abstracted to the generic polar concepts of yes/no, positive/negative. When combined with initiating/responding, one has the generic dynamic ingredients of new social human encounters; positive/negative/initiating/responding.

Every adult in this culture, by the time he/she is signing up for a program in family therapy, has had multiple new meeting experiences. Each will recognize the factors involved.

The trainers then designed a bare-bones and rich exercise, calling for the mix of ingredients, in behavior, without words. They wanted the new group to conjure up and play out the essences of new meetings, a systems issue—the very situation they were in—and to do so in a way that would draw on their own previous experiences. In so doing, the leaders gave people the generic roles in new meetings, which may have been similar to or different from one's usual and ordinary entry behavior in new situations. The trainers did not wait to find out at that time what "normal" entry behaviors were. They created roles for the trainees to fill, as analogous to those prevailing in all new meeting situations.

The trainers extracted the essence of the situation, connected it to the essence of what they wanted to see happen in a way that actively involved the trainees and connected the data to systems concepts derived from the trainees' own experiences. They had made the situation the issue.

Metaprocessing the Process

What's happening and what else is happening? The process of training through designing analogic exercises is only as good, complete, thorough or holographic as the quality of thinking and energy put into debriefing, evaluating, and keeping one's eyes and ears open. If in training we look to trainees to discover in an exercise only what we originally planned, then we cut off new ideas, new information, resources, creativity and integration.

The author has learned over the years that in paying attention not only to that which fits the mind's eye image, but also to that which does *not* fit, one can discover hidden treasures and new ways of seeing and doing.

Let us now take a look at the same two exercises and discuss them from an overview position, commenting on the process, and analyzing what generic processes are involved in doing each exercise.

The First Exercise: What Was Happening?

By the one simple move of setting up a scene of "silence" at the very beginning, the trainers had surgically interrupted each person's automatic entry behaviors, and the exchange of the usual verbal societal cues relating to status, position, relationship! Impressive! No person could program his/her behaviors to *assumptions* of roles and status—all definitions of relationship. No one could ignore relationships by chatting about the weather. There was no way to refer to outside events, or contexts, or data.

The new group members were caught. There was no way to avoid participating in what was occurring now, as long as one had basically agreed to obey the rules and lend the situation an "as if" trust (Bernhard, 1975), for no real concrete thing or being prevented anyone from talking, moving, leaving!

What was being called upon. Let us look at this experience now beneath the surface, from the vantage point that time and overview afford us, for our human minds cannot consciously focus on surface and substrata simultaneously. We can only describe behavior, give it meaning, and look at what principles of mind and of system are operating, sequentially.

When new people enter a new setting and elect to obey the chalkboard "Silence. Do Not Talk" instruction, they have accepted on the level of behavior the rules of that context. They are "doing" the instruction. In so doing, new group members must then rely on nonvocal data processing (or avoiding, as the case for some turned out to be!). The meanings given to those nonvocal data by each person are direct, associative, impressionistic. It is the only way anyone can make any sense of these people new to oneself. Eliminating the usual verbal exchanges also removes the guides we have been socialized to use in our meaning assigning through verbal exchange. Taking out of use one's basic social channel of communication for sense-making forces people to use other mechanisms.

And what else was happening? While the leaders were quite cognizant of the ability of their "Silence" instruction to cut out the usual social verbal interactions, they were not aware* of the importance of the flipside: that in eliminating word, they were triggering and activating whole different processes. They were completely unaware that silence also heightens each trainee's sensitivity to and acuity in recognizing and deciphering that paraverbal information. People still size each other up, whether they use words or not. Visual and

---

*F. Duhl, personal communication.

other synesthetic information is checked against an associative file of contextual and behavioral core images.

That first evening, the author was aware that in the absence of word communication externally, one has several choices. One can increase and attend to one's own internal verbal dialogue, the internal chatter. One can pay attention to internal stimuli and fantasy and daydream, removing oneself. One can get very focused on external *things*, avoiding people. Or one can attend, see and hear, both internally and externally, in the way we each did before we had words or verbal modes of communication.

Our first language is direct and synesthetic. Later socialization instructs us in how we should be and in how others' dress, posture, looks, behavior should be interpreted, and we begin to interpret information contextually on several levels at once: synesthetically, affectively, cognitively, contextually.

Omitting verbal language in an exercise concerned with a first meeting of adults has a powerful novel shock effect! It interrupts our basic cultural rules about social behavior. It interrupts our patterned way of behaving, allowing us to look at the underlying rules we took for granted. *They stand out in their absence.*

Silence in a usually verbal context creates an uncomfortable void. Although no one is ironclad to obey the written instruction calling for silence, it is assumed by those participating that, given the context, this powerful instruction is already part of the program one signed up for! (Yet stop for a moment and think, image, consider the data-bank of information from previous experiences that go into making even that, or any other assumption! *What if* the chalkboard instruction had been left over from some other class or group!) Thus, in the midst of one's discomfort with the covert acknowledgment, if such there be, that one is actually agreeing to go along with this uncomfortable game which takes away one's sense of stability through words, one is expectant at least that there is some "sense" to it!

The Familiar has been made Strange (Gordon and Poze, 1973) and one is agreeing to stay with it. That which is strange can always be compared to the familiar. Silence with strangers is familiar enough. It is that instruction and behavior in this context, a new training session, boundaried by the institute, that is strange. In such a setting as this, one is in conscious awareness of the usual expectations of first such meetings, which are to talk, to size each other up, and to see whom one can connect with in some way. We each locate ourselves contextually in some way to other group members. These expectations are perhaps in some way related to the basic human need for contextual information ascertaining safety or threat to survival.

Silence with strangers happens in public settings. This setting is not public. Additionally, unlike subway riding or airport settings, where one is en route to a chosen context and can get lost in a book, this *is* the chosen context, and the rules and expectations mitigate against getting lost in a book. In this context, unlike subways and airports, one is not free to ignore the context! The dissonance set up between the socially patterned expectation and the actuality creates a tension in each person. One must use other equipment than words to gather information here.

One's earlier equipment has been working for so long out of sight, and under cover, that it rubs its eyes, startled, to be called upon to come out in the light. It does not know what to do all by itself anymore. It has worked as an undercover agent with or against words for so long, that it feels awkward and exposed alone. To make one's wants known directly or to respond directly entirely without words belongs to a period of life lived long ago, before one learned rules of social interaction and appropriateness. It is almost as if this earlier and relied-upon base equipment for communicating had long ago been ordered not to show itself, except perhaps on very special occasions, and this is certainly not one so catalogued. A situation such as this is not even listed! Some people are irritated, for there are personal rules, as well as social/cultural ones, about "staring" at other people. Yet how else could one get information? Another conflict between expectation and actuality—and no way to comment on it!

In debriefing, one doesn't comment in words upon what was directly perceived about another synesthetically, for that is open acknowledgment of breaking these social rules, compounding the crossing of boundaries.

Boundaries? Boundaries between people? Information? Ways of processing information? Information crossing the boundaries? Rules? Breaking rules? Patterns? Interrupting known patterns of behaving and images of behavior? Core images? Core images and safety? Safety and threat? Pattern breaking as strange? As threat? These are basic phenomena in human systems, delimiting the way that information can or cannot cross boundaries openly, according to the patterns, images, and rules of the culture that we each carry with us in our minds, through the roles we each play, and the contexts which define both.

We are talking about individual people obeying rules in groups while experiencing many unruly phenomena! Yet all are systems phenomena. The hologram is there, contained in the bit.

Metaprocessing: The trainer/trainee interface concerning the first exercise. Trainers did not yet ask the types of questions that would also begin to unearth all of this information, these ideas, for that was not their focus or intent at that time. They asked generally about the experience itself and related it to new meetings. They listened to some of the flack of annoyance and irritation the silence had stirred up.

They also did not ask what specific people had learned of others during the silence. Indeed, to have asked new trainees directly at that time about specific observations and the meanings given to each other's behaviors while waiting would have been a breach of more than convention. It would have been a breach of the barest beginnings of the "as if" trust assigned to this new training setting. Crossing such boundaries on the leaders' parts would have completely destroyed the assumed contextual social contract for safe relating, already shaken by the types of exercises themselves.

There are tolerances for novelty, for absorbing the familiar made strange, beyond which one must defend oneself under threat of giving up one's sense of contextual reality completely. Brainwashing and other mind-changing techniques are based on how mind works under that type of stress (Conway and Siegelman, 1978).

Training programs in mental health arenas themselves carry in that title expectations of context, the least of which is that one's basic sense of psychological safety and of self-in-the-world will not be abused or destroyed. Played with? Expanded? Hopefully. Cajoled? Piqued? Perhaps. Challenged? Seen contextually? Indeed.

Yes, even training programs which change the context and the rules and the paradigm and the way of teaching, and which make them strange, must honor the metacontext, the metarules, and the metaparadigms and values underlying how people learn, grow, and change in a coherent manner. The issues of safety for nondefensive, integrated learning thus were raised the very first evening.

The trainers did not know what they had begun to unlock, although all the elements were there. They had merely wanted to stop some old social patterns from getting started, and to have a new process of meeting begin, in a novel and a different way, so that trainees would be open to each other and new ideas. They had made the familiar strange so that something new could happen. They succeeded in more ways than they ever knew!

The Second Exercise: What Was Happening

Meanwhile, in the midst of the trainees' uncertainty and search, and while the trainees were off balance (and while elevating trainees' nonvocal information processing to the forefront, of which the trainers were unaware), the trainers introduced the second exercise.

In this exercise trainees are faced with empty abstract verbal concepts, to fill out with their own images to enact: positive/negative/initiating/responding. They cannot be "themselves." They must be themselves—their version of behaviors. One's usual new entry behavior is thrown completely off base. Each person has to enter by someone else's rules and game. It feels safer. It feels unsafe.

What was being called upon. The process of finding internal meanings to fill abstract word concepts can best be stimulated by asking trainees for active positive and negative initiating and responding behaviors. Trainees must then fill the void of those image words, those concepts, by searching their own world of images and memories, and by metaphoring their own idiosyncratic, synesthetic translations and notions into those concepts.

Enacting without words those indwelling meanings allows each trainee to employ a unified modality of message sending, from the inside out. One is not being called "negative" in putdown or blaming fashion. One is asked to be *one's own version* of negative or positive. How to initiate or respond is left to one's choice from those many internal snapshot and movie albums that accompany one's dictionary of behaviors.

As adults, the meanings we originally gave to certain behaviors have long ago become attached to words representing the categories of positive and negative, initiating and responding. Reflexively, these behaviors become meanings we will enact when presented with certain words and conceptual categories. These meanings enacted become ways of trying on varieties of metaphors of identity.

The underlying assumption is that we each have and know versions of negative behaviors, of negative initiating and negative responding. Equivalently, it is assumed we all have and know versions of their positive counterparts, that can be teased apart from their transactional contextual embeddedness as free-floating roles we can play.

Each trainee can "go inside," calling on his/her own images to fill assigned generic categories with personal, idiosyncratic behaviors. In debriefing then, from one's own experience in such an exercise, trainees can move to the abstractions and generic concepts drawn from these examples quite smoothly and easily.

In dividing up the group of possible combinations, trainers ensured that all would be enacted. And by asking each person to switch roles, from the positive form of initiating and responding to the negative, and vice versa, each trainee had an internal role comparison of positive and negative behavior as well as his/her experience in different contexts now and in the past. In such a situation, myriad past concepts are called upon to be brought into the present, through their essence of positive and negative behaviors. Trainees can become aware through this type of exercise that categories can contain subcategories of differing behaviors, all of whose meanings are equivalent. Each person's negative responding may be different. Each is responding negatively.

In addition, trainees further become aware, as they switch roles, that each role can be a partner in some reciprocal dance, and that staying with repeating one set of behaviors continually is difficult when there are different responses to it.

The trainer/trainee interface concerning the second exercise. Any exercise can be and is a whole world. One makes choices constantly. However, if the debriefing questions or comments had been at a different level at that time, they, the trainers, could have underscored the principle of equifinality—or many ways of getting to the same place. And those ways of getting there had not only to do with personal, synesthetic meanings but with social and cultural rules and backgrounds.

The initiator/responder exercise raises, for both men and women, not only family values and the rules with which each grew up, but also the rules, roles and values of the larger culture. For instance, being physical varies in different cultures. Many women in this American culture state, when debriefing this particular exercise, that it is exceedingly difficult to enact negative initiation physically. And the type of physicality used in positive initiating is felt to be sex related as well.

That first evening, two women had indicated that the cultural constraint in this society against women being aggressive, particularly physically, had been well ingrained in them through constant family, school, and peer group repetition. Each had found it impossible to use any impacting physical motion, positively or negatively. One of them had been the woman who felt "guilty" being physical; the other had been the woman whose way of being a negative responder had been to fold into a heap. This could raise interesting questions about the possibility of connection between depression, withdrawn avoidance behavior, and cultural rules about sex roles and physicality.

If we move from asking about personal rules to asking, "Where did you learn to learn those rules?", all levels of system can be brought into the room, raising hypotheses concerning direct connection between individual images and behavior, acts performed, and the cultures one inhabits. It is the inclusion of all data that lends coherence to our system dances.

What else was happening? The trainers had successfully connected the experiences of this exercise to the generic issues of new meetings. They had successfully cut off old ways of socializing. However, somewhere in the search for analogic meaning they had not also realized that the real people in the room needed ways of getting to know each other that were also new, rather than being kept from knowing each other except through roles in exercises.

The sense, however, of the overall good will and eagerness in the persons of the trainers, in addition to the interest in the novelty of the total experience, established a sense of excitement about this new process of learning about people, families and human systems in this unusual way.

The sense of trusting skepticism (a compressed conflict), emerging from the total nature of the evening's activities, thus became a system precursor for that group. Initial reactions of cognitive excitement and interpersonal guardedness were set in motion as system formers.

A training setting is a system, as much as a family is a system. Trainers set the tone, the structure and the metacontextual rules. How trainers are with trainees and how trainers respect trainees' interpersonal needs in a learning setting about human systems is a message about how to understand human systems. The message concerning process is process. In this setting the lack of congruence between values and theory-as-espoused, and values and theory-in-action, is evident.

For the author, this beginning kindled the timbers of a far-ranging search for processes which were congruent with value positions, as these surfaced, within a humanistic and generic general systems theory framework.

Metaprocessing the Generic Processes: What Else Is Happening?

Let us now approach these two exercises in Polanyi fashion, moving from that which has been focal to that which is subsidiary. In that exploration, let us heighten our awareness and understanding of some of the processes involved in the doing of such exercises as I make sense of them. These subprocesses of mind exercised during the doing of experiential, action-filled role enactments play a crucial part in each trainee's integration process of his/her own life events, as well as integration of life events with systems constructs.

What is being discussed, described and examined in this lengthy analysis can be taken as generic for all other exercises of a similar nature, wherein nonverbal information gathering and enacting is called upon, for the way the mind must make meaning with verbal information is different from the way the mind makes meaning with paraverbal and nonvocal information. Both verbal information and nonvocal information are organized, but they are organized differently, by different processes and rules. There are different data processed.

We shall speak of processing without verbal language exchange as "synesthetic," via the senses. Such processes organize the data of the territory in ways that have little to do with conscious cognitive structures such as words, although words are usually needed to explain that organization to others.

In this examination process, we are switching system levels, and looking inside the person, and it is here that all "levels" become connected, as we speak of mind and thinking about thinking. For "levels" are constructs of mind, "hypothetical boundaries" (Grinker, 1967). In analyzing any exercise or any life experience, we can switch levels and explore the subsidiary processes supporting whatever was previously the focus of concern. All that is involved to do so is to ask a different question!

It is also useful to ask oneself when looking at exercises in this way, "Which level are we looking at, and what information does this level offer us?"

Thus, as we move now to discuss not the interactive aspect, but the subprocesses of mind involved in doing these exercises, we will be looking for information about generic processes which are interactive, in my usage of the term, that allow trainees to "use both sides of their brain" (Buzan, 1976), to include all data, as well as to "go beyond the information given" (Bruner, 1973a) in the learning process.

SYNESTHETIC LEARNING: SOME THOUGHTS ON OUR FIRST LANGUAGE AND ITS IMPORTANCE IN UNDERSTANDING SYSTEMS

Each of these exercises, as well as many others utilized at BFI, either analogic in nature or metaphoric, calls upon trainees to enact scenes and situations without words, as a way of heightening how much knowing there is of a nature that has nothing to do with words. Words are about. Experience is. Interactions are. Systems concepts are about.

Enactment without words, as we see here, can be very powerful for all involved. In addition, as we will also see in the subsequent chapter on spatial metaphor, such nonverbal enactments can be utilized to illuminate system and/or to intensify the sense of theater, or both simultaneously. Such "strange" ways are novel enough to allow us to see and understand in a different manner. Yet such ways of knowing are generic to us all as enactors and as receivers, interpreters, every day of our lives.

Let us pause and examine these generic ways of knowing, in greater depth.

Exploring the Known

We human beings are amazing, yet ignore ourselves so well. We are wonderful to behold when we stop hurrying around long enough to stand back and take a good look at ourselves. At such rare moments, we can remember and raise to consciousness the very amazing phenomena which we usually and continually take for granted: our human capacities 1) for conceptualizing relationship between one thing and another; 2) for creating symbols and rules expressing those relationships; and 3) for externalizing those expressions and rules.

To the best of our knowledge (that is, to the best of our human ability thus far to think about thinking in all species), we are the only species to have ever inhabited what we call the planet Earth to be able to conceptualize and to communicate with one another by symbolic language, thought, metaphors and objects that can be externally represented.

Although perhaps loving and intelligent, as John Lilly believes them to be (1975), dolphins just can't paint. Imagine if you will, the human race without spoken or written language, or tools!

However, the infant hears, sees, smells, touches, feels, tastes, before he learns language. Soon children begin to catch on and find out that there are rules concerning what they are supposed to think about what is seen, heard, smelled, felt, touched and tasted, and how one may or may not use one's body. They learn these rules through behavior and through language. Children learn language and become enculturated (Lidz, 1963; Bruner, 1966, 1973a, 1973b, 1976; Piaget, 1952, 1965, 1976, 1977a, 1977b) by language and socialized by rules. They learn the social boundaries of their cultural systems, with one's family as the first and most meaningful culture.

Yet before that happens fully, the infant has already a great understanding of his world, for there is inborn in each of us the structure, or the capacity, for sensing, and for "knowing a betweenness" that precedes language and those early rules. The normal infant is born with the capacity to discern the betweenness, for instance, of hand-mouth actions, the reaching, grabbing, pulling, and bringing something to one's mouth. This basic capacity is not limited to physical actions.

The brain/mind capacity for making connections between something and oneself, between someone and oneself, and between events, objects, persons with each other, is so fundamental, so basic, that we never think about it in relation to ourselves. Yet Piaget's lifetime works, as well as those of Luria (1976), Hunt (1961), Bruner (1966, 1973a, 1973b, 1977), Brazelton (1964, 1969, 1981), Thomas and Chess (1977), and myriad others, keep exploring the capacities in infants and children for organizing and giving meaning to experience.

Each adult, if I am not mistaken, each one of us, was once an infant, a toddler, a child, who also had a "knowing of betweenness" which preceded words. This knowing of betweenness, which we can call the metaphoring process, as Jimenez suggests (1976) (see Chapter VII), comprises what we can also call "understanding." Without it, there is no meaning-making and no meaning as we know it. We call those who do not have such taken-for-granted mental capabilities defective in some way.

It is somewhat circular. Understanding itself implies relationship. "There is no such thing as one thing" (MacDermott, 1974). Each thing or item, each bit of behavior, or word, event, object or person, stands in relationship to another "something" in a context. Relationship, however, is dependent upon each individual's human ability to perceive and to assign that connection, that relationship. The mind only notices the differences between one "thing" and another, to which we assign meaning and relationship (Bruner, 1973a; Bateson, 1972, 1979).

This internal meaning-making capacity begins to be exercised shortly after birth, as researchers have discovered. We each began to associate certain phenomena with other phenomena: bottle with milk; this face with being picked up. We know a betweenness. We have metaphored connection, relationship. A certain face "means" comfort, another face "means" fear. By six to eight months, we get upset with faces we do not know. This "stranger anxiety" has nothing to do with words or verbal language expression. It has to do with perception and cognition of relationship, with recognition of differences, with Strange and Familiar.

The original connections we each make, then, the linkages in metaphoric meaning, are made actively, synesthetically, via the senses, before verbal capacity. By the time we have language, we have solved many complex problems and have a well-established sense of certain human and nonhuman systems and of context, all paraverbal and organic, synesthetic, and connected as "schemata" (Piaget, 1952). Such images or schemata are the base of all personal meaning for each of us. They form the inner context for understanding, by which we make sense of the world, and upon which we continually build our sense of safety, sanity and reality.

The particular equipment or "wiring" and physical condition that we are each born with contributes to the distinct personal as well as communal meanings we each give to experiences. We call our unique constellations of meanings our "reality." That same capacity for metaphoring betweenness/ relationship allows us to create symbols and objects, thus expressing those relationships externally in spoken and written words and things and metaphors. We also create relationships internally, in dreams, in juxtaposing past, present, and anticipated future, in combining wishes and images with actions, in creating all things and ideas not of nature itself. And all of these capacities exist in and comprise our timeless minds.

The multitudinous events and experiences we each have over developmental time are contemporaneously available, in some miraculous way, in our minds, though mostly out of conscious awareness, as deep hypnosis and brain research have shown. Meanings and information are transposed and transformed in many ways, not just in images of word sounds. There is, for instance, a memory that muscles seem to have, which context evokes. In everyday life, our muscles and bodies tune into and adapt to the context continually. Repeated contexts create repeated patterns of body movements. We can walk in the dark in rooms we know and never bump into the furniture or walls. And in another type of memory, musicians know the translation and transformation of heard music into the finger positions which can elicit those sounds on their instruments, without their thinking about it.

The normal infant, toddler, or young child establishes by this metaphoring process basic meanings of personal safety, comfort, distress, and so on. By the way in which a young child is touched and carried, by voice tone and intensity of touch or tone, by facial gestures and expressions, in combination with other contextual phenomena, by all of these signals we each begin as child to make meanings of core significance to us before we know a word of language. We are making the beginning *meanings* of relationship.

As children learn language they do not learn the words that describe how they experience others. They act their experience and later use imagistic metaphor to describe their internal worlds. Adults are amused by descriptive poetic metaphors of children, as if such metaphors are less real than the literal category words for internal states that adults use.

Children experience disparity between how they are and experience and how they are supposed to be and experience. As children we cannot escape developing an overlay of other meanings which relate to the spoken and unspoken rules of relationship of the family, the society, the culture. These rules are transmitted in many forms, verbally and by behavioral patterns.

As the child is instructed in what is OK and not OK to see, hear, taste, touch, smell, think and feel, he not only learns the rules of the culture, but also learns ideas about being. Yet, while these rules of the family relationship or wider context are instructions for behaving, according to externally derived programs for order, they do not necessarily have anything to do with the information metaphored by one's own sensorium and meaning-making processes. The meanings assigned by earlier internal synesthetic "knowing of betweenness," of relationship, often are quite separate from the external rules of relationship imposed from without. How one actually experiences the person called "mother" has nothing to do with how one is supposed to experience her, or how mothers are supposed to be.

We each then metaphor on at least two levels of meaning-making at once —the synesthetic, which gives us basic information about the rules of access and our sense of self in relationship to other persons, and the cognitive, concerning the contextual rules of relationship and rules of order.

These two levels may be related to what are called right and left brain functions (Ornstein, 1972). Synesthetic metaphoring and meaning-making are personal, idiosyncratic, coherent, yet often nonlogical by analytical logic. Cognitive metaphoring and meaning-making begin to be contextually consensual, following external rules of order. The first type of meanings often get buried in the overlay of the second, or can be conflictual, as described in Bateson et al.'s double-bind theory (1956).

As children, we monitor our basic sense of trust/distrust, connection/ autonomy (Erikson, 1950) synesthetically, as we also learn the ways of our family. We learn how we are supposed to be for all these other people, how we are supposed to behave. We learn the "yesses" and the "no's." We learn the positives and the negatives about ourselves and the world, according to "them." We learn limits, boundaries, labels, systems. We learn how our family "works." We don't know we are learning all that, at the time, at all. We are living our learning.

As children, though, we are in a peculiar position. We know a lot more than we can express in words. We are reading systemic behaviors all the time, and may only learn how to express this knowing verbally years later (Piaget calls this "vertical décalage") (1977b, p. 816). We monitor how people are with us by their voice tone, gestures, facial expression and lots more. We do not know, however, that others, like mother, father, sisters, brothers, are doing the same thing with us. We cannot know that adults and other children give meanings to what they see and synesthetically experience with us—our touch, our gestures, our facial expressions, our tonality, and our movements —as we do theirs. We really cannot and do not see or hear ourselves as they do. We do not realize that we send and transmit data which they metaphor into *their* meanings of relationship. As children, we cannot conceptualize "fit." We experience it. We cannot conceptualize a transactional world in which each person is the data for meaning-making in each other's lives. Each of us, as a young child, is at the center of the world which exists only for us (Piaget, 1952).

While we now have language by and with which to learn and understand such different rules, we still monitor all physical behavior for its congruence with the spoken rules. The verbal rules tell us cognitively what we can or cannot do in certain contexts, and how we must behave here. They denote what our roles in each context are supposed to be.

However, the synesthetic knowing still monitors our interpersonal relationships. Direct experience combined with observing others' behaviors tells us what is safe and what is not, what is play and what is serious (Bateson, 1972), what the context is, and what our role can be. Many of us then forget just how much we know without words, and how much we rely on this other kind of knowing.

In most cultures, we learn to use our cognitive verbal language and our symbolic and logical metaphoring capacities to carry us out of our moment-to-moment physical world through "reading, writing and arithmetic." By the time we reach adulthood, we carry with us vast amounts of nonverbal and paraverbal data, metaphored into connecting schemata of human relationships. These schemata, these understandings, are based on continuous synesthetic metaphoring overlaid with the connections metaphored through verbal language, interconnected with the learned expectations and rules of the culture—the cultural metaphors of organization and operation. Personal schemata are so interrelated and embedded within other interlocking schemas that they are taken for granted as "reality," as "the way it is." Such amassing of schemata, of core images, becomes our "assumptive world view" (Parkes, 1971), our epistemics (MacLean, 1975). These coded schemata comprise the substrata to how we now think, what we now think, notice, talk and do not talk about in relation to other people, ideas and events. They form the bases of self in the world and the meaning we each give to our life.

By the time we are adults in new situations, the synesthetic cues we have metaphored into meaning long ago are read, checked, noted, and tucked away. They influence our words, voice tone, body posture, and sense of relationship. Our words then talk about other data, and we stay within some boundaries of role as consensually (or even idiosyncratically) defined for each particular context.

Exercises such as the ones described here bring the synesthetically derived theater-of-our-lives to the fore, and cause us to reinspect what has been taken for granted about behavior and about meanings. Such renewed inspection allows for integration of our understanding of behavior in context, for changing options, for updating assumptions, for finding multiple behaviors in any one category, and for becoming multicentric. The timeless and flexible mind can be teased and stretched.

Synesthetic Metaphoring in Exercises

How Behavior Means (Scheflen, 1974), an area of study which looks at behavior from the outside in, deriving a conceptual epistemological map of territoriality and assigning labels to behavior patterns observed, is matched then and coexists at BFI with an approach that asks *how meanings behave* (Duhl, B. S., and Duhl, F. J., 1980), wherein interpretations enacted by each person allow for the connection of epistemics, or personal world views, with consensual categories, or epistemology.

How Meanings Behave

Each trainee enacts his/her own version of the generic combinations. In boundarying and delimiting each role and in asking each person to fully inhabit one such metaphor of approximation at a time (i.e., try on the role of a positive responder), trainers are intensifying each trainee's experience. Each is being asked to assume this one metaphor as a metaphor of core identity, *as if* it enveloped all of one's attributes and ways of being: "Be a person who is always, in every way and fiber of your being, a negative responder." To do that without words, one must caricature and heighten one's behaviors so they will be recognized as fitting that metaphor. One's own flesh and blood human actions fill out the boundaries of that generic and abstract concept as one begins to enact one's own images of how one's meanings behave. Each person creates and lives fully his/her image of positive initator or negative responder. Each is being negative responding or being positive initiating.

Eliminating the use of verbal language compels each person to make his/her images known through action, gesture, facial expression and body behavior, employing physically known stances of consensual meaning within the general culture, as well as those idiosyncratic to one's own imagery and meanings, or to particular earlier personal cultures one has inhabited. Behavior cannot be "hidden behind" as words can. The unified version of message-sending can then be checked with varying versions of message received. In such exchanges individual, family, or group systems issues are enacted and debriefed. Hidden messages in the message-sending are difficult, for only one level and type of language is there to interpret. If there are two messages received, both are metaphored from the same data and the different metaphored meanings derive from different people who interpret the behavior.

The origin of such varying metaphors can be explored for total sequences of behavior. As researchers of nonword communication processing have pointed out (Bateson, 1972; Birdwhistell, 1952, 1971; Condon and Ogston, 1966; Goffman, 1963, 1971; Hall, 1959, 1966; Scheflen, 1974; and others), behavior is. Experience is, words are about. And experience is always in context. Our bodies are. And our bodies, our expressions, our physically nuanced behaviors also speak a language of metaphor to others by their combinations and juxtapositions, sequences, cadences, and repeated patterns. Each bit of behavior, like frames of a silent movie, can be metaphored into meaning only by locating sequences of movements in context. Traditional Siamese dancing may be graceful and stunning, and appreciated as pure flowing form and grace. Its meaning in relationship, in gesture, is lost to those not steeped in the culture. It is an aesthetic experience, like ballet, carrying no consensual message.

Anecdotally, I am reminded of being in a Bush-Negro village in Surinam in 1972, with a Danish guide and Bush-Negro boatman, watching funeral proceedings in the village. Villagers were moving to the beat of a drum in a wide circle around the coffin. Close by the coffin, a woman was moving rhythmically, waving a thick handful of long twigs over the coffin. I asked our guide what she was doing, and she replied "Keeping the evil spirits away." I wondered about this, and I asked her to ask the boatman, whose village this was. She did so in the local dialect, Taki-Taki, then turned embarrassed to me and said, "She's keeping the flies off the coffin!"

We must make meaning! In this case, our guide jumped to the context of funerals—with the assumption that all behaviors were part of the funereal symbolism. In a strange setting, she ignored the behavior as having a meaning familiar to her, as if that would be inappropriate, and placed it into the on-going context, as part of those proceedings.

Conversely, if we have not experienced a context or culture containing some form or variety of the particular behaviors being experienced, we cannot give meaning in the appropriate metaphor. That is, if we have no contextual set for a series of physical behaviors, gestures, we cannot interpret them accurately, i.e., consensually, according to their particular agreed-upon essence. We interpret them actively, idiosyncratically, assigning meaning, feeling, idea and/or experiencing confusion, non-order, uncertainty. Sometimes what we assume "means" fits the people and context. Sometimes it does not.

Thus, as we enter different roles in an action exercise, our metaphoring processes synthesize the multiple contexts we have been in, in which we have given meaning to others' behaviors and to our own. We carry the meanings from those places into our present context, where the roles we each take become parts of total systems processes. Additionally, we continue to interpret others' behaviors by our synesthetic screen of meanings, which we carry as core images. Our experience in the theater of the role then operates on several levels, which are worthy of examining.

Self and Systems

As we fill and enact the role, we pass previous experiences involving other people through our minds. The timeless mind is contextual as well as fanciful. In our role relationships, we are part of transactions. Our metaphors of identity can be looked at through our roles in terms of the parts they play in larger systems, or played in the systems in which they originated. Thus, as the trainee becomes more curious about self-roles in context, he/she is examining many contexts, many systems, which he/she has inhabited. In so doing, trainees are beginning to look at the ways those other contexts were organized and the ways that they functioned, which influenced the trainees in behaving in certain ways. Over time, trainees begin to recognize the times in which those behaviors were not elicited and to note differences in external and internal contexts. The self as psychological system, composed of thinking, feeling, sensing, imaging, and acting aspects, becomes available to be examined, as people explore "What did I learn? What did I find out?" in debriefing exercises.

COMMENTS ABOUT EXERCISES

Where an exercise will lead depends not only upon the exercise, but upon the focus of the trainers at that time, the purpose for which the exercise was planned, the data and material evoked by the participants, and the ability of the trainers to fit responses into situational, contextual maps as well as conceptual ones. When trainers are not afraid of answers, but have a wide metamap, they can help locate and weave together themes. If the exercises contain generic human situations, there are probably boundless numbers of ways in which material can be explored: all the ways I have thus far mentioned and innumerable others as well. All it takes is asking different questions. Such exercises as the ones addressed here can introduce another metaphor—people-as-storytellers, elaborating the history over time of the changes in one's age, stages, places, contexts, and the cumulative experiences stored in the timeless mind, woven into a tale. Such personal stories are the teller's condensations of experience, embodying the coherence and meanings of one's life events, one's sense of bondedness, connectedness, separateness, and purpose.

In the first evening of BFI, each person as system and part of other systems, each person as storyteller, each person as a theater full of experiences upon which to draw as actor and approximator, was evoked.

SUMMARY THUS FAR

We have covered a great deal of territory in this exploration as we have crisscrossed back and forth, under and around the paths through the hologram of these two first-night exercises. It is time to review here where we have been and the significance to the author of choosing these first-night exercises as the ones to explore when discussing generic processes.

While other analogic exercises which I could have chosen could have explored family-as-system, I purposely chose ones that look at interaction generically. In addition, I chose a system level, group, that is not family, that does not have the bonding qualities that family has. Without such intricate bonding and belonging, it is easier for us to look generically at how new systems, like new dating relationships or new training seminars and programs, get started. There are certain generic processes involved in each such situation.

In professional training groups, there is usually no expectation of strong interpersonal bonding of any significance; thus, there is less at stake. Yet, while we can more easily look at the idiosyncratic differences that each one always brings with him/her into such situations from previous contexts, we can also begin to become aware of the role of safety for disclosure in a learning setting, when the learning model draws upon inside-out material.

Beginnings of programs are interesting because they are system formers. Whatever happened that evening influenced what was to come over time, as the group and trainers became a total human system themselves, with varying subsystems and self-organizing, self-regulating patterns.

The examples of the first night exercises examined as under an electron microscope were thus chosen from myriad numbers of systems-exploring designs as a way of making several points at one time, concerning training in integrated and multicentric systems thinking:

1) I have wanted to paint some pictures of the generic methodologies present at the beginning of BFI from which all other discoveries flowed, positive and negative: the valuing and use of analogue, theater, stories, metaphor concerning all levels of human systems, the need for safety, congruence and integration in the way we trained.

2) I have wanted to communicate, if possible, the power and pull of this kind of learning experience, and to begin to explore the mixture of types of learning ongoing in any one exercise. In such an examination we can see that, for instance, one exercise can be cognitively exciting, affectively engaging, synesthetically distrusting, physically disconcerting as well as playful, imagistically mind-expanding, and socially pseudoconnecting—all at the same time!

3) In searching for the source of so many "reactions," we come to realize and to underscore how such designs call upon our associative metaphoric mind (Samples, 1976) to tap into any and all other contexts, where aspects of any role-to-be-enacted might be found waiting in the wings, for an invitation to join in the play. The associative mind gives personal definition in making behavior mean the role. That is, in such exercises of generic categories, one invests into each behavior a chosen conscious meaning. The associative mind, a filter through which all designs and roles must pass, connects what is ongoing to other contexts. This cross-contextualizing capacity is an integrative one. It closes the horizontal décalage (gap) that Piaget speaks of: that knowing of principles in one situation which have not been recognized as isomorphic to other situations.

4) When we then speak of the associative metaphoric mind, we can highlight the timeless quality of mind, for in an active engagement, each trainee

generates his/her "now" data out of all the screens-of-the-past-in-the-present (Duhl, B. S., 1973). From these internal raw data of idiosyncratic meanings of behavior come generalizations about categories of behaviors and about individual differences.

5) When we can take the time to explore an exercise fully, we can perhaps share the author's delight in discovering that no exercise does one thing, that the questions "What else is happening?" and "On what level?" are perhaps the most important questions for trainers to ask and to pass on to trainees. The same questions are useful in other settings, like agencies, institutions, therapy, and in daily life.

6) Once we realize that there are so many levels, we are free to examine a wide range. One can look at the conceptual metaprocessing, and designing of the exercises themselves on the part of trainers. We can explore what is actually involved in doing exercises. We can look in depth at debriefing exercises, wherein meanings begin to emerge. From there we can explore subsidiary processes of mind wherein meanings live, hinting at contexts/situations where idiosyncratic meanings formed when self was a part of other systems. And lastly, we can examine transactional aspects of any individual role from many different vantage points and positions.

If we review the main headings of this approach, as questions, they would look something like this:

a) What do you want trainees to learn?
b) What kind of situation best exemplifies that principle? Or what kind of exercise essentially is a metaphor for or analogic imitation of a real situation?
c) What is the manner by which you will have trainees do the exercise?
d) What does that type of exercise design and the manner in which it will be done "do for/to" the trainees, as individuals? As a group?
e) What types of questions will be asked during debriefing?
f) What will you do with the answers? And what will you do with the answers that don't fit what you had in mind?

7) No one can grasp the full implications of any act while it is occurring. Yet it seems relevant to underscore the importance of first events as potential system precursors, system formers (Gray, 1976). The processes set in motion on any first night begin to define the ways in which people are to relate and, unless attended to, can create problems in one arena while in the process of solving others.

8) The tenuous quality of the safety to risk self-disclosure that first evening led the author to raise questions about the quality of the learning environ-

ment as well as the cognitive and thematic content to be explored. The question "What else is happening?" allows the delicate balance of trust/distrust prevailing in such a seminar to be addressed.

The question of safety/trust was not addressed directly and broadly while the author was a trainee. Experiential exercises, in drawing upon each person's own interpersonal life experiences, raise issues of exposure and disclosure. Such role-enacted interactions in the group system of the trainees require real connection of the people in the room if they are to be free of defensive learning and open to new integrations. The real people behind the role enactments need routes for new connections to other group members besides the roles they play. Attention must be paid to this need and processes developed to meet it (Duhl, B. S., 1976b).

9) Thus, it has been my wish to share an important experience that changed the direction of my life, through giving me permission to use everything I brought with me in the process of my learning and participation. Over time, I was able to help create a context where others could do the same, where no one had to censor aspects of self, but could draw upon rich inner resources to reinvent systems thinking, integration, multicentricity, and new behaviors.

In 1969, the trainers did not know what a demon-goddess they had unleashed, for generic processes and questions have a habit of sticking around. Explorative processes do not lend themselves to being wrapped into neat little packages. There are always untucked edges sticking out. Organicity, which begins to develop a cohesiveness and a coherence as more and more "what if's" are explored, spreads out beyond pigeonholes. Linkups which connect one's internal experiences from the inside out with epistemological conceptualizations are never complete. The processes of mind engaged seem to be all of them. Yet generic gestalts are possible that feel and think whole.

In 1969, the trainers would have spoken of the importance of concept or issue, action and analogue. They would have spoken of the importance of trainees' being involved in an exercise conveying conceptual material. However, they would not have spoken of action and the use of nonvocal information processing as essential to engaging both sides of the brain (Buzan, 1976; de Bono, 1970; Deikman, 1968; Gazzaniga, 1968; Ornstein, 1972). Nor would they have spoken of that active engagement of both sides of the brain in many forms in an atmosphere of respect and safety as a key, if not *the* key essential element in the organismic integration of mind necessary which allows us to go "beyond the information given" (Bruner, 1973a) to multicentric systems thinking.

For all of these considerations, the first-night exercises are significant to the author. However, while I am sure that the generic aspects of looking at the exercises can be followed, I am also aware that one example of an exercise does not necessarily do the trick. Rather, as I mentioned earlier, one example is experience, two allows for comparison, and three allows for the sense of patterns.

SOME LEARNINGS ABOUT SEQUENCING

Let me now present several other N's of experience in analogic designing to explore multipersonal systems called families, so that the reader may have several from which to catch the sense of pattern in designing, and some of the types of situations that one can explore.

Before we examine these other exercises, however, let me add some words of introduction concerning our sense of sequencing of exercises, which evolved out of the author's learnings from these early years: While it is necessary to interrupt the usual social patterns in ways that allow for new learning and new ways of looking, it is also necessary to connect the members of the group so that these new ways of looking can be connected to the interior of each person in terms of his/her own life. This same principle holds for people called clients, students, or patients.

Thus, we have found it important to first connect the people in the training group from the inside out through first utilizing exercises which explore metaphors of identity and approximation, as illustrated in Chapter VII. We then move to those highlighting metaphors of organization and operation of systems. *Thus we progress from self-as-system to self-in-system to systems-in-context.*

When people feel comfortably connected, they are free to inspect all aspects of ways of thinking, feeling, interpreting, acting, seeing. Thus, we will work from the trainee's sense of self to the contexts and systems in which that sense of self developed.

Exercises which tie into the themes of system interface, heightened since 1973, of vulnerabilities and defenses, learning styles, boundaries and core images, allow us to move from the individual person to any level of system. Trainees then can look at ordinary families and those seeking help, or other human systems, with a map that can go from the person to the entire system, without losing anyone, or from the entire system to the persons, without being reductionistic. When there is a general map inclusive of all aspects of human beings, the clusters of behaviors can be seen analogically as the bits which project the entire hologram. Exploration of these themes of system interface is beyond the scope of this current work and comprises the author's next project.

FAMILY-AS-SYSTEM EXPLORED

At this point, with the preceding as background, in order to underscore and highlight analogic design as an essential tool for exploring family-as-systems, let us explore briefly some of the ways in which we have used analogic designs to illuminate different types, levels or aspects of systems.

I offer these now not as cookbook recipes for analogic exercises, for I am sure there must be books full of them from the National Training Laboratories in Bethel, Maine, and other places. Rather, I mention them now as exercises highlighting multipersonal systems, as a range of ways in which we approach the multicentricity of stance in the trainee, and as ways of exploring consensual metaphors of operation and organization, and as one of the routes to analogic thinking.

Examples and Samples: Multiproblem Families

An interesting exercise designed to demonstrate one way of understanding "multiproblem families," while the author was a trainee, emphasized the importance of escalation of issues that families had to deal with.

The trainers asked several group members to role play a lower economic class family of the type in the area served by Boston State Hospital. The trainers' design then called for events to happen to this family, one after another: The father deserted the family. Mother applied for and received welfare payments to take care of herself and the children. The school counselor called to say the son had been suspended for smoking in school. Another child needed an operation. The welfare worker threatened to have welfare payments taken away if mother did not return a small television set she had purchased. Another child in grade school was doing poorly and found to have a learning disability, and so on. We each took parts and played out the scenario, building upon our awareness of the total context of these families.

In the debriefing of how it felt to be in those roles, trainees discovered and expressed the impact of feeling out of control, helpless, trying to cope on all fronts at once. They reported the sense of lack of resources, and of enormous amounts of energy going into sheer survival.

Trainees then generalized that when people feel threatened around issues of basic survival, there is competition for all resources and a sense of deprivation with not enough of any resource. Trainees associated to similar escalated crises in their own lives. Empathy for those in such situations, as contextually harassed, rather than as noncaring and incompetent, began to grow, as we reexperienced and discussed bombardment to our sense of stability. The system interfaces between family and other system entities, such as schools or the welfare department, were highlighted. We became aware of the prevalent inability of families in such situations to focus and to feel any sense of control over their lives, pointing up the need for focused step-by-step problem-solving with competency enhancement as a goal.

Deviancy as Generic Issue

Other such contextual analogic exercises drew on drug-related issues such as alcoholism, or on school/family interfaces, or family/police interfaces. In a grant-sponsored training program* developed and taught by BFI faculty for Family Service Agency social workers concerning issues of alcoholism in families, alcohol was treated as a type of deviancy, in order to help promote attitudinal change in the case workers.

In a series of exercises, originally designed for this exploration and used ever since in varying ways, trainees are asked first to role play a "normal" family, choosing some very usual topic to discuss. At one point, as the family "gets under way," the trainer, who has arranged a predetermined signal with one role player, signals that person to become deviant in behavior in some way. The rest of the "family" members do not know of the prearrangement. They then begin reacting to whatever the deviancy is, in role, but "from the guts."

When the exercise is debriefed, there is a spontaneous and very real element to the range of feelings about the deviant and deviancy! The sense of confusion, betrayal, annoyance and anger comes through. The system reactions can be looked at also, as a whole. Again, trainees become aware of context and transactional processes. As they then relate their own reactions to deviancy in the exercise to people who use alcohol excessively, trainees begin to make connections between their rules for behavior, their bias, and clinical practice.

In a sequential exercise, group members are again instructed to break into groups and to form a family per group, decide who they are, decide on their general context and an issue they have to deal with. The instruction is then given, "One of you will decide to start drinking alcohol. Your reasons will be your own."

Trainees play out such a situation, and derive reasons why they might want to drink from the ongoing transactional processes in the family situations they are enacting. In such an exercise, trainees are drawing upon personal and professional experience. However, as they try on the roles and debrief them,

---

*United Community Services, 1971–72. See Epilogue.

they combine the sense of such situations from the inside out with an exploration of the entire systemic process.

As role players in such contextual and issue-laden analogic exercises, trainees begin to feel what it is like to be on the other side of the therapist's chair and begin to ascertain what types of internal processes lend support to an individual's becoming alcoholic. Generalizations concerning alcohol as a regulator and substitute for more substantial connecting processes are often drawn from this exercise. Trainees then begin to raise questions concerning what ways each person could be touched or moved that would allow for change in individuals and change in the whole system.

Subsystem Exercises

In other types of exercises generic aspects of subsystems are explored: dyadic relationships, triadic relationships, multiperson alliances.

In a dyadic relationship exercise, two-thirds of the trainees are asked to pick partners from among themselves, nonverbally. Without words, they are asked to negotiate a place in the room that they would like to have and call their own space. After they have done that, the remaining one-third of the trainees are asked to decide which of the pairs each would like to join, to choose such a pair, and to negotiate their way, again without words, into each dyad.

Again, in debriefing, trainees become aware of having had to make needs and wishes known without words. They have to work much harder at that, and as a result, they have to attend more carefully to each other to understand what each wants. As such, in a very short time, each dyad builds a sense of exclusivity that can stand for any courtship, friendship, couple.

Into that a third person comes, and bumps into the boundaries of exclusivity previously set up. Upon the internal imagery of each person involved and the meanings privately assigned by each member to this dyadic relationship depends the outcome of the attempted "intrusion." Some dyads do not allow a third person to enter. Other dyads quickly welcome a new person, and still others truly allow negotiation into their space.

Such exercises are rich and can be provocative of, as well as evocative of, many sorts of experienced systems issues for each trainee, as well as illustrative of issues in families and other systems.

In an exercise concerning family and alliance building, generic issues arise. In the first several years, a nonverbal form of "Farmer in the Dell" was used to build a family.

Starting with one person, the entrepreneur then chooses another, negotiating the "marriage" without words. These two then decide on a metaphoric "amount of time," still without words, before "having children."

Of course, without words, it is sometimes hard to be precise, and so the misunderstandings of signals become symbolic of daily life misunderstandings. "No words" becomes metaphor for the lack of discussion between real life partners, which usually leads to enormous assumptions and misunderstandings.

In any case, the instructions then are to "choose" (have) a child, to decide on "time between children," and to "choose several," stopping when they feel they have "finished their family." The whole exercise can then be debriefed by the group on many levels. Given the universality of this situation, one has only to limit the choice of questions to debrief and the focus at any one time. Individual feedback is immediately made analogous to real life situations, by trainers and trainees alike, through the generalizations drawn.

Focusing on Focusing and Interpretation

In another very simple exercise, two trainees are asked to have a brief verbal argument, while others watch and listen. We will then ask, "What did you hear?"

It is amazing how many adult trainees respond with evaluative and judgmental precoded interpretations! Trainers will ask the observers again, "What did you hear?" And again—until trainees begin to respond with what they actually heard.

We will then ask, "What meaning do you give what you heard?" So often, trainees (and practically everyone else) interpret without tracking what was actually said, which does not allow them the option of being free to help the arguers be clearer in their own communication processes.

The same type of exercise is done, asking trainees, "What did you see?" and "What meaning do you give what you saw?"

As I became aware, such exercises also aid in re-walking trainees through different Piagetian stages of cognitive and self-knowledge development (Piaget, 1952; Alschuler et al., 1975; Duhl, B. S., 1978). Asking "What did you hear or see?" requires trainees to pause momentarily at the pre-operational stage, in which we all are capable of describing events. "What meaning do you give?" brings trainees into concrete operational thinking where hypotheses are posed from data. And asking trainees to underscore the system principles operating draws upon formal operational thinking.

The Therapist/Family System

Analogic exercises highlighting systems issues for the trainee's eventual roles as therapist and consultant began in 1969 and have remained a source of rich exploration. One of the prime methodologies begun was role playing many types of systemic situations.

One such generic process, which emphasized interviewing as information gathering and exchange, has been in constant use since the author was a trainee, for when trainees enter a training program in family systems therapy, many still have a hard time not thinking "pathology," not thinking in we/they terms of one up/one down, of the usual medical, psychiatric and psychological models. Family therapy originated as part of the field of mental health. Mental health was/is seen as the opposite of mental illness. Mental illness however takes on a different twist when seen as systemic and contextual adaptation. It is akin to asking, "For what type of context is this behavior appropriate? In what types of contexts/situations are these sets of thoughts and actions fitting?"

The idea that one could look at the interactive, transactional and intergenerational schemas of family members and find the problem arising within the transactions between members was (and still is) a new idea. Originally, the following exercise was designed to steer trainees away from specific conventional and prefabricated ways of thinking about people who seek help, toward thinking of them contextually.

The Job Market Exercise

In heightening the metamessage that interviewing is contextual information gathering and exchange, the leaders created a number of almost ridiculous (at that time!) job situations: two people needed to go to live on the moon; two trapeze artists needed for a circus; men and women needed for an escort service; aquanauts to live under water; balloonists to go across country together; tennis players for a team.

In each situation, one person is to be interviewer. Other trainees, two persons in teams, choose which jobs they will apply for. All trainees have a chance to be both interviewer and interviewee. In each of these situations, because they are fairly extreme and removed from usual daily life contexts, the interviewer as well as the interviewee has to stretch somewhat to consider the total context and to assess what skills, interactive attributes, and personal qualities are most needed to fit each situation.

In addition, each trainee is applying for the job as part of a two-person team, and each can only be hired as a team member. It is difficult for any player to enact any of these roles without thinking afresh. It is impossible to act on some assumption of knowing automatically what would be "right" and required in these jobs, as well as fitting oneself with a teammate. One has to think and act creatively, transactionally, instantaneously, with regard to all aspects of the situation, presentation of self, and self as desirable team person, all without rehearsal. Interviewers also have to be on their toes, to become aware of which questions will give them the widest range of information in the same arenas.

For trainees, this exercise is always important. When one begins to think simultaneously of self, of team issues, of skills and tasks in context, one is thinking systemically. The stretch that one has to do mentally is to quickly puzzle solve how to find out what the image of job and fit is for each side of interviewer/interviewees. Such rapid sorting and acting take in all the levels and metalevels of systems thinking holographically. Biological and physical attributes, such as stamina and general health, become important aspects of person in each of these off-beat job situations. Personality attributes in terms of disposition are important in stressful dyadic jobs, as are character attributes, such as responsibility and trustworthiness. Careful interactive teamwork or ability to fit with another and with a task must be assessed, and so on, to say nothing of actual skill and performance capacities.

Anecdotally, it was during this exercise as a trainee that the author experienced that kind of delicious "aha" that feels so rewarding, integrative, and permission-giving all at once. For in the midst of doing it, it occurred to her that everything she had ever done or knew about could be useful in thinking conceptually and systemically and in working with people. Everything she had ever experienced could be utilized in some way for connection-making with or about other people and how they worked. No part of her experience, interests, capacities nor diverse arenas engaged in need be shut off. It was as if the barriers between compartments of mind rolled down. The process over time then became one of discrimination of not what to use, but when and when not to, and how to do so effectively.

Rent-a-Family

In another series of interviewing exercises, trainees interview ordinary families, which we call our Rent-a-Families. We pay them to be interviewed by teams of trainees and to give feedback about each interview. While these exercises are not analogic designs of the usual role-taking sort, they are analogic in a different way. The emphasis here is on information evocation and integration, focusing on how ordinary families work, love and play, and organize themselves. In that sense interviewing a Rent-a-Family is analogic to any system interviewing. In addition, trainees have an opportunity for rehearsal and feedback about their styles, from "consumers" who are not seeking help. This is a luxury not possible with families seeking care.

Trainees' Families as Clients

In an important series of analogic exercises, trainees role play their own families of origin as coming into therapy around an important family issue, and are interviewed by other trainees.

For the past several years, the author has started her supervision groups with some version of this exercise. Basic questions are asked of trainees: What issue or what kind of issue would have brought your family into treatment? How would the idea of therapy have reached your family? Who would make the decision? What kind of therapist would your family need? With whom would the therapist have to connect in order for therapy to have a chance?

Before possibly role playing the family situation, the trainee must answer all of the above questions for him/herself and spatialize and/or diagram the family dynamics, as he/she perceives them. The role play then ensues, and comparisons are drawn between the presenter's sense of family and the interviewer's. For many trainees, this becomes the first time they have actually thought about the processes any family undergoes before a member even makes a phone call or the family walks in the door of an agency or office.

Trainees again learn interviewing as an interactive exchange, needful of respect for each person in the situation, and the need for interventions fitting both individuals and the whole system.

When trainees have the opportunity to interview ordinary families such as their own and Rent-a-Families, so that they can find out how normal families work, they can approach the task of facilitation and therapy of those who do seek their help from a broad range. In interviewing families to find out "what's wrong," they can begin to assess individuals and families as if along a continuum of issues and conditions ranging from discomfort to jeopardy (Duhl, B. S., 1978; Duhl, B. S. and Duhl, F. J., 1981; Duhl, F. J. and Duhl, B. S., 1979).

INDIVIDUAL ATTRIBUTES AS SYSTEM COMPONENTS

As the program progressed, BFI began to expand and develop the range of exercises to find the themes that linked in an integrated manner through all levels of human system, as well as all levels of mind, intrapsychic, interactive, transactional.

Exercises highlighting individual biological attributes as part of individual learning styles, which influenced and shaped systemic interactions, became another category of exercises which began to link the trainee to individuals in total systemic transactions (Duhl, B. S. and Duhl, F. J., 1975; Duhl, F. J. and Duhl, B. S., 1979). The author's development of boundary sculpture in 1971 (see next chapter) became a major tool for varieties of exploration about personal styles and preferences, as components in larger systems (Duhl, F. J., Kantor, and Duhl, 1973).

In another such type of exercise, trainees are asked to form family groups and to assign themselves family roles of mother, brother, and so on, and an age. That one role and age assignment stirs up enough image material from which to work.

Each family is then asked to simulate waking up in the morning, in its own "home" in the room. (Hopefully, one has a carpeted room in which to do this exercise!) All are asked to "Lie down, go to sleep in your most comfortable position. It is morning. Wake up, and get up in your usual style. Do your own usual morning routines, in your style of being, without words."

In such an exercise, trainees discover how their different ways of being, called "style" become grist for the interactive family systems mill. How people go about being themselves, coping with mundane daily life, becomes grouped under a category of information-processing styles. Trainees learn that all is not structure of roles and contextual constraints, but that personal attributes are key phenomena in such structures and roles. Functional autonomy and dynamic interaction seem to come together in exercises of this sort.

CONCLUSION

It is hoped that these additional family-as-system exercises, while not presented in depth, have served to stimulate the reader to think of his/her own setting and program and what is needed there that can be explored analogically, through an exercise designed for that purpose.

Over time at BFI, by continual experimentation, we have found ways to draw upon all categories of analogic exercises in order to combine content, process, skills, themes, and tasks in the training setting in a manner which is reflexively coherent (Wideman, 1970) integrative and systemic, all at once.

Some exercises call on analogic or metaphoric thinking before entering the exercise, as a part of it, while others call upon those capacities during the exercise, and others afterwards, in debriefing. Over time, trainees begin to listen, think, talk and act metaphor and analogue, as well as to think analytically. There is no embarrassment about the use of either. The senses are tuned to be able to speak "the language of impact" (Duhl, F. J., 1969) of whomever trainees work with, and to analyze what is occurring. They have been trained to think associatively, using all of themselves, to capture the metaphoric essence of whatever is of importance to the people with whom they then work. The total process is a holographic one at this point, wherein each bit contains the whole and can be directed to any part. We will explore further certain aspects of this process in the next chapter.

The analogic exercise of family-as-system provides the mechanism for a here-and-now experience as common metaphor for the group of trainees. The now information is a moment-in-life, without history or depth. It is our meaning of the moment. It has no past or future, until each trainee infuses it with meaning, images of contexts, situations, people, systems, ideas, wishes, dreams, that we each bring with us all the time. At the same time, the wonderment of our human capacity for metaphoring is that there is no limit to the amount of metaphoring we can do. We can create new experiences and new memories and transpose, transport, and transform data and images from one arena, context or form to another.

In this here-and-now experience, trainees are generating the data on many levels. Trainees are finding out about who people are at the individual level of system, as well as at varying types of group levels of system, and the amount and type of hierarchy within each system level. As each person connects this event to other experiences through questions, either woven into the exercise itself or raised in debriefing, trainees become aware and find out about who people are in family systems and work systems. Some of the people they are finding out about are themselves—in varying contexts and over time.

Trainees, then, are information gathering and analogically problem solving on several levels and arenas simultaneously. The multiple roles and ways of being and acting each person has and plays in various contexts and systems can be elevated from subsidiary to focal awareness. Categories of experience are generalized by individuals and in the group. How much one is the same in different contexts and how much one is different and in which ways, gives clues to how that might also be so for the people one will be working with, as clients. Thus, grounded in one's own personal experiences, each trainee's assumptive world view gets transformed to a place in a larger map. Each begins to invent a general systems metaphor and way of thinking.

Analogic exercises which cover wide ranges of situations, in addition to utilizing experiences of each person in the room as resources, create many such N's of experiences, giving trainees the opportunity to search out many types of "fit" in the similarities, differences, patterns and metacategories of types of experience among themselves and among clients.

Trainees who go through many 1-2-3-plus experiences begin to map their theories from the inside out, into patterns which connect as they locate the generic categories which group their singular and idiosyncratic variations of experience. Conversely, they learn to recognize patterns of human interactions in a variety of ways. In tracking back from those patterns they learn how to find the connection of the patterns with variations of singular individual behaviors and experiences. Perhaps most important of all, such continual exposure to varieties of analogic exercises in which generic questions are asked both in entering the exercises and in debriefing, connects for trainees personal individual behaviors with human systems theory, when there are integrating themes. In such analogic exercises, one discovers how one's own behaviors and those of others derive from contextual settings, as well as one's inner world, and are given individual idiosyncratic meanings. The principle of equifinality—of many ways of getting to the same place—is "seen" and experienced.

Trainees learn respect for each individual view of a situation as a valid view of system, "correct" but incomplete. Each explores the views of the system from the "outside" as well. Such diversity of experience is critical in training therapists to work in an open systems model with other human systems. Only by understanding multiple meanings can each trainee not lose touch with each person's essential human core while working with and within the whole context. Each trainee needs to be able to approximate many persons' vantage points, as well as to see the whole pattern fit together, as if he/she were outside it. One cannot approximate and know multiple stances, multiple meanings, without the multiple opportunities to practice, to "get into" those stances.

Thus, training through analogic exercises, in a context that will consider family-as-system as well as family-as-theater, is critical to training in multicentric systems thinking and the type of therapy which keeps touch with each individual person involved.

As therapist, trainer, teacher and agent of planful change, the more experiences one has had in life the better and the wider one's scope will be in knowing the ways of the world and the people in it. The differences between an "old pro" (Kramer, 1980) and a novice consist in the range of variation, the numbers and types of experiences the former has had, that the latter as yet has no map for.

We attempt, through analogic designs, to help our trainees become "Old Pros" sooner.

Sculpture and the Theater of the Mind | X

I was his younger sister, aged 10. I stood by silent, helpless and heavy, as I saw my brother pick up my father from under the table, to carry him home. We moved in silence. Father was drunk as usual, and it was my 12-year-old brother's task to find him and bring him home.

My stomach was tight, and I felt as weighty as the load my brother was carrying. The lights were low, capturing the mood and emotional tone as projected and described by my brother, the sculptor. We were a well-to-do Indian family, living in Malaysia. We had moved, for business reasons, from the entangled matrix of the extended family compound in New Delhi. Here we were isolated and exposed among strangers. The helplessness felt intense.

There was something grippingly stark and awesome in this, for I was in a very delicate and special place: standing inside someone else's private and existential image.

Another time, I was a butcher, one of the few people that this woman stopped to see on her way home. As a newly divorced parent of one, her network had shrunk, and I was one of just about ten people in it—the edge of trouble and craziness.*

These were early forms of "sculpture," David Kantor's invention (Duhl, F. J., Kantor, and Duhl, 1973), which perhaps also could have been called theater-in-the-raw—no rehearsals, pure, fast and quick essences of the dramas of our lives. More involved with interactive patterns than psychodrama, with the world of words removed, its images and meanings are the sculptor's, drawn from his/her internal gallery, metaphored into a reality in external space and enacted by members of the group. Each player searches the images and feelings within self, and screening them, finds the essences that accompany the

---

*According to Ross Speck, M.D., Family Forum, BFI-sponsored series, 1969–70. During the discussion of his interview of a commune in front of an audience, Speck stated that when an individual's network contains less than ten people, that person could be expected to become agitated, edging towards disorientation and craziness, due to the lack of enough people resources to meet ordinary grown-up human needs.

sculptor's descriptions, poses and directions. Once enacted, actors debrief the whole experience. Observers comment; the ensemble together discovers key themes, personal wishes, wants, bondedness, conflicts, contextual restraints, patterns, possibilities.

Then and now each person becomes an actor, a player, in someone else's drama. We enter each other's lives, and discover the rich interior images we each carry, the condensations of our life experiences, where environments and spaces as well as people hold special tones and sensations, special meanings, forces, ambience. We discover new and rich ways of externalizing our internal spheres of meaning, memories, and maps. Each representation of our real life dramas and situations becomes raw data from which to learn about self, others in the group, families, systems, contexts. Here, the first questions are not, "What did you learn?" and "What did you find out?", but other versions of those: "How was it for you to be in that role, in that position, that interaction, that sequence? What was happening for you? What did it evoke in you?"

In that early development of family sculpture, in a class of 14, we became knowledgeable, from the inside out, about 14 family systems, making it a very crowded and populated room. And yet, we had explored the essences of each trainee's personal sense of family and family system in dramatic form in relatively short amounts of real time. We had explored and learned system through our participation in the creation of those dramatic essences in moving spatial and kinesic metaphors.

As Kantor first developed one form of evocative family sculpture in depth, the private family dramas in our minds became theater. We sculpted our aesthetic and symbolic impressions of the physical and interpersonal contexts of our lives and the dynamics of living in each of our families, giving these impressions external form and shape in the staged time collapse of theater. We illuminated relationship and began to discover the forces in each character that helped move relationships in the way that each did.

We were deeply involved in the dramas of our ordinary lives. We began to catch sequences and patterns. We invented system, from the inside out.

Now, some 14 years later, many of these evocative experiences are still vividly available, to be run on the screen of my mind and to be reintegrated, reexamined and conceptualized in still a dozen other ways.

"My family" means my sets of images* and conceptualizations of my

---

*Again, I am using the word "image" generically, as a generic sense construction, to include all varieties of synesthetic metaphoring, wherein we translate, transform, and transpose from one sensory modality to another. Thus, I am using image to encompass various modes of phenomenological representation.

family, just as my sister's family means her sets of images and conceptualizations of the same group of people, of which I am one. The family in my office similarly means my set of images and conceptualizations of them at any given time.*

Sculpture, as it was first developed in depth, became a rapid metaphorical idiom for presenting the symbolic essences we carry of the people who gave and give our lives meaning, in our sense of relationship with each of them and they with each other. The symbolic essence we portray is guided by our private aesthetic valuings of each person and context—our idiosyncratic sense of fit, order, bonding, comfort, dynamism, beauty, balance.

In the evoking, in the doing, in the discussing, in the thinking about, such spatial representations rapidly allow new information to come forth, all filling out and expanding images and conceptualizations.

A LOOK AT ORIGINS

The birth of sculpture took place during the Spring semester of 1969, the first in BFI's history, when founders Fred Duhl, David Kantor and Madeleine Gerrish were leading the group. There, in what perhaps can be described as a characteristic fashion, David Kantor recalls himself as impatient and bored with the way in which material concerning a family they were discussing was being handled.** He wanted to "try interacting with that material in yet another way." As he recalls it, he started to describe a board game idea that he had been thinking of, on which there would be wooden figures representing family members, that could be moved around, using spatial distances between figures to represent relationships. As he began to talk about the board and figures he said, "Here, let me show you what I mean," and live family sculpture was born. For instead of continuing to describe the family members linearly, by language, Kantor moved to the language of pantomime and the spatial metaphors of theater, dance, and spatial relations to carry the ideas and images he had formed of the family they were discussing.

In that spontaneous happening, and yet drawing upon his background in psychodrama, Kantor chose several people to represent the family members they had been discussing. Telling each player a little about how he "saw" each member, he then placed each in positions of relationship to the others,

---

*Some years ago, Ray Birdwhistell, M.D., of the Eastern Pennsylvania Psychiatric Institute, produced the *Hillcrest Series*, four interviews of the same family done within two consecutive days. Not unlike the Japanese film *Rashomon*, or Lawrence Durrell's *Quartet*, each family therapist interviewer (Don Jackson, Carl Whitaker, Nathan Ackerman and Murray Bowen) drew forth a different image and sense of family and sense of "problem" from the same unit of people.
**Personal communication, March 1981.

utilizing horizontal physical space to represent degrees of closeness/distance, and vertical space to represent power/helplessness. He asked players to employ certain gestures, capturing and externalizing metaphorically the organizing meaning Kantor gave to his perceptions.

He started by asking father to stand on a chair, finger pointing, and frowning to indicate his authority, anger and displeasure with his son; mother to stand 10 feet away, pointing to the daughter, trying feebly to get father's attention by a halfhearted wave; the younger daughter at a distance, oblivious to the whole scene, reading a book; the son standing back on the other side, shielding himself from father. As mother tries to get father to pay attention to daughter, he "yells" at the son. Mother then runs to protect the son. Father "yells" at her and she runs away as the son hides again. Father again turns to the son, as mother points to the daughter. And so on.

Kantor thereby quickly represented his internal images, his sense of how each person seemed to be in relationship to each other. And he told each what to do when, in what repeated sequences. Thus, all could "see" Kantor's image of relationships in the family they were discussing. Each person in the room had a common external metaphor against which to compare his/her own private internal understandings and images of the family they had been talking about.

Thus, family sculpture became an unusual mix—a concrete and enacted event, yet simultaneously a representation of abstract conceptual as well as intuited and known phenomena, in context and time. Sculpture became a metaphor of meanings, and of the dynamics of interactions.

The idea took off at BFI among faculty and students, as well it might, and training was never the same after that! Sculpture expanded in many directions. Kantor's quick casting of characters in a stylized moving sequence was immediately recognizable. It was intuited in every cell of each person. Each trainee and trainer immediately grasped and understood this powerful metaphorical language and presentation that captured the dramatic essence of known and lived sequences of everyday life. Indeed, we already operated within this modality and had since infancy.* Our sensorimotor learning and knowing precede and are the basis of all other learning; metaphoring, through imitation and play (see Chapter VII) is our connection-making apparatus at work. "Show me" follows close on the heels of "doing."

When BFI trainees briefly presented sculpture a year or so later to other family therapists from the Northeast, at the Boston-based Society for Family

---

*America's most pervasive and thriving communications medium, television, owes its beginnings to the silent movie, not as technology, but as a medium understood by all: actions without words, in spatial metaphor, denoting relationships.

Therapy and Research* and at major BFI-sponsored workshops in 1973 and 1974, sculpture took off completely.** It unleashed and provided a vehicle and channel for the restive creative energy in people in this new field who had been struggling with linear language to present the multiple, simultaneously occurring and interconnected phenomena of family life, in and among members, across, within and between varying types of boundaries. Sculpture captured the imagination of those who were looking for a modality for the creative exploration of and experimentation with ideas about family relationships.

Sculpture, or spatializing, as I now refer to this medium, became the idiom by which to express experientially that which is experiential, and which has first been perceived and given meaning experientially, before it is given conceptual or theoretical meaning. Sculpture and spatialization provided the means of organizing, defining, and expressing the verbally inexpressible: the idea of simultaneity, of betweenness, of action and relationship in and over timespace. The medium fit the message.

Sculpture and spatializing also allow us to incorporate and interconnect in juxtaposition contextually dyssynchronous events. In our timeless minds, such events are often fused in their meanings, constituting our inner sense of reality and coherence. The mind makes meaning from the way in which it sees connection and pattern of disparately occurring phenomena. Our minds create *"fit"* and the sense of order.

The form of sculpture enacted by Kantor that first evening was a spontaneous one, both from the inside out and the outside in, depending on who and where you are. In his metaphoring process, Kantor, as trainer, imaged a production inside his theater-of-the-mind. He asked others to enact and make manifest his internal image of a third "party," the particular family being discussed (a modality still utilized by us in training as well as in therapy). For the observers, it is an "outside in" experience, of information transmission of a point of view. It allows them comparisons, conceptualizations, judgments. For the sculptor and players, it is both inside out and outside in.

---

*Boston, 1971. It was at this meeting that social worker Peggy Papp, a former actress, first saw a quick sculpture in another of its emerging forms: quick, static, photo-like positioning of members highlighting their structural arrangement; quick stabiles similar to single drawings for animated cartoons. The modality appealed, and she began popularizing it in this static form, later "adding" movement and renaming it "Choreography" (Papp, 1976; Papp, Silverstein, and Carter, 1973).

**The 1973 and 1974 workshops sponsored by BFI were host to over 100 family therapists each year, and explored a plethora of ways of utilizing spatial metaphors to grasp, represent, and explore meanings and images of, and potential change in, system interactions. Constantine's article (1978) is based on notes and materials developed by the author and others for these earlier workshops. By 1970, we also discovered at the Orthopsychiatric meeting that Virginia Satir was using various body positions of people to explore basic "communication stances" and fixed relationships.

SCULPTURE: THE LANGUAGE OF THEATER

As a trainee, and later as a trainer, I like others felt this medium to be a bottomless, unending wellspring, forever generative, forever fresh, capable of flowing in all directions and of being used for many purposes. When I was invited by Kantor to teach with him for two years at BFI and, simultaneously and concurrently, by Jeremy Cobb to co-lead seminars at Boston State Hospital, I found myself with the opportunity to invent multiple ways of using this spatial metaphoring process until, within a few years, it became not a modality but a fluid and fluent language, spoken as easily as "verbalese."

It is a generic and native metaphoring language of form, gestures, movements in space, known by all of us, used and translated constantly by each of us every moment. It can be raised to an art of translation and transformation by people who would more fully understand the taffy-pulling interconnectedness of human beings with each other.

However, while it is a familiar language, it is also a strange or estranged language for us as adults. We are uncomfortable speaking it consciously. Like people well inducted and assimilated into another culture, we are a little ashamed of having known this first language so well. It is the language of children, of play, of imitation, of delight in the discovery of being and of meaning-making, before others impose their meanings on our behavior. *It is the language of finding out how behavior means, and how meanings behave.*

For most adults, it is the language of theater, of exhibition, self-consciousness and discomfort. Often we are not aware of what we are "saying" to others, or are uncomfortable talking about such paraverbal, nonvocal and contextual messages, expecting that blame and/or ridicule will accompany that which is undertaken as the very beginning of an exploration.

As adults, we are all actors, but not necessarily informed, intelligent, cognizant ones. Yet, where in this culture does one have the opportunity to be a "fair witness" (Lilly, 1972) in becoming truly cognizant of oneself as a message-sending actor? Where can one experience and observe oneself as system member while others are doing the same, without penalty?

In the world of theater and dance, pantomime and all forms of paraverbal spatial metaphoring are used, in aesthetic balance, in presentations of relationship. The world of theater helps communicate the interconnected drama as well as the zaniness, absurdity, and humor of and in our daily lives.

Yet theater is but a fine and refined tuning of what we in daily life do, know, and struggle with. Theater but highlights the essences of meanings already known to us in some form. Theater reflects the configurations of our behaviors, experienced by us in real time, in another pacing, with other people. Theater takes us into the land of strange and familiar—enough that is strange, novel, and new to capture our attention, awareness and interest; enough that is familiar that we can feel and recognize, to create coherence of events and messages, spoken and unspoken.

Sculpture, then, took us into the world of theater, where, as consummate directors, we staged our images and fantasies of relatives, relating and relationships.

Sculpture also returned us to the world of our inner thinking, that private dialogue that takes place within self, that inner commentary on the current scene and context. It returned us to the world of our childhood, when we first became aware of what we liked and didn't like, and where we *knew* that beginning sense of differentiation, of discrimination. Sculpture returned us to the inner world of images, of preferences, of opinions never spoken, known but never made public.

As adults we call sculpture "theater." As children, we used to call it play. It was what we did for a living. We imaged, we created, we played with actions, words and life scenarios as we played with crayons and fingerpaints. We said "what if," and "make believe"; we entered the world of playful imitation when we directed and said, "You be the mommy and you be the daddy, and I'll be the baby," or "You be the Cowboy and I'll be the Indian." Sculpture reawakened the sense of the inner "I" who discriminates, knows, sees, and who has a certain inner set of aesthetic rules, very private ones, very idiosyncratic, which guide the sense of how relationships ought to be, could be, should be.

And sculpture provided a most interesting idiom for the exploration of images and of human systems of all sizes and shapes, and of concepts *about* systems. New questions raised new searches, new information and answers. Our original "metaphoric mind" (Samples, 1976), which orients us in the world, in space (Piaget and Inhelder, 1956), in our explorations (Pearce, 1976), and in our preverbal knowing, is revitalized and reawakened in the playful drama and dramatic play of spatializations. And the wonder of it is that we have all been there before. We have all created theater-in-our-mind, as child, if not now.

Thus sculpture belonged to honored traditions. However, the traditions were out of context. Theater and play did not belong in the serious field of education, training, professional systems thinking, psychotherapy. What did theater have to do with knowing how families work, and how human systems work?

We had entered the world of theater and play—to focus and learn more about life and living.

Let us explore that world for a moment, for its importance in training generic and multicentric systems thinkers.

FAMILY-AS-THEATER:
THEATER IN TRAINING AND THERAPY

The role reversal and alter ego techniques developed by Moreno for use in *Psychodrama* (1946) had been some of the first in the world of psychotherapy to offer trainees and clients an opportunity to be both inside of self and an outside enactor *with* self.

In early psychodrama (dramas of the world of mind/soul), Moreno had participants take their internal tape recordings of the mind and give them an external audition, in a performance, a hearing, with an audience. That audition was to take place in dialogic form, with the author of the scripted internal dialogue and another participant. In such dialogues, the protagonist of theater is the inner voice of want, wish, the "I" who is pushing for something different, who would grow, develop, be. The antagonist is the voice of the oppressor, the one who stops growth, movement, thwarting emergence of competence and confidence. In psychodrama, the actor first takes the voice of the protagonist—the push for differentiation and integration.

In role reversal, one takes the side and voice of the antagonist—the person one *sees* as outside oneself restraining one from being the way one would like to be, from doing what one would like to do. The author of this dialogue steps into the shoes of the antagonist, speaking the words of the original characters, while one's co-dialoguer speaks one's own words as protagonist. It is a powerful step toward decentration, when one can begin to see oneself from "outside."

In alter-egoing, Moreno lends support to the protagonist who is unaccustomed to speaking his own cause for survival well, who is too frightened, or untutored in being in touch with the inner "I." Alter-egoing, or doubling, offers other optional dialogues of inner thoughts, feelings, sensation, meanings to such players. This support of ego-centrism in the Piagetian sense of a developing and separate sense of "I" is fostered again by borrowings of the "aside" from theater.

Such vocalized dialogues bring the intrapsychic, psychological self alive, externalized, to be explored in new ways in training and therapy. Such inner dialoguing, externalized (which also takes place in the Gestalt therapy approach of Fritz Perls and the Psychosynthesis of Assagioli), allows the originator of the script to become aware of the inner system of "parts of psychological self."

When/if such dialogues are viewed contextually, participants become aware that their internal dialogic system is often populated with the characters with whom one has lived and interacted, and been impressed by, in one's own particular idiosyncratic mix of meaning-making and definition.

Yet the meanings we give to our relationships, the data for such inner dialogues, come from more, much more, than the spoken word. Kantor's sculpture, extending psychodrama, translated the dialogues *into the meanings of the dialogues*—in action, in space, as such dialogues represented the *distance regulation* messages sent and received by family members.

In addition, he included not only the disapproving gestures, the intensities of tone, the ways in which members moved and when; he included the knowing that is nonverbal, the generic and metaphoric issue of boundaries, of self and others in contextual and interpersonal space over time. Such essences of experience do not inhabit the world of words. They inhabit the world of image, of sense, of aesthetics. And that world is the world of theater.

Sculpture allows us to enter this world of theater to explore our images, and our thoughts, through the most complete, untapped, unschooled and original part of ourselves—our inner sense of personal aesthetics. It is through that experiential, aesthetic sense that we somehow give weight and value to external and internal phenomena. We metaphor those weightings into meanings (right brain). Only later do we try to make sense and weave coherence of the meanings we derived or gave to our perceptual world with reasons, explanations, or theories (left brain).

Sculpture allows us the opportunity to join the right and left sides of our brain in joining our aesthetic sense with our sense of reason, through the full vehicle of theater. Theater is more than image. It is also the world of form, of order and sequence. And the world of theater is where the idiosyncratic human trait of being able to bond psychologically in varieties of ways is played out. Not only are human beings capable of being bonded to certain persons, evoking great emotions in life dramas with each other, but human beings are peculiarly able to be psychologically bonded to certain ideologies, concepts, theories, images-of-human, myths, and beliefs about people and the purpose of life itself.

Not only are we capable of remembering and juxtaposing past and present, but we human beings are also oddly able to image an as yet nonexistent future, be it the pie one is going to eat for dinner, an unformed masterpiece in clay, a nonexistent machine, or an unheld battle in a war. We are able to feed that image forward, to plan for making that future happen, to create its being. Once upon a time, this book did not exist. We dream what does not exist, create it, then receive, react, incorporate and "bounce off" the fact and wonderment of the existence of our creations, only to begin the process anew. We are indeed marvelous creatures.

In the creations of theater, then, the vicissitudes of daily life are reflected to us, as well as the universals of bondings, of imaging past and future, of aspiring, hoping, wanting, and planning, making something happen. These universals are the stuff of dramatic conflict and resolution. They are also the stuff of the drama of ordinary family life.

It seems, then, that in the introduction of sculpture, historically, we had come full circle from another tradition and age: from psychological, systemic dramatists to dramatic system psychologists.

SYSTEMIC DRAMATISTS

Indeed, in the ancient Greek dramatists we find some of the first systems psychologists and systems thinkers of the Western world, whose themes are as fundamental for us today as they were for their actors and audiences in Greece, who struggled with them.

The emphases change, but the themes are the same. After all, it was the 5th century B.C. Greek playwright Sophocles who made famous Oedipus' complex family story, in which he unknowingly kills his father and, equally unwittingly, marries his mother. However, Jocasta is as much married to her son as Oedipus is married to his mother. In the 20th century version, Freud reawakens that legend by "inventing" and analogically labeling an individual "complex" honoring only one member's part of that family system's transactions.

The Greek dramatists not only captured the psychological and ideological themes of importance, but also captured the awareness of the multiple roles each person plays in life, in his/her private and public spaces, and in relation to his/her own inner sense of self and purpose. The personal bondings, the social rules of order, the invisible enacted loyalties and disloyalties which give human life meaning are masterfully captured by Aeschylus, Sophocles, Euripides. They, and Shakespeare later, fully caught in their plays that, while one person inhabits one body, he/she *is a different person* for each other with whom he/she is in relationship.

Each son or daughter "sees" his/her mother and father quite differently from the way the father and mother "see" themselves and each other. Romeo's trusted and beloved friend, Juliet, is seen by other family members as the enemy. We decide relationship both by outer constructs of role (who one is for another according to the cultural status hierarchies of that context) and by the inner experience of fit of personal preferences (of who each other person is for oneself in his/her way of being). The dramatic tension in ordinary family life comes from the many roles we play in our own and each other's lives, both symbolically and in actual process.

Each relationship then *is the betweenness*, that essential something that brings vitality, intensity, and unique meaning to human life. Like snowflakes, no two betweennesses are exactly alike. Relationships in their fine tunings are infinitely varied; they come with the range of difference for which our unique fingerprint is also a metaphor. Each betweenness, each relationship, has its own fingerprint.

The dramatist, like a systems theorist/therapist, must find meanings and patterns, and must represent varying points of view, varying types of betweenness. He/she must have a sense of how each character acts, believes and speaks, and thus how each plays a part in the whole enterprise. He/she creates connections by the juxtaposition and sequence of contexts, actions and behaviors, intent and meanings.

The Greeks and Shakespeare exemplified in action, commentary, and metacommentary each author's profound visions into the complexities and ironies of human nature in play with the forces beyond any person's individual control. The plays were the playwrights' inner metaphoric images of the external world, remetaphored again through and into the vehicle of theater. In Greek theater, the story was first told by a chorus, and then with one, two, and later three actors taking all parts while the chorus commented on the whole.

The Greeks highlighted the relationship of man to Fate and to each other. From those beginnings, dramatic theater—or the portrayal of conflict, of dynamic differences—was born, which has continued to portray and communicate messages about human beings and the human condition to this day.

Drama is in the juxtaposition of symbol, meanings, and behavior. The closer behaviors are to the desired symbolic meanings, personal and consensual, the greater the harmony. Drama occurs in the mental space "between" symbolic images of what should be, one's sense of what has been, and what is occurring now. Drama is the betweenness of symbolic meanings and actions.

What constitutes theater, then? We can define it as inner images organized by an imager, externalized, carrying extracted and heightened essences of perceived and known phenomena, in a cohesive set of messages, within a coherent set of relationships, comprehended by an audience.

SYSTEMS THINKERS/THERAPISTS AS PLAYWRIGHTS AND DRAMATISTS

That task of organizing images, of selecting particular components from one's reality, and metaphoring them into a play which tells a connected and coherent story, is also the task of systems theorists and therapists, trainers and trainees.

Family systems theorists and therapists are not unlike dramatists. As plays reflect the cultural themes and images-of-human of the author, so theories of human systems reflect the observations of human life within the experience and image-of-human of the theorist/therapist.

We all know that home movies are boring. They seem to just go on, without purpose, without particular focus. Cinema verité, too, is tedious for us, for it has no plot, no definition. It just goes on. Somehow, though, human life is like that. It just goes on, and without each of us to give it focus and meaning, it is boring, tedious, unending, and happening. It has been doing so for millions of years.

It is our human capacity for symbolic meaning-making that focuses and organizes our experience into what we call our reality. Each human being has a mind that searches for relationship, for betweenness, for connections, for meaning, for patterns, to organize the "bloomin' buzzin' confusion" (James, 1950) of the simultaneous ongoing cinema verité of our lives. Like the playwrights, each individual as person first, as theorist/therapist later, selects from all that bloomin' buzzin' confusion those themes and patterns seemingly most cogent, important and interesting to organize and explain one's experience. Like playwrights, theorists too select what is in the hypothetical unit called system by what they include. Omission defines what is not included or is outside.

Our learning set, the culmination of our previous experience and personal aesthetics, frames the way in which we approach coding events, adding to the "professional deformation" that Bruner speaks of (1973a, p. 226). This is as true of the dramatist as it is of the systems thinker or scientist. It is no less true of the developing trainee in human services and systems thinking.

Each systems thinker/theorist/therapist frames his/her hypothetical punctuation of life according to his/her inner perceptions, images-of-human, and world views, extracting essences and thematic patterns from the plethora of data lived in the run-on sentence of life. Through abstract language, these essences are heightened and contrasted by theorists, thus mapping the territory that the playwright/dramatist/therapist walks. Thus is epistemology colored and shaped by one's personal aesthetic preferences and one's epistemics (Kuhn, 1962; Bruner, 1973a, 1973b).

In theater, when the playwright, director and performers succeed, essences of relationship are heightened and contrasted, and the dynamic tension within which life is lived is organized into a comprehensible whole. Each participating or observing human being of that culture can recognize him/herself and his connection to that play, to those themes. Each viewer is able to approximate that which is happening on stage to the degree that he/she is able to enter that way of seeing and thinking, for each brings his/her own inner theater-of-the-mind to the play (as each theorist/therapist brings his/hers to the plays of life). Each observer must be able to metaphor, to carry from one place to another, the experience which is happening between actors upon the stage and the experiences inside him/herself and to make meaning of them. When that occurs, we know the person has "entered the play." He/she can approximate and feel with the characters and can understand their relationship. Although watching from the "outside in," one then understands from the inside out. Trainees in systems thinking need to be able to do both, in order to keep in touch with each person while seeing the whole perform.

Without such abilities to approximate and feel with, cognitive "translations" are needed, which "explain" meanings and what is happening, from the outside in. One stays detached, outside, knowing the system but not the people.

DRAMA IN SYSTEMS THEORY

Drama is conflict unfolding.

The height of drama occurs when innocent intention is betrayed. The tragedy of paradox and irony occurs when one innocently makes one's own worst thing happen, especially when trying to avoid it, in the process of ordinary living, as in the Oedipus story. Resolution in drama comes when "crooked talk" becomes "straight" or congruent, and "crooked" or fixed relationships become fluid. Theories of human family systems and family therapy speak to these same issues.

Americans at the Chinese theater do not understand from the inside out the drama and significance of what is happening; we need a cognitive translation. We are told. We make up an explanation based on our previous experience. Or we tune out, and disregard the theatrics as sending messages of any importance.

As theatergoers, it is of little significance if we do not comprehend and tune out. As facilitators of other human beings, it is most important that we have ways to tune in—to know human relationships from the inside out. As facilitators, we hopefully help crooked talk become straight, in "the language of impact" (Duhl, F. J., 1969) of each person's aesthetics. It is most important that we consider others as we consider ourselves, as real actors in real life dramas.

The use of the world of drama and theater in training systems thinkers allows us to explore the epistemic lenses and personal aesthetics that color our professional theories. Systems theories, even the most scientific ones, are our professional myths, the best we have at this point in time, for how human behavior organizes itself. Each of us brings our epistemic theories into the room, covered by the label of epistemology.

Each theory of therapy, systems variety, talks to a version of resolution in the drama of "crooked" talk and "crooked" relationships between people becoming "straight," so that people can get on with the everyday cinema verité of their lives, somewhat more in charge of themselves. Theater offers us many ways to tune in. Theater offers trainers, trainees and clients many ways of seeing that shift their "assumptive world view" (Parkes, 1971).

The trainee who can approximate many roles, metaphoring connection, enters the lives of people as the empathic audience enters a play, from the inside out, discovering the systems of systems, of relationships, and building constructs which go "far beyond the information given" (Bruner, 1973a).

As each individual within a family has its own story, its own sense of drama, and its own sense of how the family works, so does each individual trainee carry into the training programs images of family systems and family stories.

We must be aware how the *theater-in-our-mind* frames the dramatic stories and organizes the data of our own lives as well as those of the people who seek our help.

For, as we each make coherence of life, family dramas and systems, we later carry into the room with our therapist person our individual aesthetic and epistemic person.

We each have a frame, a way, which we have metaphored into being, formed from the myriad interactions of self in the world. We are each born with capacities, a context, and a *tabula rasa* of meaning, of understanding. We configure our understandings as we experience the interaction of self in our contexts in the world. We learn-to-learn and build our epistemic theories of experience from all that we interact with and touch externally and internally. We are each authors, dramatists, and playwrights of our own version of life. Yet most of us are not aware of the organizing principles of our personal epistemic theories, or of our versions of drama, and how they shape our epistemology.

As the aforementioned Hillcrest Series (see footnote, p. 215) so blatantly yet subtly illustrates, *the family data are not the family data, but how the therapist sees, evokes, and organizes the family data.* We cannot know how our epistemic version of family system distorts our lenses such that we recognize and look for in other families our personal version of life or its opposite. And, we cannot transcend that which is unknown to us. We cannot look at that which we cannot see. We cannot know how our epistemic theories of experience contribute to our "professional deformation" (Bruner, 1973a), unless we are given the opportunity to bring them under the spotlight for scrutiny. Nor can we know how our avoidance of looking at our own families and contexts keeps us out of touch with the very real human actors in the dramas unfolding before our very eyes in our offices, agencies, classrooms, institutions.

Sculpture and spatialization allow for this looking, for the beginnings of this transcendence in training and therapy. The medium is a many-splendored mechanism by which personal epistemic versions of family and other systems can be put outside the self to be explored, examined, questioned, later compared and grouped. That which is covertly intrapsychic (in the mind) becomes overtly transactional (across, in and among members). The spatial metaphor of sculpture gives form and shape to the dynamic interaction, the theatrical essences, of messages meant, sent and received by component members. Drama and system become one and the same.

Sculpture creates an "N-of-2 plus" experience for many people—a second look at the first opinion.

FAMILY-AS-THEATER: EVOCATIVE SCULPTURE

While Kantor's first sculpture was a quick "outside in" version, he then went on to develop an elaborate form of "evocative" sculpture in depth, from the "inside out," as a fuller theatrical form in which trainees metaphored their image of their own families, spatially, as in a pantomimed play, without words. Other trainers at BFI began to try on, try out, and experiment with the new medium of spatialization, and also joined Kantor in exploring this extension of psychodrama in the metaphor of *family-as-theater*.

When Kantor began to develop this form of sculpture,* he was interested in how normal, ordinary families "worked," in keeping with his *in vivo* research with normal and schizophrenic families, and the generic questions he and the BFI faculty were pursuing about families. He was also interested in how each family member and the family as a whole used space as territory, how the family defined that territory at the interfaces within the family, and with outsiders as well. Additionally, Kantor was interested in the ethos, the feeling and the aesthetics of both contextual and interpersonal space. He thought that the enactment in spatial metaphor would serve well as a way of exploring those concerns.†

In our training sessions, the same questions that concerned Kantor were raised for us as trainees, as generic questions with unknown answers. In that sense, we were all on a search together, in exploring how families worked and how families used, defended, conceptualized, and gave meaning to space. Obviously, as members of families, we all had information in some form and degree. We thus were on a search to find personal answers as well as broader conceptual generalizations inclusive of all our individual answers. We were

---

*For the original description of this form of sculpture, see Duhl, F. J., Kantor, and Duhl, B. S., 1973.

†See Kantor and Lehr's *Inside the Family* (1975) for a full explication of Kantor's theory of family spaces and organization.

all searching for what I later termed metaphors of organization and operation, with sculpture as a major tool in that search.

With sculpture, we began exploring space and assigning meanings to family members. We selected spatial distances to represent emotional and hierarchical distances and relationship.

The guidelines for this newly developing form of theater-in-training, which evolved from our explorations, began to include those for defining the context and its inhabitants. We developed procedures for setting the stage, for selecting dramatic personae, as well as those outlining tasks for monitor, sculptor, players, and audience. We created the family-as-theater, discovering how aspects of mind work, and a new vocabulary with which to question, search, uncover, explore, and even facilitate change in family and other human systems.

Aesthetics and Physical Metaphor

It is interesting to note that we use words regularly to represent the aesthetic sense and feeling of physical space. We speak of "dark and depressing" rooms, "cheerful and warm kitchens," "cozy corners." Novelists and playwrights rely on such phraseology to present their image, their meanings. Every play begins with such instructions:

> The room is fairly large, homely looking and cheerful in the morning sunlight, furnished with scrupulous medium-priced tastelessness of the period . . . (Cerf and Cartmell, 1941*).

In our verbal vocabulary, we already use many phrases representing physical and spatial relationship: "I felt very close to him"; "he's a drag, a weight around my neck"; "she kept herself at arm's length"; "he turned his back on me", and so forth. Everyone speaks such metaphor in everyday language to capture one's image of reality.

With sculpture we began to "speak" a different kind of metaphor to bring the same reality to our cognizance: the vocabulary of the theater. In so doing, we discovered the other side of ourselves that had not been valued in this culture for its ability to contribute to knowledge, understanding, and exploration of conceptual material.

As I now begin to describe the process of sculpture with words, we should not forget that sculpture originated as the *solution to problems of verbal*

---

*Beginning stage-set descriptions for Eugene O'Neill's *Ah, Wilderness!*

communication. Sculpture was Kantor's solution to the problem of *talking about* simultaneous family *interactions.*

Let us now investigate this spatial process and its generic underpinnings. Let us discover how presenting human events, images, interactions, systems in an enacted theater form facilitates integration and multicentricity in trainees. We shall begin by exploring this earliest form of sculpture developed in depth by Kantor and the BFI faculty, for from this seedling which took root germinated many other versions, which we shall examine in a moment.

EVOCATIVE SCULPTURE

Context and Process

Consider the training room large enough, with movable chairs and space to walk around. There needs to be room for the enactment, the metaphoric space of one's scene to be laid out as a stage set is laid out. There needs to be room for the players in that set and there needs to be room for the audience to observe.

In the place of the playwright, Kantor had and has the creator, the *sculptor*, who was/is aided in his task of evoking and externalizing his inner imagery and memory by the sensitive guidance of a *monitor*, in the place of the director of a play. Instead of working in clay or stone, the sculptor was and is seen as creating his inner image spontaneously, directly, with real people. The players in sculpture are like actors in improvisational theater. And in this theater-in-the-round, the audience plays an observer/commentator role.

Setting the Stage

In this most complex and comprehensive version, the fullness of such a process recreates externally one person's *core images* of specific and generic family experiences or processes in their contextual space.

The externally constructed stage set image involves the evocation and mention of remembered tones, textures, ambience, and atmosphere of the actual physical space, as well as of the experiential and aesthetic meaning given those different physical locations in one's home. Such symbolic metaphoring is not meant to capture the concrete memory of exact details or to attest to accuracy of memory recall. Sculpture is not to be realistic, but as memories are dream images, this type of sculpture is meant to evoke and to then externalize felt experience in symbolic form: the meanings and experience of living in a particular context with particular people called one's family.

The Monitor's Role

The monitor is a guide, one who stimulates data with his/her questions and who sets up the search for definition. It is the monitor's job to facilitate the sculptor in clarifying his/her* images, to bring them from the fuzzy edges of awareness to external space to be tried out. The monitor must also protect the sculptor in this process and keep the sense of dignity and respect around the aspect of disclosure of self-in-family-system taking place. The sculptor has only one job at this point: to reexperience, evoke and re-present his sense of the contextual and interpersonal spaces of his family.

The monitor asks the sculptor to think of a time in his life when he was younger and still living with his family of origin. The monitor then asks the sculptor how old he is and where he is living at that time. She may also ask what year it is. These three questions already organize and locate the sculptor in the contexts of his life-cycle, family space, geography, and in relation to world events occurring at that time.

The monitor then asks the sculptor to set the stage for this particular scene and cast of characters. She asks the sculptor to pace out a space, metaphorically representing the living context, and to describe the *sense* of size and shape of it as he goes. She walks with him, pacing him, asking the sculptor questions about the actual physical type of space in which the family lived and the emotional sense of the space in which his *image* of family lives. Literalness begins to give way to metaphor. The "stage set" that begins to take form is the external representation of internally felt and remembered moods.

As they walk, the monitor asks about the sense of the boundary around that total space and, metaphorically, of what it is made. Questions as to whether there is easy access to and from the outside world through the "boundary" raise other questions about metaphors for its texture and type. The sculptor may describe walls of ribbons, heavy curtains, one-way windows looking out, high steel panels, and so forth. How family members enter and leave this space is explored, not only through which boundaries and when, but with whom in charge of entries and exits in the family space.

The monitor asks about the feel of different areas of the house, and the quality of such spaces, as well as who "owns" each space. Some spaces in families belong to everyone. Some supposedly belong to all yet are controlled by

---

*From this point on, in this context, for ease of reading I am imaging the monitor as female and the sculptor as male, and so will use the appropriate pronoun for each.

one member—as in "the living room was mother's." The weaving of physical and interpersonal space begins to occur through metaphor.

The aesthetics of brightness (light, dark), intensity (color), temperature (hot, cold), atmosphere (dense, clear, dry, wet, hot, cold), texture (rough, smooth, prickly, soft), form and shape, which represent the *feel* of one's sense of context, are asked about, and answered by the sculptor, often through metaphor: "We walked on eggshells; it felt gloomy like a dungeon in the cellar."

Though these might sound like strange questions to ask about one's early (or current) environments, this is metaphoring we all can do, because we have all experienced our own contexts in all of these ways.

As the sculptor is answering these questions, his eyes become glassy, as he begins to turn inward, reentering the original environment internally. *He is entering a type of trance state*, as the myriad inner images cross the screen of his mind. The search is on for the appropriate aesthetic equivalents of the original with which to "paint and light the set" here. When sculpture was first developed, in that huge barn of a room at Boston State Hospital (described in the "first night" exercises of Chapters I and IX), Kantor and others actually adjusted lighting to help create the desired mood and tone, as the sculptor began this intense reentry into his original environment.

The early literal answers mark the beginning of the sculptor's inward trip as he remembers and *has to notice now what he previously took for granted as "home."* He has to make focal that which was subsidiary (Polanyi, 1958). As he continues inward, he is able to become more and more symbolic and metaphorical, in touch with the feeling, ambience, tone, texture, and qualities of the space and the experience of living in that space.

Such aesthetic and emotional awareness and descriptions are usually reserved for poets and playwrights. The medium and form of the spatial metaphor of evocative sculpture allow each of us to reach the poet inside ourselves.

As in our childhood make-believe, with minimal or no props and much imagination, each person in the room begins to have a sense of the feel, the ambience of this metaphorical physical and interpersonal space of the sculptor's.

Casting the Characters

The trainee involved in creating such a situation is then asked to populate it, calling on other trainees to play the parts of the people who had lived the original version. The sculptor scans the group for an actor to fill the role of one of the well-known people in his life. As the sculptor searches the faces, a person is chosen for each part.

We became aware very early that often a selected individual reminds the sculptor of the original character in some paraverbal modality, such as voice tone, looks, or expressions. This associative connection is most often out of the direct awareness of the sculptor at the time he is choosing someone to play a member of his original family.

The monitor tells the sculptor to give each character a thumbnail description of him/herself, using the present tense, "you are," as in "As my mother, you are a small woman, though very energetic." Such instructions put people into a here-and-now setting, yet put the sculptor deeper inside his trance-like imagery. Each character is told of characteristics that stand out as predominant to the sculptor, as he begins to think/see in condensed images. The monitor then asks the sculptor to position the first character in relation to himself, using space to represent emotional distance, with questions such as: "Do you feel your father as very close to you? Distant? What amount of space represents that distance?"

As in Kantor's original quick presentation, vertical space is often used to represent power, or aloofness to which authority is attached, in which the "father" stands on a chair or platform when he is "in the home," or in relation to the sculptor only.

Additionally, information is requested by the monitor concerning specific gestures and movements, representing how each particular family member is remembered and was experienced by the sculptor at the general time being described. The sculptor seems to stare inside. He has to become more specific and differentiated at this point. He must search for and tease out from the many blurred and fused images the essence of how he perceives this person. He extracts essences, in stylized symbolic form: "My mother's typical gesture for me would be one of smiling, her head to one side, reaching out to me. I would take her hand and move in next to her. We were fairly close at that time."

Discovering the System-as-Context

As each person is added to the scene, the sculptor is aided by the monitor in paying particular attention now to the interrelatedness of people. In this form of *self-as-center sculpture*, while the sculptor remembers how each person appeared to him, in relation to himself, he is challenged to be more focally in touch with how each family member also related, gestured, and moved from, to, and with each other person in the family. Thus, the sculptor/trainee must think systemically: how the whole functions and is dynamically interacting, all the while focusing on his private and personal view of the whole family. He may not talk *about* them. He must recreate them, in active interrelationships.

Questions such as "While mother is frowning at you and begins to turn her back on you, where is she in relation to father? And where is father in relation to you? If mother is 'out of the picture,' how do people realign themselves?" force the system-thinking issue. One cannot think unidimensionally or linearly anymore. One must create system with dynamic interaction of the component parts. The monitor can ask about family roles at the same time in spatial terms, such as: "To whom does each go to talk about personal issues? To get permission to do things? Who is 'in'; who is 'out'? Who controls the center space of the family? Any and all family processes can be explored in this manner, as the patterns of the family are revealed through the sculptor's eyes.

The Roles of Players

As this form of sculpture developed, so did guidelines for the players, devised to keep the process from becoming too literal, or from being taken over by any or all of the players. For instance, the players are instructed to ask questions in the first person to get ideas of behaviors and relationships with each other family member: "Am I . . . angry with father as well as mother? Do I comfort you or seek you out in any way? If I am 'outside' the rest of the family, how do I get 'in'?"

Players are asked to be pliable to the sculptor's positioning and instructions, and to check out one's own sense of gestures and connectedness with the sculptor's sense of that family member's way of being. Each player is asked to *be* the family member, to enter into his/her shoes and to enact the part as the sculptor has described it. Thus, they enter and try on total metaphors of approximation: "If I were his mother, how would I be? What goes with being his mother?"

Then, the players are instructed by the monitor to be aware, as they stay in role, of the range of feelings and thoughts that get stirred up in relation to the ongoing action, postures, sense of self in the midst of these others, in the context of this physical space. Such impressions, thoughts, feelings, are to be saved for feedback time when the entire process is debriefed.

At various times, players may be asked to act differently, in different variations of evocative sculpture, when seeking options to a pattern or options to the role as conceived by the sculptor. Players at times are also asked to be ready to enact their own options for those roles, still using the data the sculptor has given.

The monitor asks the players if they feel themselves as whole persons in their roles, and if things make sense to them. They are asked to keep aware if any such puzzles as they might have are "solved" during the process and during debriefing. These queries, their answers or lack thereof, are to be raised later as part of the feedback process. Trainees, as players, are stretched to feel and think into the roles they play, using life experiences.

Big gaps in one's sense of oneself as a player often point out "grey areas" or lack of information on the part of the sculptor about that family member and his/her role or interconnectedness with other family members. One by one the cast of characters is added, each in relation to the others, with appropriate gestures. As each character is chosen and joins the group, the sculptor is adding information and fleshing out the story and shape of that particular time in his life.

Invariably we became aware that each sculptor, without conscious awareness, chooses a scene or time containing some "unfinished business," some deprivation of information still awaiting fulfillment, some painful or unresolved puzzle awaiting closure.

Silence! and Action!

At this point, as the trainee/sculptor has presented the fullness of his/her images of context and interpersonal space, and the players have a sense of who they are, the ensemble, including the sculptor, is asked by the monitor to use no more words. The "family" is then asked to put the actions of this story into motion, so that a sense of the family's interactions can emerge: the patterns created by rhythms, sequences, pulls and tugs of movements and ritualized behaviors. The symbolic essences of these interactions surface, for each player and for each person watching, as each assigns meanings to them.

The dramatic conflict of the family emerges as the action begins and continues. Speeding up and slowing down the sequences illuminate the stresses and strains in the family, the missed connections and missed moments of an ordinary family "dance." How people use time and energy in that family space emerges as of critical importance, as contributing to issues of connection, disconnection and the emotional distance regulation of members.

The Role of the Audience

In the early days, the audience, those trainees watching, would try to push for closure, for a happy ending or therapeutic breakthrough, which was not the purpose of this exploration, as it may be in psychodrama. Out of such learning-as-we-went, a framework also developed for the audience, meant to increase their activity while observing. These guidelines also serve to protect the dignity of the sculptor and the respect for the process.

Audience members were and are asked by the monitor to tune in and *pay attention* to: "What gets stirred up in me as I watch this sculpture? What does this remind me of? Who are these people in my life?"

Observers are asked to hold the associative answers for the debriefing period. In this, audience members are asked to consider themselves as private people first, rather than as professionals. In this self-observation process we are asking trainees to shed light on the subsidiary processes of mind which are basically analogic in nature. Observers are also asked to watch what the sculptor and other individual members each bring to the scene that contributes to getting that person into some type of "knot."

This sculpture is also expected to be a training process. Observers are asked if the monitor is clear in her choice points, in guiding the process. Does each observer understand the monitor's rationale for her moves and statements and way of monitoring? The monitor in sculpture is analogic to the therapist guiding a therapy session.

The audience then has the task of observing the sculptor and his sculpture, the monitor-as-guide, as well as the interaction of monitor, sculptor, and players. A range of questions is thus available for audience members to consider, about the data the sculptor presents, the process itself, and the manner in which the process is handled.

Questions given to the audience members ahead of time alert them to these overlapping dimensions:

1) What got cut off or truncated in the sculpture that you think should have been expanded? What else would you do? What would you do differently?
2) Do you have new thoughts about how this family operates as a system?
3) Can you risk telling the monitor what made you restless and/or uncomfortable?
4) What feedback will you give to the sculptor? The monitor? Players? What feedback will you not give to each of them? Why?
5) What does this tell you about your own knots?

In addition, the audience members are reminded that they have a special vantage point, from which they can see what others perhaps cannot see, and thus they may have a sense of the total ensemble from the "outside." As such, audience members are often asked for metaphors which would grasp their images of the essences of the "family" in this sculpture. Sometimes they are asked for a metaphor capturing the total *process* of the sculpture inclusive of the monitor's direction of the event. Hence, the spatial metaphor now becomes a stimulus for a verbal metaphor capturing the whole system. Thus, each participant has to recreate and remetaphor the portrayal of a family and translate it into another image of the whole.

After the feedback and discussion have been concluded, the monitor guides the players, sculptor, and audience in "de-rolling," in returning to each one's own skin, here, now.

This then concludes a bare-bones outline of the process of evocative sculpture. Let us continue now with some comments about what happens inside that framework.

DISCUSSION OF EVOCATIVE SCULPTURE

All the elements of multipersonal systems can be experienced and observed in essential raw or stripped-down structure, dynamics, and transactional patterns, while simultaneously all the elements of each person as a functionally autonomous entity can be experienced and observed.

When the sculptor chooses an event or time to portray, it is usually representative of a transitional point, before or after some change in the family, either by loss of a member, a move, or change/crisis of another nature. The monitor, in such situations, may move the sculptor either backwards or forwards in time, asking for an example of the structural arrangement of members of their stylized processes with each other before or after this event, still using space as the regulator of relationship. The drama in the family is inherent in the placement and movement of people in relationship during an important crisis. As the sculpture is put into motion, it takes on a life of its own.

Sculpture is an activator of the timeless mind. The recreation of the context and mood of one's earlier living quarters re-evokes behaviors long ago learned in that context, as fitting both physical and interpersonal space. Movements long remembered in the muscles, but forgotten in the conscious mind, get set into motion, as the context and conditions evoke restraints on action and relating for the sculptor. Small movement cues, indicating stances or attitudes of relationship contrary to what the sculptor originally indicated in his verbal description, are taken note of as they emerge and are discussed in debriefing.

The actual experience of enacting such a scene is a powerful emotional event for the sculptor, who reexperiences the same internal feelings and dynamics as in the original context. He knows this play. He's been there before—except now the sculptor can be an observer as well as an actor. Sometimes we ask another person to actually stand in for the sculptor so he may watch "himself" with his family.

The ethos of the family culture—the feel of it—emerges from the inside.

Individual meanings and behaviors now have a context in which to be understood as fitting and coherent.

We can look at the parts. We can look at the whole. We can look at change points. We can, if we choose, experiment and experience how any intervention might affect any part, any member, and/or the whole group.

When one does such enactments with trainees, or with families, all people in the room are privy to the same information at the same time. All have tasks in the process. And there is the constant generation of material from inside each person involved. The feedback from all members is essential in this process.

In the clinical arena, this form of sculpture can best be and is used in couple's groups, in multiple family therapy, and in family therapy. In the latter, asking teenage children to take the roles of their grandparents—their parents' parents—allows them to see parents as former children.

The Importance of Debriefing and Feedback

As Kantor and others at BFI developed this form of sculpture, the debriefing of participants became as important and impactful as the enactment itself. As stated earlier, the first question was not "What did you learn?" but "What did it feel like for you to be in that position, that role?"

In such feedback, even from brief enactments, comes the individual experiential components of system transactions, and the joining of psyche and system. That which is inside each person or intrapsychic becomes joined with actions in transactions. The intent/action/reception/intent/action interchanges among members become vividly clear. The personal aesthetics and the sense of order of each family member emerge as the "view from the other side" of those relationships originally set up by the sculptor. The view from inside others is often the information which has been missing for the sculptor, especially as it relates to how the sculptor was perceived and experienced by those other members.

In addition, players give feedback to other players as family members, regarding their impacts on each other. In this self-as-center, hub-of-the-wheel sculpture, the sculptor, through the debriefing process, becomes but one of several centers.

We are all actors in someone else's version of the play.

Each player, including the sculptor, experiences self as actor and receiver. The differences between intents/actions/impacts begin to be explored. Each describes the many views from the inside.

The sculptor who had set up the scene and prescribed the original action often tries to "correct" feedback which is discrepant with his own world view and memory. He so sees the players as the "real" people that he expects them to report on their insides either 1) as he has heard in the past; or 2) as he has imagined each to feel; or both. In any case, he wants to keep feedback familiar. When players take on the gestures, positions and movements previously requested by the sculptor as those capturing the essence of each original family member, the sculptor hypnotically "sees" each player "as if" he/she is the original cast character. The gestures which "stand for" the whole of the original versions are seen as the whole person here. Thus the bit projects the hologram, hypnotically.

The moments of feedback are crucial moments for the sculptor—and the time at which the trance "breaks," and something new is possible. The sculptor is then asked by the monitor to just "hear it," to "let it come in." The monitor suggests that that which is discrepant can also offer information as yet unknown to the sculptor, perhaps available to be checked out with the "real" cast of characters.

Feedback from each player, then, from inside the experience which the sculptor himself set up, is heard with the potential for possibility, for accuracy. The players "are" the real members, yet they are not the real members. Feedback comes from each as part of the results of the sculptor's own controlled experiment. The sculptor cannot not hear what is said, for it is as if his own voice speaks to him from outside. For the first time, the sculptor has a gap now between his image and his sense of possibility. He is decentrating (Piaget, 1977b), as he begins to hear and to consider information he has never heard before.

Since one sculptor's players are often another sculptor's audience, trainees learn to play all parts, and in the roles of players they become more and more comfortable and "authentic" in each one, searching self for an accurate handle to "How do I feel in this position, in this role?" Such feedback of players cannot fail to be contextually related to the enacted experience, and as such it is "kept honest." Players get into this experience. They do not want to do a poor job of being someone's brother or mother. And, it is hard to have a personal and particular ax to grind with someone in the midst of a role enactment of a member of another's family.

The Importance of Simple, Radical Questions to Players

Questions asked of the players in debriefing, such as "What was it like for you to be in that role, that position? What was your experience?" are radical questions. The very posing of such questions sets the framework for acceptance of all the answers as valid, and all as incomplete. Incomplete also includes the views of the observers, who saw all the actions, yet knew not of the meanings for individuals. The only valid view as full view would be one that includes all information, a generic holistic systems view. Such a complete view includes intrapsychic phenomena as part of observed transactional events: the personal and interpersonal dramas of life, in the apersonal world of human systems.

A sculpture of this sort rarely ends with the sculptor seeing his world in quite the same way. The cognitive dissonance or discrepancy in the feedback process between what is known and what is new information sets up a search, a question, reaching for a new answer inclusive of the sculptor's and each player's experience. "Real" information, often affirming comments made by a player, later results in mini to major paradigm shifts, wherein the sculptor/trainee no longer sees himself-as-center of system, but as self-in-system, a self as member of system.

Such discrepant (that is, non-matching) images of the sculptor's "reality," constituting a "grey area," are left to the sculptor to ponder, search, explore. We know he will. He is free and invited to bring new or illuminating information from the external world about family members back to the training group.

The Importance and Pitfalls of Feedback from the Audience

The audience is asked for feedback. As the non-enacting observers of the entire sequence, the audience early tended to be critical and judgmental, and to speak in what I term "the first person accusative" to the sculptor, relaying how he *could* have made life easier, different, more acceptable to himself, *if only* he had had the sense to. . . .

We then instituted the rule that stated that all audience feedback had to have an equivalent of the player's feedback, starting with a statement of what had gotten associatively stirred up for each observer during the enactment, as plays and movies also touch one's center. Then, at that point, the observer was free to continue with observations, not criticisms. This rule constituted the first major inroad towards maintaining the safety for trainees to take the risk of exploring family contexts, space, unfinished business, and the right to have had one's own experience in life, with one's own point of view.

For audience members, such a role drew them in while at the same time making "fair witnesses" of them (Lilly, 1972). It gave them permission to be human, not perfect. It gave them a way of staying, as well as greater freedom to search for a metaphor fitting the whole. With such a rule, each audience member is at liberty to overview the whole as well as to connect with each player and sculptor, with what I call "short-term empathy." Each of these abilities is a key to becoming generalist systems thinkers and therapists.

As we began creating more sculptures, we became more acutely aware of and discussed the pitfalls of this type of sculpture in a training setting. All related to safety and to inhibiting the process of exploring the sculptor's perception. They included: the move towards catharsis, as in psychodrama, promoted by anyone, demanding it of the sculptor as a way of taking care of oneself; fairy tales, including the nonvalidation of the sculptor's perception along with the "happy ending" syndrome; voyeurism, in wanting something to happen to entertain the audience through drama, comedy, or titillation; and overliteralness, not utilizing sculpture as metaphor. This last sometimes came about by the sculptor defining a space in "real" terms, with "real" chairs and so on, rather than schematically, poetically, or analogically. Or, at times the sculptor would take the sculpture as a real event recreated rather than as a dream image, representative of or an exception to a more general pattern in the family. Such pitfalls are addressed as they occur.

The multidimensionality and simultaneity of experience represented by the feedback from this active spatial metaphor led Kantor to use the word "multicentric"—to represent the simultaneously different existing "centered" views of the same event. For in such events, each person is data for the other, subject for the self and observer of others, and object of other people's observations and feelings.

Impact of Sculpture on Trainees

The introduction of this form of sculpture opened a veritable Pandora's box of riches, still untamed. It opened up the world of the right brain, of pantomime, of imagery, of action, of raising questions and answers in new and fluid forms, about aesthetics, bonding, interaction, systems, interventions, hierarchy, and lots more. Family-as-theater became the way of exploring and expressing family-as-system and mind-as-hologram.

Feedback from trainees concerning this and similar evocative forms of sculpture has never been pallid or tepid, including comments made months later. For example, one trainee in 1978 reported several weeks later that the feedback of feelings had been "most important" to him: "It gave me feelings about people who never let me know what feelings were. The feedback filled gaps for me." He further stated that knowing that those emotions were possible in "cool" people allowed him to see his parents differently: "I have much less anger and understand those people much better. They didn't have control of the scene as I thought they had." This trainee had new information about families—his and others—to carry with him as therapist. He can believe feelings in parents are possible.

This particular trainee could also see the impact of his parents' deaths in his tendency or pattern of exploration/avoidance. "I'm still afraid people around me will die, or be taken away. It connects for me." The external pattern was analogic to the internal fears and vulnerabilities. He was aware that the same pattern of exploration/avoidance went with him in his style as therapist.

In each of these statements, the trainee's sense of self expands to include new information which not only updates information locked in at a much earlier age and stage of development, but which is also accepting of and inclusive of the previously held information. When that happens, one's mind takes a leap. One switches paradigms. One is thinking, in this arena, at the next level of logical type (Bateson, 1972). When people's world view or sense of "reality" changes, their behaviors and feelings change, from the inside out.

The modality of sculpture soon became the source of discovery of myriad ways of using kinesic-spatial metaphoring to explore meanings, expectations, actions, systems. Through evocative sculpture and other forms, we found ways of giving expression:

1) to the "betweenness" of human relating;
2) to the sense and feel of family and other human groupings;
3) to the internal world of idiosyncratic meanings with which we live our lives and fill abstract language;
4) to relationships over time; and
5) to the personal aesthetics of relationship, those senses or personal rules of form, correctness, order and ambience by which we measure and monitor our total sense of *fit* of self with others and self in the world.

We gave form and motion to abstract concepts. Closeness/distance, inclusion/exclusion, omnipotence/helplessness, fusion/disconnection and many other ethereal constructs became multidimensional continua, filled with idiosyncratic behavioral and contextual definitions. We began to explore what I term individual and consensual rules of access and rules of order, in powerful, graphically dynamic ways. We began to find out how families work without having to ignore any aspect of human experience. We grew towards multicentricity, knowing systems, knowing relationship, from many insides, inclusive of the views from inside those who were "outside."

The validation of the process of sculpture, in capturing the internal essences that accompany external behaviors and gestures sculpted, occurred one evening in 1974, when a trainee invited his mother, stepfather (since age eight), his sister and brother-in-law, and his wife to watch him create his sculpture. He chose a period of time when he was age 10 and his family had moved from one house to another in another town, where he felt quite isolated. He had felt his mother to be pleased with the move. And he had experienced quite a few "grey areas" about his stepfather, not knowing much about him.

As the feedback concluded, concerning "What was it like for you to be in that role?", the young woman who had played mother in the sculpture reported how ambivalent and torn she had felt between moving where her husband's new job was and wanting very much to stay where they had been. The mother of the trainee turned to this young woman and exclaimed: "How could you know that that's exactly how I felt then! He [her son] gave you no information like that and he wouldn't have had it to give!" The stepfather then concurred with his player counterpart that he had not been very available as a father, and filled in information missing for his 33-year-old stepson.

IMPORTANCE OF SCULPTURE FOR THE AUTHOR

As a trainee and a trainer, I have been fascinated with the modality, the process and the potential of sculpture/spatializing. I have found myself freed up to legitimately experiment with and try out and try on roles and positions in relationship far different and discrepant from any I have ever lived, to discover their meanings in particular contexts. I have found opportunity to "see" how others "felt," and to "feel" how others "saw." I have tried on short-term empathy, by approximating others' lives and then returning to my shoes, carrying my new cognizance with me. As a trainee, with sculpture I could be "audience" to an entire scenario and draw my own impressions. Then I could listen to how/if each player's presentation of the view and experience, when debriefing each role, filled out and matched what I had observed, intuited and concluded. I could be one of those players, or creator of the entire drama, the sculptor, wherein I instructed others in their expressions, gestures, movements, to match those active and alive in my theater-of-the-mind.

When one is sculptor, startling new information challenges the mind's eye image as soon as action begins, as the sculptor faces his/her image role as system member, and as he/she then listens and receives comments from inside others.

I was exhilarated by this new modality, which seemed to unite both sides of my brain. I could "see" dynamic interaction. I could "see" system, in many shapes and forms. I felt compartments of mind flow one into the other as an entire new world of internal imagery opened up. The back-of-the-mind daydream type chatter began organizing itself into vignettes concerning people, ideas, relationships. I began to look inside to "see" what was occurring "outside." In the beginning, the types of images startled me, as irrelevant, irreverent or absurd. Then I began to pay attention, and with that, I discovered an incredible resource for myself as person, therapist, trainer. The inner screen pulled together as metaphor what I was seeing, hearing, experiencing, in ways that words could never do for me. Words still have to be translated by the perceiver/receiver into relationship images.

The medium of spatialization had stirred and restimulated in me an entirely different way of knowing. And it offered me a way to access and to express the verbally inexpressible, metaphoring process (see Chapter VII) in three-dimensional space simultaneously, with energy/motion, over time in spatial metaphor. It allowed me to express differences-in-relationships, in dynamically interacting ways.

I got hooked then. I still am.

GENERALIZATIONS

The process of sculpting itself exemplifies for me how the mind works, while the medium provides us with ways to represent, comprehend, compare, and group many individual versions of relationship and system.

Piaget and others postulate that all thought begins with sensorimotor action (Piaget, 1952). Sculpture is thought/action. With sculpting, there is always new information about self, about others, about families, about systems, about contexts, about how we think and make sense of the world, and most of all, about the many simultaneous views of any situation. And one can always ask new and different questions of the same raw data.

The awareness of the aesthetic rules that each person tries to make manifest became clear to me through spatializations of many types, as people expressed personal preferences with a well-defined certainty.

It is in our individual versions of relationship where subtle nuances show up as those differences which make so much difference. In couples, in families, in nations, individual versions of bonding, of relationship are what the fuss is all about: who is what for whom and in what ways, against images of what should, could, or needs to be, and the tradition of what was. Sculpture, as we developed the idiom, allows for the presentation of such multiple organic images.

When information internal to every member of a system is available and information about the whole is also available, developing a map from the inside out, about part/whole relationships called human and family systems, becomes almost a given, in a challenging, exciting and self-expanding way.

All concepts and theories are grounded in the experience of each original theorist. Sculpting provides the walk of experience through each territory, in ways that trainees are challenged to conceptualize, to create theory anew and to create new theory.

Intent/action/impact transactions debriefed from all directions and parties in a common experience allow for the holography of systems to emerge. As one begins to understand the contribution of each member to the ongoing-ness of total transactions, one begins to link differences of ability to cope with similar events and issues within different human systems to questions concerning individual uniquenesses, resources, context, and experiences. One learns that there are optional reactions to almost any event, and therefore choices of actions which could influence patterns in any family or other unit we choose to call system. One learns conversely that certain types of situations, contexts or events seem to evoke certain types and patterns of emotional and behavioral responses within an expectable cultural range.

LEARNING-TO-LEARN AND ANALOGIC PATTERNS

In that early form of evocative sculpture, we did not move to create interventions, to interrupt patterns. That came later. We used it then to begin to understand system, our own and others'. And we began to understand much more that influenced us as we continued. The analogic connections between sculpted real-life scenes and one's type of approach to certain contexts became examples of the learning-to-learn of our timeless minds. Certain events and contexts are lessons in coping and establishing patterns of information processing.

For example, the woman trainee who had been ill for a year as a child, with a complication of measles that led her to be deaf and almost blind for most of that time, sculpted that period in her life. She included her tendency as a child to cross the major street outside her home totally unaware of danger, as her deafness and near blindness gave her no information. She had never had a mishap and could not understand then why her mother got so upset.

She realized with a sudden shock that she approached many situations as an adult that others would think of as dangerous, completely unaware of that potential. She said she "had not learned to look into situations, to see danger" and possible consequences. She had not felt fear as a child, crossing the street. She did not have the sensorimotor pattern for processing as "dangerous" information which aroused no sense or prior experience of apprehension in her. It seemed she had no map for other types of socially "dangerous" situations.

Another trainee's family of origin sculpture revealed how she could control her family members and their activities by the way in which she moved slowly, by her pacing and timing. She still tended to do that with people who moved and responded faster than she did, with whom she felt pushed and uncomfortable. We discovered direct and analogic types of pattern "replication" in such ways (Bloch and Rosenthal, 1964).

We became alerted to the power of ghosts in the family through a trainee's sculpture which included a player in the role of her dead twin brother, lying at the feet of her mother, who prevented the sculptor from ever getting close to mother. The ghost represented the mother's grief, constantly aroused whenever the alive twin wanted cuddling and connection.

We had started out to explore space, and its meaning to family members. We discovered "spaces" we had never dreamed were there, for we had begun to tap into what I term the *"themes of interface"* through the medium of sculpture: the realm of learning styles, vulnerabilities and defenses, core images and boundaries, key aspects of each of our lives. And we had begun to tap into the connection between each trainee's epistemics, and experiences in his/her family of origin and growing up, and his/her epistemology, his/her world view as therapist.

Sculpture and spatialization then began to form a bridge between epistemics and epistemology.

SCULPTURE AS COGNITIVE ORGANIZER

Thus, at BFI, it was not just sculpture as a theatrical form in training that was new. Sculpture provided the bridge by which trainees could make a paradigm shift, to see individuals systemically as interacting members in varying contexts, some of which they carry in their timeless minds. Sculpture became a cognitive organizer of systems thinking, as well as the language for externalizing one's sense and images of relationship of all kinds. And sculpture puts the tools of equivalent views into the hands of each user, be it trainee, therapist, family member, agency worker, teacher. Each becomes a researcher, an authority about, and an author of* his/her own images of people and events in the world. From new images, new combinatory play (Piaget and Inhelder, 1958), come new conceptualizations.

Kantor's first "Here, let me show you what I mean," in that particular context and time, became a move that was itself a new system former (Gray, 1976, 1981), for it opened the door to the right side of the brain to be developed. The inner metaphoric mind which works on hunch and image was freed up to work towards the same understanding as the linear analytical left brain mind. Feeling, sensing, hearing, seeing, imaging, acting came together with thinking, and thinking systemically. The medium became a necessary link fostering integrated knowing.

With the exploration of the idiosyncratic differences that make for in-

---

*With thanks to Mel Bucholz, hypnotist and friend, for this usage of authority/author.

dividuals and betweennesses came the appreciation of possibilities for developing processes which foster harmonious uniquenesses.

And in each sculptural process, each trainee owns the results of his/her exploration for him/herself, fitting the data organically into his/her evolving map. Each creates and "sees" relationship systems and enjoys the process. The combination is unbeatable.

SCULPTURE: THEMES AND VARIATIONS

A note for the reader: As we now begin to explore a number of different types of sculpture, it is my hope that the reader will take the liberty, risk and time to try out and take part in these forms of spatialization. Indeed, any spatialization or sculpture is much more informative, and more fun, created and experienced, than read about. And the doing allows you, the reader, your own sets of discoveries and your own inside-out knowing.

The language of sculpture and the forms developed at BFI keep growing. As words can be used to create different forms of poetry, novels, plays, stories, books, newspapers, so has the language of sculpture and spatialization been used to develop a variety of forms, all serving slightly different purposes, and highlighting different aspects of the hologram. And indeed, as with verbal language, there are always spur-of-the-moment conversations, repartee, and momentary definitions.

As we now examine other types of spatialization, let us remember that *any such procedure is a solution to the problem of talking about multiple, simultaneous interactions, or to revealing covert intrapsychic meanings and images.*

Boundary Sculpture

During the first year of teaching at Boston State Hospital's Center for Family Therapy Training and Research, in 1971, Jeremy Cobb and I were struggling with the issue of a repeating "fight" between two trainees, both easily in their fifties. The man was a reserved British pastoral counselor, in the States for a few years of training, and the woman a rather energetic and somewhat scattered children's teacher/therapist, daughter of missionaries and married to a minister.

As group leaders, we had asked them to settle their differences outside the seminar. They said they would try, and failed, if they did indeed try. We had asked if we could mediate, and they said there was nothing to mediate. The fight took the form of a kind of bickering, but we could not ascertain what the goal or purpose of it was. He found her irrelevant, with a presumption of knowing things she didn't know.

Their fuss would erupt at various lull points in the seminar, between exercises, at the beginning of the session, in a most disruptive way for the entire group. After several weeks of wishing it or they would go away, we discussed at a faculty meeting our attempts and our dilemma, and decided to see if we could do something with their disruptive dispute.

At the next meeting of this seminar, the author and Jeremy Cobb invented boundary sculpture, which has become a most useful and extraordinary tool in training, therapy, agencies, organizations and business for exploring and giving definition to the intangible and overlapping boundaries of two or more persons or systems.

That day, I asked the pastor to describe and outline, by walking around it, his sense of his personal territory. He chose a 9' x 12' rug. Again, as in the earlier form of sculpture, I asked what constituted the boundaries to this space and he said that there were no walls or boundaries, that it was an open space. When asked where he would be within his personal space, he said he would be sitting down on a chair, in one corner, the furthest from the group. I then pointed out that inside his space he had defined a smaller space that was very much his, to which he smiled and answered, "Always."

I asked how someone could come into his space. He replied that they could just come in. Since there were no walls, or doors, I asked if I could "just jump in," which I did. He responded that he would prefer that I didn't do that, that it would cause him to "feel affright" and that I should just come in.

I then went back and walked towards him at my usual pace. He said that was too fast, and asked me to stop about two feet inside the rug. I pointed out to him that he had just described another boundary. He said, "A second boundary. You're on the second boundary."

I then asked him to reverse roles with me for a moment and to show me how he liked to be approached. He moved slowly, at an even pace, halting every few feet, before continuing towards me. He said, "The newcomer has to make signals that he is approaching, and if he doesn't, I resent it." And we discovered how his holding out his arms to shake hands was also a boundarying phenomenon, keeping people from getting too close.

As we continued to explore his space and the way that people could enter or not enter, we learned that his aesthetic preferences dictated that people enter one at a time, slowly, never in groups, and never from behind. We discovered *many* boundaries inside his personal space, which became much clearer to him on his inner screen. Those boundaries related to who could come how close and when, and he had very definite range of variation. For instance, as a divorced man, his daughter was the only woman whom he would let initiate touching him or hugging him. He had had the image of himself as open, free, welcoming. In actuality, he had quite ordered and distinct ways of thinking and of moving about his space, and he really wanted others to respect his aesthetic sense of order, pacing, and privacy.

Jeremy Cobb then began to work with the teacher, attempting a similar exploration, and found it exasperatingly difficult, for she claimed the whole world was her space, and that her boundary was her skin.

Indeed, growing up in the wilds of a foreign country with her missionary parents, there had been few boundaries for her to attend to, and she first stated that she had had a very spontaneous context and way of playing with native children. We then started to make a connection with her early context and her current open boundaries. She then stated that her parents had beat her for playing with the native children. Her mother had assigned what teacher had felt to be arbitrary boundaries for her to observe, full of "shoulds." She had felt further constrained when her family moved back to the States when she was eight. She said she did not mind people coming up to her at any speed or pacing. She saw every such connection as a chance to "play." Even now, she said people in the group could get as close to her physically as her very young school students. The differences were arbitrary and artificial to her.

Jeremy tried exceedingly hard to get some sort of contextual boundary definition, and the teacher kept eluding such definition. She kept moving all over, with Jeremy close behind. She claimed no boundaries for herself, stating that any place Jeremy wanted to be was fine with her. Her answers, like her boundaries, were elusive. She said she "knew" which boundaries she was supposed to have, as those her mother told her she should have, but she didn't feel that way. She liked being close to people, kinesically. When I approached her, coming very close, and asked if that were all right, she replied that it was threatening. I asked where she wanted me to stop, to stand. She then replied that it didn't matter where a threatening person was, that that person was threatening for all time. I asked her if there were a process by which I could become less threatening, and she said that she didn't know of any, that women were more threatening to her than men.

At that point, I suggested that we put the two metaphors together, with myself enacting teacher and Jeremy enacting pastor. Pastor kept trying to avoid teacher's advances on his space or to contain teacher once she was there. Teacher kept breaking through boundaries and eluding any attempt to be contained. She was like a butterfly, flitting from place to place, all around him, and he was not able to make real contact with her or to contain her. At one point, as teacher, I got dizzy and commented that perhaps she too got dizzy in her relationships.

The real contestants recognized the patterns and the conflict immediately. As we began to talk with them about the process and their situation, we learned that since teacher's husband was a minister and they lived in a parish house, she also had no boundaries on her space, even if she might want them. Her house had to be open to all parishioners. In addition, her husband was the head of the Pastoral Counseling program, and she knew pastor outside, also. She had felt there was no reason that he should not be friendly to her.

We then discussed with the group how, without going into the content of their fights at all, we had been able to see why, at the present time, these two people could not have a conversation without conflict. Their very styles of conceptualizing themselves and their personal boundaries meant that pastor would feel "affright" at teacher's boundaryless style, and that she would feel put off and confused by his seemingly arbitrary need to regulate distances. We could see that repeated "invasions" over a short period of time would anger pastor immensely, while teacher did not recognize time and timing as important. What for him was relationship by process was for her relationship by kinesis or accommodation. Her sense of intimacy was instantaneous, where his was ordered by time and history. A group member commented that teacher seemed to be caught in the same double context with pastor as she had been caught in when very young, where she had encountered one culture that was very free and one that was quite rigid; pastor's boundaries had been described by him as open and free-flowing at first, yet had rather sharp definition upon examination. With pastor, she was encountering both cultures at one time.

The feedback from teacher and pastor was filled with relief. They saw their fighting as stemming from these differences in boundary preferences, contextually learned behaviors and personal styles. Neither of them was "wrong" or "the heavy," and neither had to try and make himself or herself understood to the other anymore, in order to feel okay.

Their conflict disappeared. She left him alone, and we felt their dispute had offered us an amazing opportunity to delve into an entirely new and related area. We had tacked directly into the storm arena with curiosity and discovered a miraculous and exciting new territory. We now had a methodology, a way of exploring wide varieties of interpersonal entanglements, disputes, differences and relationships. This new methodology more closely illuminated those personal aesthetic preferences and felt experiences we each have that are labeled "boundary phenomena" than all the talking and explaining we usually do could ever reveal. And the revelation itself showed the potentiality of also being the intervention, as in this case, for the exploration had uncovered entirely new information. Such information, as Bateson says, is "the difference which makes a difference" (1979).

Boundary Sculpture, Cotherapy and Coupling

Boundary sculptures have been part of our training program ever since, for we found they are a key to illumination of any two- or more person relationship.

Since we expect our trainees to do co-therapy as a way of understanding dyadic processes and coupling, as a way of having a mirror held up to their own processes, as a way of having a peer to explore and discuss families and therapy with, and as a way of not getting swallowed up by the first families they see, we have trainees explore their own sense of personal space and boundaries. They negotiate with each other the combining of those spaces, as well as the processes of entry and exit from those spaces. Trainees explore pacings that are comfortable, the differences of who and how many may come in when, from which direction, at what rates of speed, to which depth within the personal space. They explore what it takes to get the other out of his/her space in an acceptable fashion, as well as what type of combined space is possible for both. These are metaphoric ways of dealing with the actuality. Trainees begin to bridge and translate between types of information being processed, for all of a person's behavior is information, crossing the boundaries of awareness and meaning as well as space.

The author took this approach into therapy and found it an amazing tool which circumvents verbal masking of what is actually happening between people. Both in training and therapy, watching the enactment to confirm if the sculptor indeed maintains his/her boundaries where he/she says they are is of critical importance. There are those people who say their boundaries are two feet away from them, but actually do nothing to stop another from walking right into them. It is as if they expect the other to stop where they wish them to stop, without the sculptor making a stop signal in any way. They then hold the invader responsible for crossing a boundary! Boundary sculpture reveals such couple processes.

A slightly different version of boundary sculpture, as a way of orienting people who do not think in such terms (and how many do?) is enabled by asking people to think of an ideal space that they love, either indoors or out of doors—that they could consider their own. We ask them to let their fantasies go, that if they could have any space in the world for their very own, where and what would it be? Indeed, let me invite you to pause and consider your own ideal space and to create it in physical metaphor.

People describe and "create" physically all sorts of spaces, from ocean beaches and mountain tops to houses to space capsules. We explore the territory for markers and signals. Again, the issues of entries and exits and how people let others know about their boundaries can be explored in a rich and revealing manner.

In couples therapy, this is a particularly important modality for going beyond lip service of differentiation and respect, to the respectful differentiation of self and other, with regard for both and for negotiating the personal aesthetics of joint spaces with their overlapping boundaries—for that is the essence of coupling.

Boundaries as Perceptual Analogues

Boundary sculpture opened up another door to whole realms of new possibilities and information. We found in a BFI seminar which I was co-leading a relationship between early eyesight conditions and personal boundaries, with an "of course" type of effect.

When Jim explored his personal space, his boundary for closeness of acquaintances was about five feet away from himself. He asked people to please stop there when they entered his space. Jim wore thick glasses. I asked him how long he had worn them. He said, since age six, when it was discovered that he was exceedingly nearsighted. I asked him whether his vision had changed in the ensuing years. He answered that it hadn't changed markedly. Standing about 20 feet away from him, I asked him to take off the glasses and to tell me when he could clearly see what I was doing with the expressions on my face. I walked toward him, smiling, grimacing, frowning, and so on. He said he could see and discriminate clearly when I was at five feet! Clearly his boundary had formed at the distance at which he could discriminate smaller cues. Piaget states that decentration (a type of differentiation) requires perceptual activity (Piaget and Inhelder, 1956). If there is no perception, there can be no perceptual activity.

An N-of-1 means nothing, except as a possibility that there is a new question here—something to pursue with other people who have worn glasses since childhood. Over the years, we have found a fairly close correlation (not researched, but personal contact!) between boundary phenomena and eyesight and other sensory irregularities in childhood.

We also became increasingly aware that, as the human being is an information-processing mechanism, how people approach oneself is one kind of information processing analogically linked to other types of information processing and learning styles. (A full exploration and explication of these topics, of great interest and involvement to us in our training program, and very tempting to pursue here, are beyond the scope of this current work and hopefully will appear in the next.)

Minisculptures

Minisculptures are very quick essences of a situation, a family as system scene, or a sense of a family being worked with in therapy. We ask trainees to quickly think of a typical scene in their earlier lives, such as the dinner table, and ask them to sculpt not necessarily who sat where, but the sense of the dynamics at the table during dinner. Each trainee takes a few minutes and quickly organizes such a symbolic "dance," using other trainees as players, sculpts it and quickly debriefs it.

The idea here is that each trainee chooses one key scene, which the others then experience, in the dynamic tension of the emotional and political pushes and pulls in that family. The group debriefs how it feels to be in those roles. The entire process for each person can take as little as 10 minutes. Yet, it is a very powerful vignette and sense of system that comes through. One can move to discuss and/or explore our five R's—family rules, roles, routines, rituals and resources—from such a quick enactment. One can discuss or explore structure, processes, context, myths—whatever seems to be relevant for trainees at that particular curriculum time.

Historical Sculpture: From Pre-birth to Network

During 1971-1972, also during BFI teaching, I began to wonder if we couldn't use a combination of minisculptures and Kantor's in-depth version to get a sense of the key themes, the intergenerational themes in a person's life. With that, one evening while planning to sculpt a trainee's family, I stated to David Kantor that I was going to try a new idea that evening.

I asked the trainee what legends she had heard about her family from before she was born, about other siblings and people on the scene before her. Such legends could be about those in her immediate family, about grandparents, and about "who" she was supposed to be when she was born. What myths and legends were there surrounding her birth and infancy?

With that information, I asked her to begin to populate her world with people, one at a time, in relationship, with gestures and motions, to each other. We were not attending to the quality of the living space in as great detail at this time. Rather, I touched on it for a general sense of ambience and tone, comfort and atmosphere.

Choosing significant times or events in the sculptor's life-cycle, for example, a time before age eight, between then and 15, between 15 and 20, 20 and 30, we sculpted her family at those times, adding or taking away significant members and contexts until we reached her present-day network. We then needed to use players to represent the needs or demands of entire institutions in her life, as well as significant people.

When we reached the current context, as she moved to touch base with all her commitments, obligations, and connections, we discovered that the key themes about work and responsibility in the family at the time she was born were still present in how she conducted her life: Her time priorities, her sense of being a workaholic, her role as the symbolic good daughter, responsive to the parents' need for positive feedback following earlier tragedies in their lives, became clear to her as intergenerational themes she was living out.

Historical Sculpture in Problem-solving

Later in the semester, a man in the seminar, a priest who had been struggling with the very serious issue of whether to stay in the priesthood or to leave it, asked me to do that particular type of sculpture with him. He had struggled for five years with an image/idea of eventually getting married and having a family.

Again, we started before he was born, and it was clear that he had been seen as the one who would lead the religious life, who would be the "family savior." He had never doubted that he would be a priest, particularly after he had recovered in childhood from a serious illness, during which time he received special attention and care from his mother, whose goal this was for him. She had told him then that God had saved him to do this work. As we sculpted time-slices, the system dynamics leading him to the priesthood became very clear. He had welcomed and enjoyed certain aspects of this life.

However, he had also felt the priesthood to be a heavy burden to fulfill, a yoke. As we brought the family context up to the present day with him at 35, we had added his wide-ranging network of demands, friends, obligations, parish, counseling recipients, the other institutions he attended to, and so on. In addition, we included the significant church superior who had just turned him down for a new position relating to a family life education project to which he had wanted to devote his energy.

At that moment, I went around to each person, playing these many parts in his current life, and asked them quietly to start beckoning to him and to tug at him as he went by. I asked him to walk around touching base with each of these contacts and obligations, and as he did so, asked him and them to speed it up, until he was racing from one to the next, and they were grabbing at him as he went by. He put his hands to his ears as he closed his eyes and shouted "STOP!" And we did.

He said everything was whirling outside the way it had been inside, but that this was the first time he had had a chance to interact with all the parts of his life at one time. He was dizzy. He felt intensely as he sometimes felt at the end of the week, like an automaton who raced from need to need.

We debriefed the sculpture, with players giving feedback on their experience. Not only had the themes of the past family flowed through into his future, basically unconsidered and unchanged, but players expressed their experience in role, that their sense and condition of well-being demanded that he *not* think of himself.

We ended there. The whole process had taken some 45 minutes. Three weeks later he came into the seminar, saying he had made his decision to leave the Church. He is now married, the father of three children, and very happy. He is still very busy.

The above incident brought home the power of sculpture as a problem-exploring tool, which frames the "eventshape" (Auerswald, 1969). All the important factors, from different timeframes, come together in the timeless mind and coalesce, forming the shape of this event. The internal world of events, images, people, messages and issues can be externalized in such an active way that they can be confronted all at once or, as in this last anecdote, confront the sculptor all at once.

Several years later, we learned that Virginia Satir had also developed a form of historical spatialization, which she terms "family reconstruction," which also weaves together the life stories, events, life contexts and processes in families over several generations. She, as we do, believes that people's behavior is contextually derived and related developmentally to each individual's ability to make meaning.

The difficulty of mind is that it is hard put to consider many diverse aspects of one's life at one time. The animation and spatialization of such a plethora of messages and events over time allow one to interact with one's juxtaposed, real yet internal intangible world in a very real way. One can confront one's nightmares, yet more eyes also see the nightmare, take part in it and talk about it. One is not alone with it anymore, and one has new information to consider.

Impromptu Sculpture

By the time the last incident had taken place, I was feeling delighted and very free to use this medium as a language. My own internal imagery had started "appearing" regularly and spontaneously, in ways that seemed to represent the dynamic tugs and pulls between people. Particularly in therapy situations, I found myself saying: "I have an image I'd like to share of what's happening here." And as I was saying that, I would get up and ask the various family members to join me as players in my image for a moment.

One that stands out in my mind as an early such happening occurred while listening to a husband and wife go at it again in their weekly argument, where he essentially was complaining that she didn't do enough for him. I realized I had stopped listening to the words, since something else seemed to be going on inside. And then I asked them to join me in enacting what was on my inner screen:

I saw him in a castle, standing by the drawbridge, with his hand on the rope. She was walking up to the moat and drawbridge from afar, as he watched. I had the couple take the appropriate positions and suggested that she start walking towards him. Just as she got to where the "moat" and drawbridge were, I told him to pull on the rope, so that the bridge came up, and she was left stranded.

With their actually pantomiming this, they both nodded and said, "Yes, that's about what happens." And then they amended it somewhat and reenacted it *their* way! They had entered the metaphor and taken it over, adjusting it to their sense of experience.

I have found that, with the use of sculpture in this way, there is never a mistake. There is only new information. Clients, trainees, children—all take over the image if it does not fit and "correct" it, enacting it their way, which then gives one, as leader, missing information as they take charge of their own process presentation. The therapist/facilitator loses nothing. The sculpting of an idea or image, with the bodies in motion, is far more effective than verbally stating it as metaphor, for the others are in charge of their own information and exploring it for themselves. And it gives them the same tool for expression as the therapist. The mystery of "systems" disappears. Their seeing themselves as system eliminates blame and singular causality, offering them many options.

One-person Sculpture

Individuals are contextual creatures, who usually grew up in families and carry them around inside. Most times they come into counseling or therapy by themselves, without the rest of the cast of characters. For such times, I evolved a way of sculpting an individual's total family system, using the client, myself and anything else in the room. (One time, the cat became a baby.)

In this process, as the client is exploring a particular time in his/her life, I have "stood in" for each family member, asking the client to position me with gestures and movements of that person in relation to him/her. With each family member, I then ask the client to reverse roles with me for a moment, so that I can check the accuracy of my approximation, while the client is experiencing the beginnings of multicentricity, not available via feedback from other players besides myself. As we move on to the next person and positioning, I put a chair or lamp in the appropriate place of each family member, as a symbol for where each one stands in relation to others, spatially, facing the appropriate direction.

In one such sculpture, the client who always had seen herself as the "bad girl" and "depressed" sculpted her family at age three. At that time, they had moved, father had gone to the army, both of mother's parents had died within the previous six months, she had lost her "nanny" in the move, and a baby sister was born after the second grandparent died!

As we had sculpted the scene, laying down the chairs as each grandparent died, "leaving" the nanny behind, "losing" father, "gaining" a sister, she suddenly saw the lack of interaction with her, and the emotional desertion of herself by all other important family and household members. In her momentary role reversal as mother, she felt her mother's sense of loss and depression and mother's need to be attended to in her losses when she had to attend to a new baby and a three-year-old.

Her experiencing the total situation was the beginning of change for her. She saw her family at that time as a multiproblem family, with all of the stresses of such families, and not enough resources to stay on top of the number of changes occurring so closely together. Her sense of self as target, as patient, shifted markedly, as she saw and understood at 33 the total system she could not have seen and understood at three.

System Map Sculptures

In this variation, a family or group can rather quickly portray alliances of who does what to, with, and "against" whom, over time, or at any given time. One can achieve a very rapid sense of the structural relationships over time, in one's own or another family, organization or agency. In addition, one can project such a sequence into the future.

We use this form of sculpture very effectively at BFI in supervising groups of trainees, who see families in other agencies. In addition to audio and/or videotapes, the trainees will portray by this method what they see "happening" in the family systems with whom they are working. They sculpt how they see the family/co-therapist interface, whom they see themselves allied with at various times, and different subsystem variations. In such ways the supervisor and other trainees can experience how each co-therapist sees the family differently, as they discuss and design goals, processes and interventions. Trainees will often sculpt the organization of the agency. One trainee, a head nurse, utilized this method of sculpting to explore, in supervision, problems within and among her teams at the hospital. We then planned interventions from the information gathered.

In another situation, I had two trainees diagram and sculpt the administrative and clinical power structure of the drug center in which they worked. Such an exploration was necessary to determine how they could intervene in the larger system which prevented them from doing effective family therapy by changing client appointments without consulting the trainee/therapists.

One can also ask family members to sculpt themselves this way, presenting their images of their family. This form of sculpture is a particularly effective way for children in families to "speak," for it is in a language they already know. They can say what they cannot say in words,* for often they either do not have the words or are unattended when they try.

The form that we have often used with entire families, which becomes a form of multiple perception sculpture, is to ask the least involved or least targeted family person to sculpt who is close to whom, who allied with whom in the family, and then to move on to ask each other family member in turn to do the same, each from his or her own perception. One asks the identified patient, if such there be, to do his/her image of the family, as the third or fourth sculpture, neither first or last.

With one such family, the mother in a divorced couple with four children, kept saying: "No, that's not the way it is!" when each of her children put the only son, eight years old, next to his father. Father was present at the session. We assured her that she would get her turn, that each had his/her own perception of how the alliances were arranged. The boy had put himself by his father, as did the father, too. Since the mother wanted the boy to go with her while she and the girls went to another country for a year, she had been particularly diligent at not seeing or hearing previously how the boy saw himself. When it was her turn to sculpt the relationships, she put her son, also the youngest child, literally under her arm, huddled in close to her. However, since she was the only one who put him there, she could not ignore the information that had been expressed by all the others. On the basis of that information, a compromise was worked out. The son would spend the summer with mother and the girls overseas and come back to live with his father in the fall, for the remainder of the year.

Such sculptures cannot be argued away or verbally disqualified. These same multiple perception sculptures are useful in various types of groups,

---

*Piaget refers to this as "vertical décalage" or gap in time: knowing at one age what one only has language or verbal explanation for years later (Piaget, 1977b, p. 176, 810).

agencies, organizations, and work settings for exploring differences in views of any situation.

From Here to There: Present to Future— or From Problem/Knot to Ideal Solution

In training and supervision, as well as with families, the trainee/therapist of a family sculpts a problem or knot that he/she sees and is unsure how to deal with, giving minimal verbal explanations. The sculptor then gets feedback from the training group or family quickly as to how it feels to be in those positions, with those gestures. The trainee hears what does not fit, new information, and possible new options.

In this type of sculpture, any individual, any group or family member, sculpts the situation as now perceived, and then sculpts an "ideal" solution. Feedback from those enacting roles/positions offers information about that experimental solution in terms of its acceptability, new knots, and so forth.

This type of sculpture can be done to preview any thought/image of possible interventions and arrangements or interactions of people with each other. Often with families or work and other groups, it serves to clarify, in ways that words cannot, solutions deemed acceptable by different members. The sculptor is then free to find the commonalities in each version and to work towards compromises. Each "family member" is also free to be asked, as the trainee/therapist asks him/herself: "What would be the steps from here to there, from the knot to the solution?" In simulations or in therapy, the therapist and trainees/clients negotiate a facilitation plan.

In training situations for facilitators in human systems, this particular form of sculpture avoids many hours of trial and error with clients, for the trainee can try out with other trainees, rehearse, and approximate metaphors of operation and organization, which system sculptures are. Through feedback, a likely solution emerges. At the very least, glaringly inappropriate suggestions can be discarded ahead of time. Additionally, therapists can ask real family members to sculpt how they now "see" their issues, and how they would like them to be, cutting through all kinds of "verbalese." The key issues for each are: "How do you see the knot? And what do you want?"

"Resistance" of clients then often shows up as the therapist's word for having wanted something the client doesn't!

Definitions/Images

It has been my experience that when any two or more people are arguing heatedly about any word or concept, they have a different image of the meaning of that word or concept. Even in the simplest language, particularly that bandied about in the mental health profession, the words of relationship conjure up different images for different people.

Whenever I hear such disagreement, I stop and say, "Show me what you mean." This may occur with trainees, or indeed, among faculty members, and almost always between couples and family members. Again, such clarifications can often serve as holographic bits of the relationship, defined by the parties themselves.

I am reminded of a couple we were seeing who were arguing about a car ride from Washington, D.C., to Boston, in which he said she wasn't close to him during the drive home, and she said she was. She said she had sat near him and talked to him the whole time he drove. He insisted she wasn't close.

I asked them to stand up, and asked him to show me what his version of close was. He held her by his side, skintight from shoulder to toe. She said she was suffocating. I asked her to show me her version of close. She took his hand, standing by his side, and allowed about six inches between them. He said that was too far away.

That brief scenario encapsulated their entire relationship for them, for then they saw all their differences as hinging on that concept of closeness, as a basic bodily and aesthetic preference which was different for each of them. The six inches and the intensity he wished also translated into his wish for her to be intensely involved with him, to be fascinated by his ideas and thrilled with where his mind went. And she wasn't. She was interested, but not engaged or fired by his conversation. Within a couple of sessions more, they decided that they knew what the issue was and now they had to see if they could work out compromises of value to them both.

With that experience, we began playing with trainees and at workshops, with varieties of words, exploring those which are concepts capable of being enacted by one person, those that must have two or more people, and so on.

We ask participants to pair up, and we list some words on the board or newsprint: joy, anger, sadness, pensiveness, anxiety, depression, peacefulness, and so on. We choose different words at different times. These are examples of some words in the first group, representing emotional states possible to have by oneself, just by reading a book, thinking one's own thoughts or daydreams, or watching TV, which is some sort of outside stimulus yet without another "real" person present.

We invite participants to choose one word at a time from such a list, not in the order listed, and to enact them, by being that word. Partners are to guess which word is being enacted. Invariably there are misread states of being, most often between pensiveness, depression, anger, and sadness. (Which ones are misread in your family and work contexts?)

We then list another set of words, such as: loving, independent, needy, close, aggressive, dependent, schizophrenic, distant, assertive, responsive, and so on. Again, we ask them to enact and guess different words. Again, partners find that not only are their versions of words different, but their interpretations of each other's enactments are often wrong. One person's "loving" is guessed by another as "needy"; "independent" is often seen as "distant." And one person's "responsive" is another person's "aggressive."

Participants in this type of exploration become aware that these are words of relationship, that it takes at least two to tango, and that schizophrenic is a word that means an inability to communicate with another in usual or consensually meaningful ways.

Consensus Sculpture

Quite at the opposite end of the polarity between individual expression of meaning, and simultaneous meanings of many people, is the group consensus sculpture, or composite sculpture, useful in any organization, agency, school, training group, or family. In this form, the leader asks all group or family members to be sculptors to themselves and players for each other simultaneously as they quickly sort themselves in relation to each other on some issue of importance. The resulting tableau may or may not be a moving one. The leader then asks all to look around and asks whether there is consensus as to whether this is the way each person sees the group, and what observations and comments anyone might have on this constellation. The leader may then select individuals and/or subgroups with whom to explore discrepancies.

This is particularly useful in large organizations where people tend to get lost in the structure, in relation to the flow of information or authority. It is also useful in training groups for leaders to be able to match their assumption and inner sense of how group members relate in toto to the group's own sculpting of such phenomena. These procedures allow for new information and updating of previous impressions.

This form of sculpture, used by Jeremy Cobb as an aid in an organizational development consultation, offered one executive the information he needed about the shifting power structure in the organization. Upon seeing the placement of people in relation to a new manager, this executive decided to leave his position in the firm. The composite sculpture gave him instantaneously data and information he could get in no other way, that his ability to be effective was now sharply curtailed.

Group/Family Metaphors

By this time, it is probably obvious that there are probably 1001 ways of conversing in this language and as many forms as there is imagination to shape them, for the lines between sculpture, spatialization, and action metaphor become rather arbitrary and thin after a while. It was through the "habit" of playing with sculpture that we began to invent action metaphor warm-ups such as the "Be an Animal" exercise of Chapter VII. In this sense, there is no limit to where one can go. And the more one does, the more one learns to learn to think metaphorically, analogically, in new and different dimensions.

One of our favorite forms of group or family metaphor was one that came out of Kantor's original sculpting. When this is done from the outside in, the therapist or leader thinks of a metaphor which captures his/her sense of the entire family or group, such as "A Three-ring Circus," "A Masqued Ball," "A Speeding Train." Each metaphor is then quickly sculpted and put into action, allowing an imagistic, kinesic sense of the whole to emerge. Speeding up and slowing down the movement allow essences to come through. Questions can be raised, metaphorically, such as "Who is the ringmaster of the circus? Who are the performers? Audience?" and so forth. Key issues in this form of sculpture are overview, circularity, and moving all members to the level of metaphor.

When this type of metaphor is created from the inside out, the family or group member will sculpt his/her own metaphor for the unit, also without necessarily assigning one-to-one roles of family member to metaphor part. In training groups, we have used such metaphorical representations of family systems to raise the issues of "change" and "influence."

Particularly since there are no distinct family role functions, we will ask one group to observe another group's metaphor in action, and then to change it in some way. Then we will ask them to debrief that experience from both sides—the changees and the changers. Next, we will ask them to begin again with the original metaphor, in action, and request that the other group influence the metaphor group. They then debrief that.

The contrast in the feedback is remarkable. In most instances, the metaphor group has felt coerced in some way, when they were changed, as if they had been "worked on" with no respect for their own ways of being. They report feeling moved "with" when influenced, as if the changers had to truly stop and pay attention to what the "metaphorees" were doing, and to get in rhythm with them in some way in order to influence them. That in itself becomes an analogue for therapy as facilitation, as working with, rather than "on," people.

Let's Go to My House

A final example of sculpture, which again returns us to an original spatial concept of Kantor's, yet developed by Fred Duhl and myself for an Orthopsychiatric Institute conference,* is the House Tour (Jefferson, 1978).

---

*Washington, D.C., March, 1975.

Mbst everyone has heard of house tours, in which participants pay a fee to go through various historical houses or contemporary ones with special features or occupants. Our version of a house tour is to pretend one is leading such a tour of one's own growing up or current home, for several other people.

The tour starts by walking down the street to the house or apartment building, with a verbal description of the surrounding environment and context, in the present tense, no matter what age one lived there:

> Here's the big park I play in. And this is my friend Billy's house, next door. We play in his backyard because ours has laundry lines and cement in it. Here we are at the front walk. We come up to the wood porch. Ours is a two-family house, and Mrs. Jones and her married daughter live upstairs. They own the house. We are not allowed to play on the porch. We go in the door on the right.

The personal aesthetic and emotional quality of each place, space and room is emphasized. One enters the house, describing each space/room as it is approached and entered, and its special meanings, including hiding places under the table, or the place at the top of the stairs where one listened to the grown-ups at night.

The tone and ambience of the furniture and spaces, reflecting the meaning of the space itself, are commented on. Mention is made of the people who occupied these rooms and some key or typical events that took place in each room. The sculptor in this case literally walks people through the imaginary house, outlining the space as he/she goes. Again, memory evocation of core images, illuminating aesthetic preferences, exploring, shaping the physical and interpersonal context in which our learning-to-learn took place, is a key issue in this type of sculpture.

Additionally, within an ongoing training group, inviting others into one's early home introduces them to the self one "was" in ways that have validity as each sees the world through the eyes of the sculptor/tourleader. For the tourleader/sculptor, this is a different type of experience than in evocative sculpture, where the monitor is responsible for pursuing and evoking clarity. Here the sculptor/tourleader must do it for him/herself in ways that communicate to the guests one's personal sense of the total environment. Such a gliding between inner imagery and communication with others is the task of skilled therapists.

Trainees take turns within their groups of threes or fours. Each "visits" the houses of others. They learn to actively visualize, as they listen while walking through the house—a quality indispensable to them as therapists if they are not to lose touch with the people who inhabit such spaces. In this exercising of the theater-of-the-mind, the body, in action, helps the mind create the images of the words that each hears. Each person grasps the sense of each family and each space, from the inside out, as each walks through it in pretended activity.

In spatializations such as these, as well as many others preceding, not only are one's imagery and sense of different living contexts sharpened, but that very sharpening opens the door to whole sets of new questions.

As we go on many tours of people's lives through their images and through the stories they tell as they spatialize, we begin to become aware of the shaping influence of the total context on any family and the individual members—the geography, ecology, economics, culture, ethnicity, religion, accidents of history, genealogy, sex, birth order, and genes, all factors which come to bear on how life is lived and what life means. We become aware that sculpture quickly captures the rules, roles, routines and rituals in any family's (or other human system's) life, and can reveal points of departure for thorough examinations.

Such sobering considerations give us pause when we try too easily to simplify the variables that make human beings, human life, human history, human capacity and potential the intriguing puzzle it seems to be and to have been, in one form or another, since human life began.

SUMMARY

Sculpture and spatialization then are ways of keeping generic questions open while "answering" others. Spatialization, after all, in the family systems movement, started out as an answer to problems in communication. Kantor and others using action techniques struggled with what interactional image they wanted to get across, to communicate, and each developed methods to do so. Each technique of spatialization invented has been the momentary answer to a question.

We started out wondering how to rid ourselves of the disruptiveness of two people in our seminar, and invented what we now call *boundary sculpture*, a generic and metaphoric process for exploring the intangible betweenness of two or more people.

I started out wondering how my internal images related to what was happening and "discovered" *impromptu sculpture*, a way of communicating my internal "assessment" of interaction through action metaphor.

Others had wondered how different people "saw" the same situation, and invented *multiple perception* and *composite sculptures*.

I had wondered how themes and patterns did indeed carry forward in families over time and "created" *historical sculpture*. And so on.

It becomes apparent to me that a technique is not a solution, but a process derived by a searcher with a question. Techniques, then, are not just answers to a problem, but also byproducts discovered en route to someplace else.

Some techniques are also processes for exploring generic questions. Spatializations are this type of technique: processes for finding solutions to other and others' questions.

Theories, too, are the human answers to human questions, the "best" explanations that we have or will accept at any given time, a map for guiding our seeing, our explorations. Each current theory is today's "answer" to yesterday's questions.

In most fields, when theories and techniques are taught, the original questions are left out, and the humanly derived, constantly evolving theories and techniques are often presented as closed systems, as final answers. The result is such that students and trainees become receivers of answers, technicians, rather than competent searchers.

At BFI we feel that final theories as answers to questions concerning being human, growing, developing, surviving, and living with others cooperatively and/or exploitively are far from in. This is the first time in history as we know it that we have had the possibility of information from many views simultaneously. Not just through theater can we approach simultaneity, but also the technology of many television cameras and computers can present to us the cinema verité reality as seen (though not as given meaning to) from many positions. The 180-degree films of Cinerama-type movies are attempts at that presentation on a movie screen of the reality we live.

In our search, we have tended to ask generic questions and to develop generic techniques or processes that allow for new information, new experiential ways of seeing. And even when we may not be asking generic questions, but specific ones, having generic questions in the background of our minds allows us to perceive generic issues when they emerge spontaneously.

Generic techniques illuminate human betweenness, the relational aspects of our lives, from the inside out, without necessarily dictating any particular solutions to new questions. Solutions can be evolved fitting with the particular people in each context. Generic techniques then are languages, metaphors, communicating meaning at many levels at one time.

Spatialization, the language of drama and theater, of image and meaning, is universal in that sense. It does not have an age limit nor a schooling limit. No fancy abstract formulas are needed. Sculpture allows the most complex sentences to be said, in ways that have a boundary around the punctuation. This boundary can also be extended into the past and future, or can expand horizontally to be inclusive of other units interfacing with any grouping. Spatialization recreates in metaphor the original scenarios, behaviors, constellations, from which theories of human behavior are derived. And with attention to a few simple rules, sculpture can offer the safety to be known, without criticisms and judgments, and to express one's view. Human systems theory does, after all, speak to what goes on between and among real live human beings. Yet the human systems theory that connects the individual experiential information with observed behaviors has not been written yet. Sculpture/spatialization allows for this private data to surface.

We move trainees to the medium of raw data, as experiencers, observers and playwrights all, as we also have them read the "plays" written by others. With analogic distance, we encapsulate and remetaphor the original interactions and look at them anew.

As anyone in the family systems therapy world is aware, not only are different evocations of a family's process possible through different interviewers (i.e., Hillcrest Series), but there are also different languages used for describing similar constellations of behaviors. One person's "undifferentiated ego mass" (Anonymous, 1972; Bowen, 1978) (already a compilation of metaphors from another arena of psychiatry/psychology) is another person's "enmeshed" family (Minuchin, 1974). These expressions are but chosen verbal metaphors for behaviors, ways of being, developed among family members over time, by which each feels unable to make decisions or to act independently of others.

Spatialization avoids the confusion of such labeling and allows us not to get lost in arguing about language and about the particular words and phrases chosen by another human being to describe what we are seeing, doing, enacting. So often, the particular label used also conjures up the particular theorist's values and techniques for "solving" the issue.

Rather than getting caught up in the language chosen, we get caught up in exploring basic human processes, ways of living, behaving and meaning, in a generic language that does not immediately require limiting or prejudicial words or phrases. We can agree to a label if we so desire, and we can also discriminate fine-tuned meanings and differentiations. Additionally, without labels, we are free to innovate and invent new interventions of congruent meaning to the members themselves.

As one becomes acquainted with wide ranges of human interacting and family forms, we realize that many types of family and individual ways of being seen as "dysfunctional" today are artifacts of yesterday, when they were traditional, expected, and accepted. We see that theories of behavior and therapy are contextual and value laden, and change over time, in keeping with the cultural, economic, and political contexts, as well as with the prevailing paradigms of particular fields. As theorists, therapists, and trainers, we are as much the children of our age, of our contexts, as are the people we speak of, help, or enter into a process of education with. Our task is to help empower others in recognizing the shaping forces in/of their contexts, and in moving towards integration, options, and flexibility in a rapidly changing world we each never made.

Sculpture and spatialization allow for the inclusion of human experience, for the contextual set, for the report from the inside, concerning pain and dis-connection, expectations and losses, love and despair, craziness and the peace of coherence.

To speak of systems speaks to "What is the problem?"

To speak of theater speaks to "Where is the pain?"

When we speak of both, we hint at the interconnected holographic totality of human life.

In training, then, we look for the generic categories that see life as an experience that we live rather than as a problem to be solved. Problems are our labels for certain types of experiences we wish to rid ourselves of, in order to enhance the quality of our living. How we look at therapy, facilitation, and problem-solving needs to be "reflexively coherent" (Wideman, 1970) with the aesthetic image of the quality of life of the participants. As Gregory Bateson stated in 1979 at a BFI-sponsored workshop, we must pay attention to "the delicate fabric of the psyche."

Our trainees explore, then, in this first year, generic tools, generic language, and generic maps for asking the right questions, for exploration, discovery, and new integrations. They "see" system and know the processes with which to derive new information—information which is different enough to make a difference to all involved in the search.

Sculpture and spatializing, inclusionary of all voices and views as they are, allow trainers to "see how trainees think." Similarly, and reflexively, sculpture and spatialization allow trainees, families and other individuals to discover and invent each human system, as if it were each one's very own idea and creation.

And indeed it is.

Epilogue

We are at a resting place, but hardly the end of a road.

I started out to write a book about a way of training in human systems thinking which provides for integration and a multicentric view in the person of the trainee.

Where can one begin such a tale, save in the middle? And that's where I began. From such a random starting place, I am now choosing to pause, without having told the full story, for sure. I have not yet informed the reader of the specific sequencing of types of exercises. I have not given language or form here to the specific courses which we teach and the interweaving of themes which we follow to fill out our hologram of human systems thinking. I certainly haven't dealt with specifics of family organization, nor with the theoretical material we cover in more traditional fashions as well as experientially. As I think of it, I am sure there is more that I have left out than I have included, which will just have to be written as the next volume.

However, somehow sandwiched in between these seemingly arbitrary beginning and ending points, it is my hope that I have been able to present a comprehensive *framework for thinking* about training in systems thinking, drawn from the ongoing search at BFI over the past 14 years. It has been my wish to illuminate some basic ways that we have found of designing, using and thinking about analogic exercises and metaphors, congruent with content, with trainees' varying ways of learning, with processes trainers wish trainees to learn, and with generic human systems thinking. I hope I have given the impression that, particularly in the field of human services, the data for the basic themes, concepts, and theories to be taught can be drawn forth from trainees' own experiences. I hope certainly that I have demonstrated that abstract concepts concerning human behavior and processes, which we struggle to grasp, can be translated directly or analogically into experiential metaphors of the human behavior these concepts describe. And most of all, I hope I have conveyed the sense of excitement in learning and training for all concerned, inherent in these types of processes.

I will feel I have succeeded if I have brought you, the reader, along with me in this exploration, and have stirred up in you new "what ifs?" I will be pleased indeed if you have been stimulated to wonder, to originate and to try your own metaphors, in your own fashion, in your own contexts. If I have accomplished some of my wishes, this then will feel like a time to pause, a time for bubbling ideas to jell, for the reader, as well as for myself.

Somewhere within this work I discussed beginnings and described how I found beginnings interesting, for the system precursors are present in beginnings. Later one can see which ones, of all those present, emerged to lend shape to a program. And that is what this work has been about.

Yet I am also ending somewhere in the middle, a useful vantage point for describing beginnings. Our process is still ongoing and happening. I have taken this opportunity to pause and take time for the creative reflection necessary to coalesce my thinking about generic issues in training. I realize that I have brought together learnings I knew about and those that I didn't realize were there. Some learnings were clear to me at the time they were happening, and others have needed a more distant vantage point. Hindsight is a new, later and different integration of patterns of occurrences that could not be perceived as a pattern at the time they were occurring. The graceful distance of timespace and a human mind are needed to metaphor phenomena over time into patterns. One cannot know before one knows. And it has been a continually exciting process to find out!

HOW ABOUT TRAINEES?

What, however, is the impact of such a way of training on trainees during this first explorative, integrative year of our two-year program, when the focus is not on clients and therapy, but on the trainee and how he/she begins to think systemically and begins to integrate personal and theoretical data? Let us turn our attention now not to processes and content, but to the "target population."

Some trainees struggle with ways of learning that are strange yet are intrigued enough by their involvement to rest judgment for a while, as connections between personal experience are made with conceptual material. Soon they are able to relax in their reliance upon the accepted processes which they have learned to call schooling or education. Our trainees are adults, expected to be competent in varieties of situations, which are interactive. Most have not been offered the opportunity to become competent thinkers, actors, competent in drawing upon their own epistemic and synesthetic knowledge.

When trainees begin to grasp the idea that our version of experiential education means that they will draw from themselves the data for their learning, trainees become captivated with the ideas of innovation, novelty, and new connections in such a way that anticipating participation becomes routine! They look forward to the creative exploration and fun of role-taking. The sense of play joins the sense of work. The ideas of metaphor and analogue become more and more overt. Trainees begin to expect to be involved and challenged, and become sensitive to and vocally responsive to tedium in the seminars.

Human beings and human systems are active entities and do not live their lives sitting down talking. Trainees expect to be active, and to pass their information through the filter of the self as they weave it into ideas.

Trainees put pressure on the leaders to keep delivering in the model the leaders have set up. Leaders, having stated they are concerned with how people learn—how they take in information and give meaning to it—open themselves to each group anew. The trainees thus put pressure on the leaders for excellence in leadership in guiding the trainees in reaching their goals, in learning how they learn, in learning how to see and act with multifocal awareness. The pressure is also on faculty to keep their creative processes going, for repetition becomes tedious for the faculty as well.

In the more usual Platonic trainer/trainee model, the trainer is the source, owner, and dispenser of wisdom and the trainee the receiver of that wisdom. That puts great pressure on trainers to be wise—and always wiser than trainees, in order to retain the status, identity and position of one who trains.

At BFI, particularly since 1973, the trainers have tried something else. To use a phrase from the family therapy field that was not yet being bandied about at that time, the trainers "triangle in" (Bowen, 1978) many types of exercises designed to connect each one's epistemics with epistemology. Such triangulation gives trainees an excuse to have a wide range of interactions and transactions in varieties of roles and metaphors, serious and playful. Each trainee then has new shared events and experiences to speak about authentically (as author). Each can draw upon such common metaphoric experiences, connecting new ideas and concepts to his/her own personal experience and to each other, person to person.

Multiple interactions within structured metaphors create material for continuous new dialogue and new integrations. Trainers do not have to know the answers. Rather, this modality allows trainees and trainers to ask, look at the same questions, and discover, find and create answers. In this more Socratic model, both trainers and trainees ask the questions. The trainees do the experiment which trainers have "tried on" in planning. In debriefing with the leaders, trainees come up with the data for some of their answers.

The trainers don't have to *be* wise, for trainees keep giving them data by which to keep *becoming* wise. Indeed, trainees even offer new and unexpected data or conceptualizations which sometimes push trainers into wisdom and new horizons before they might have gotten there on their own. Trainees who are free to challenge allow trainers the opportunity to explore new questions and to keep their conceptual system open and evolving.

We have learned over the years the importance to trainees of our emphasis on play, pretend, and simulation. Such common metaphoric, yet very real, experiences became the pardonable excuses for dropping one's "normal self," or "ordinary, natural" roles, or "proper" behavior, or core images of "I'm not a person who . . . " while trying on something different. Affectation of a role is expected, as each trainee tries metaphors of approximation.

WHAT'S IN A ROLE?
(OR, WHAT'S A META FOR?)

Multiple opportunities for verbal and paralinguistic metaphor and role enactment, while drawing on one's own experiences, analogically, permit one to reexamine whole system dances—the reciprocal and systemic interactions of which such roles are a part. One can reexplore and try on, as if it were the whole of one, many ways of being, and tuck them into the closet of one's mind, muscles and being, reintegrated. When next encountered, either in daily life or in one's work, such behaviors, metaphors, and roles are already familiar. When met again, these roles, positions, ideas, images, and feelings are known and available to be called upon to offer information about the current context and the people in it. Such knowings, if not old friends, are at least acquaintances, and never again blind dates. One can draw upon even minimal knowing to ask new questions. The strange can be made familiar, with a place to fit.

Trainees become free in a funny kind of way. Role-taking and new metaphoring free them from the literature of the field they are reading, where images and categories are set by others. Role-taking can be a place to underplay certain parts of self, or conversely, to develop unexplored, unexercised, or held-back parts of self.

Curiously, though, one doesn't have to focus on developing such a part "in" and "of" self, for the role playing has been "triangled in" as a vehicle (the third party, which takes attention away from what is really going on inside the trainee). The trainee is "just trying it on, thank you" so he/she can see how certain actions might evoke certain types of thoughts, or how a person might think and feel, in order to create certain actions. The trainee does not have to "keep" any of it. Once such a role is debriefed, the momentary role-taking can be and is discarded, and one returns to one's "I." It is not serious. Or is it?

Yes, repeated ventures into drawing forth metaphors and roles are a serious matter indeed! The "I" is changed into one who can enter into many different metaphors, many different roles, all of which call on, explore, expand, and develop different aspects and capacities of the "I-Eye," including the ability to see multicentrically from all positions.

In drawing on one's nonlanguage experiences as well as verbal experiences, each trainee expands his/her range of metaphors and roles. This repertoire becomes, as it were, an entire "resident company" housed in one person, who over time can move into any metaphor of approximation to connect empathetically with another person, to experience the world from that perspective. Additionally, one learns the process of approximating. Multiple approximations begin to foster ways of seeing that grasp images of interacting systems from each position, as well as from a view of the whole.

Thus, the methodology of training, the repeated processes in which trainees are involved, becomes as much responsible for changing the way of thinking as the particular content and subject matter. As trainees draw on experiences in their own lives and families, as well as simulations outside their range of experience, there is a metamessage to the entire process: When one tries on or explores many phenomena, many roles, one has much "diversity of instances in concept attainment" (Bruner, 1973a). One tries many metaphors of identity approximation, organization, and operation.

By playing with metaphors and roles as authentically as possible for the moment, before "taking them off" and putting them aside, one finds out readily enough that there is no right way to play a role, to see the whole, and no one right way to be. One begins to discover the complexity of fit that makes changing, evolving, living human systems. One realizes the interconnectedness of all parts: that who one is and how one behaves in which contexts seems to depend upon many factors. A new integrated way of thinking begins to develop from the inside out, which puts the trainee at the center of his turned around world of multicentric thinking.

When there is diversity of instances of concept attainment, which are linked, the trainee begins to think analogically. As Bruner says:

> It seems to be that the principal creative activity over and beyond the construction of abstracted coding systems is the combination of different systems into new and more general systems that permit additional prediction. It is perhaps because of this that, in Whitehead's picturesque phrase, progress in science seems to occur on the margin between fields. There is virtually no research available on this type of combinatorial creativity (1973a, p. 235).

Safety and competence in both the external and internal worlds derive from the ability to predict, to know that one can make the Familiar Strange and the Strange Familiar, and to know the conditions which make such sureness possible. Analogic and systemic thinking makes that ability to predict more possible. In a world which changes so fast that the technology and the newest approach to training or working with people hits the market before the ink is yet dry on the proposal to study the outcome of the last approach tried, we have been using a similar and steady approach for some 14 years now.

While I would be hard put to claim that the type of research that Bruner had in mind when he wrote the above words has been done on the BFI methodology of training, I would like to share some information from the research on learning that was done early in our career, as part of a United Community Service grant in 1971-2.*

This research found that, contrary to normal expectations in such a study process, the learning curve of the Family Service Agency social workers went up markedly and stayed up after a year, following a 15-week, 30-hour training program based on training in the manner outlined in this book, as well as didactic input from experts in the field of alcoholism. While BFI was responsible for the curriculum and training processes, the research was done independently by the investigators.

Interestingly enough, the entire training program was conceptualized, from its inception, as an intervention strategy in agencies' patterns of avoiding working with alcoholics and their families.

The general topic of the training program was Family Process and Alcoholism. Workers' attitudes toward alcoholics and their families were pre-, during, and post-tested. Workers were rated on the seeking out of such clients and on the numbers of such clients in their caseloads. Videotapes of pre-, during, and post-training interviews were recorded and scored for worker attitude and systemic views. Results indicated that agency workers were actively seeking out more alcoholics and their families to work with, feeling more effective in their work, and attributing their change of attitude and competency to the training program. This trend increased rather than decreased as the months went by.

We were as delighted as the researcher was surprised with the results of this early research on BFI's method of training, for we began to realize then that we were raising and continue to create generic approaches, rather than teaching specific solutions.

---

*"Alcoholism: An Evaluation of Intervention Strategy in Family Agencies," Principal Investigator, Harold Demone, reported by Herbert J. Hoffman and Ludmila W. Hoffman, 1974. See also exercises in Chapter IX, originally designed for this program.

SWITCHING THE FOCUS

Each major development in our training program has come from a *switch of focus* in the discovery of a process en route to somewhere else. Each such exploration expanded and continues to expand our personal, epistemic knowledge, as it also links to our more formal epistemology. Our discoveries took place from the "inside out," meeting halfway those of others which were made from the "outside in."

How we actually live will always move at a faster pace and outstrip our research about how we live and give meaning. Thus we feel we must train people in category-making, in coding events in such ways that we, the trainers, do not restrict the categories. Otherwise we train others in the questions we have already solved (and we all do that!) without providing them with the tools to approach and generate new solutions to questions as yet unasked, by us or them, or surfaced by the new contexts and conditions of living.

Again, I quote Bruner:

Let me in general propose this test as a measure of the adequacy of any set of instructional propositions—that once they are grasped, they permit the maximum reconstruction of material unknown to the reconstructor (1973a, p. 236).

I would submit that we have found some way to meet this test, to explore the maximum reconstruction processes demanded by generic education, in the process of educating generic systems thinkers.

In the family therapy systems movement, Jay Haley is quoted as saying,

Our hope has been that those who teach will have students who surpass the teacher. This isn't happening in the family movement. How to create a social situation which will create innovators? We do not yet know how to do this.*

I would propose that perhaps we have found some ways to answer Jay Haley's challenge.

And I invite you, the reader, to carry on the processes, adding your own imagery and inventions to those presented here and in so doing, to go beyond the information given in this work.

Let us continue.

---

*In *The Family Shtick,* Vol. II, No. 2, 1978; Haley's comments were made on the occasion of a tribute to Murray Bowen, Washington, D.C., September 1978.

Glossary

Analogue: A likeness, correspondence, parallel, correlate, or approximation of one structure, process, idea, or experience, to another. In training, as in life, the algebraic formula "this is to this as that is to that" expresses the concept of analogue.

Catalytic: An agent, process, or context that accelerates or facilitates changes in others. In chemistry, a catalytic agent is itself unaffected by the process. In our training process, the agents are people affected in discrete and continuing, important ways, by new information, ideas, and processes developed.

Designed experience (also *Structures for Spontaneity or Common Metaphors*): Those exercises, simulations, and planned procedures which provide a common structure within which individuals interact. In the process, each person's creativity, meanings, reflections, etc., come into play. Such experiential structures, when coupled with cognitive generalizations and frameworks, aid people in learning "from the inside out." Abstract concepts can be drawn from commonly experienced simulations and explorations.

Ecological systems: More than one co-evolving self-organizing system. William Gray, in his report to NIMH (1980), states, "Co-evolution is understandable as a necessary feature of the relationship between two or more self-organizing systems, such as living creatures and parts of their environment, for the necessary reshaping of each to occur, to conserve and extend the necessary pattern match between the two, upon which their continued existence and the growth and development to each crucially depends.

"In ecological systems, regulation is by co-evolution, while in cybernetic systems it is the result of internalized control mechanisms."

Episteme: Knowledge.

Epistemic: Of or pertaining to knowledge, or the conditions for acquiring it. Paul MacLean uses this word to mean the subjective view of science and knowledge of the self, from the inside out.

Epistemology: According to the dictionary, epistemology refers to a branch of philosophy that investigates the origin, nature, methods and limits of human knowledge. In the field of family therapy, traced to the contributions of Gregory Bateson, Dick Auerswald and Paul MacLean, epistemology has come to mean a formal world view, like a paradigm—a framework for thinking, for conceptualizing.

Equivalent: Reciprocally and correspondingly differentiated and valued; not necessarily equal, as in same. For instance, a soccer ball for my son and a leotard for my daughter are *equivalent* gifts, given each one's interests. People can be *equivalently* new to different situations. *Equivalency* is based on respect and differentiation of individual skills, attributes, meanings and experiences. For the child, "play" is equivalent to adult "work."

Ethos: According to the dictionary, "1) Sociology: the fundamental character or spirit of a culture; the underlying sentiment that informs the beliefs, customs or practices of a group or society; dominant assumptions of a people or period. 2) The moral element in dramatic literature that determines a person's action rather than his/her thought or emotion." Each family has its own feel, ambience, ethos, which creates or is the bond of connection of each member to the whole.

Hologram, holographic: Used in this work both in its metaphorical value, of a three-dimensional image projected in space (Bentov, 1977), as well as in Pribram's and others' metaphor of *the mind as hologram* (Ferguson, 1978; Pribram, 1971). Essentially, without resorting to too much technology, a *hologram* is a photographic record containing all the information needed to reconstruct an entire three-dimensional image. What is recorded on the photographic plate are interference patterns of two light sources of laser beams, bouncing off an object. An exciting fact, to this author, is that if the photographic plate is broken, each bit or piece of the broken plate still contains all the information which can be used to reconstruct the entire image of the original, when "transilluminated with a coherent light source" (Pribram, 1971, p. 147). This then becomes a wonderfully useful metaphor for organismic training in systems thinking.

Implode: To burst inward as opposed to explode, a bursting outward.

Implosion: The act of imploding, a bursting inward. Technological advances have unleashed an information implosion. We now have minute by minute more information about more things, ideas and events than any of us can individually handle, or even care to know.

Information processing styles: In this context, refers not to computer technology, but to those particular individual approaches to perceiving, giving meaning, organizing, storing and outputting data and experience that each person has. This would include thinking in images, kinesthetically, or by nonlinguistic sounds as well as verbal modes.

Integrated/integration (of systems thinking): As used in this context, *integration* refers to those conceptual digestion and absorption processes by which some idea becomes part of a whole world view and can no longer be forgotten or isolated out, as flour in a cake cannot be isolated out, once baked.

Meta: According to the dictionary, a learned borrowing from Greek, meaning: after, along with, beyond, among, behind, and often denoting change. In the field of family systems therapy, again with recognition of Bateson's usage and influence, meta is used to mean "about," as in *metacommunication,* a communication *about* communication, or *metalanguage,* any language or symbolic system used to discuss, describe or analyze another language or symbolic system. Bateson also used the prefix "meta" to refer to a higher level of generalization.

Multicentric: The ability to see, conceptualize, from many positions and to know that they all exist simultaneously.

Paradigm: An example, pattern, in science and family systems, meaning a framework for thinking.

Strange/Familiar: A concept by W. J. J. Gordon (see Bibliography) in which he proposes that learning is the process by which we make the Strange Familiar, while innovation is the process by which we make the Familiar Strange. Good teaching and therapy do both of these, and one could analyze any interventions by these concepts.

Synesthetic: Comes from the word *synesthesia,* meaning a sensation produced in one modality when a stimulus is applied to another modality, as when the hearing of a certain sound induces the visualization of a certain color. I use it in this work in a similar manner, to mean sensory stimuli which are processed in varying ways along different sensory channels, simultaneously.

Bibliography

Ackerman, N. W. *The Psychodynamics of Family Life.* New York: Basic Books, 1958.

Alschuler, A., Evans, J., Tamashiro, R., and Weinstein, G. "Self-Knowledge Education Project." Final report to the U.S. Office of Education, Grant No. OEG-0-70-2174, OEG 900-75-7166. December, 1975.

Anonymous. "Toward the Differentiation of a Self in One's Own Family," in J. L. Framo (Ed.), *Family Interaction. A Dialogue Between Family Researchers and Family Therapists.* New York: Springer Publishing Co., 1972.

Argyris, C., and Schon, D. *Theory in Practice, Increasing Professional Effectiveness.* San Francisco: Jossey-Bass, 1974.

Auerswald, E. H. "Cognitive Development and Psychopathology in the Urban Environment." Paper presented at Gouveneur Hospital, New York, May, 1966.

Auerswald, E. H. "Interdisciplinary versus Ecological Approach," in W. Gray, F. J. Duhl, and N. D. Rizzo (Eds.). *General Systems Theory and Psychiatry.* Boston: Little, Brown & Co., 1969.

Auerswald, E. H. "Thinking About Thinking About Health and Mental Health," in S. Arieti (Ed.). *American Handbook of Psychiatry,* New York: Basic Books, 1975.

Bandler, R. and Grinder, J. *The Structure of Magic.* Vol. 1. Palo Alto: Science and Behavior Books, 1975.

Bart, W. M. "A Biosociological Framework for the Study of Formal Operations." Paper presented at the Jean Piaget Society Conference, Philadelphia, 1977.

Bateson, G. "Information and Codification: A Philosophical Approach," in J. Ruesch and G. Bateson, *Communication: The Social Matrix of Psychiatry.* New York: W. W. Norton Co., 1968. (Originally published in 1951.)

Bateson, G. *Steps Towards an Ecology of Mind.* New York: Ballantine Books, 1972.

Bateson, G. *Mind and Nature.* New York: E. P. Dutton, 1979.

Bateson, G., Jackson, D. D., Haley, J., and Weakland, J. H. "Toward a Theory of Schizophrenia." *Behavioral Science,* 1956, 2:4, 251-264.

Bell, J. E. *Family Group Therapy.* Public Health Monograph 64, Washington, D.C., U.S. Dept. of Health, Education and Welfare, 1961.

Bentov, I. *Stalking the Wild Pendulum: On the Mechanics of Consciousness.* New York: E. P. Dutton, 1977.

Berlin, I. *The Hedgehog and the Fox.* New York: Mentor Books, 1957.

Berne, E. *The Structure and Dynamics of Organizations and Groups.* Philadelphia: J. B. Lippincott Company, 1963.

Berne, E. *Games People Play.* New York: Grove Press, 1964.

Berne, E. *Principles of Group Treatment.* New York: Grove Press, Inc., 1966.

Bernhard, Y. *Self Care.* Millbrae, California: Celestial Arts, 1975.

279

Birdwhistell, R. L. *Introduction to Kinesics.* Louisville, Ky.: University of Louisville Press, 1952.

Birdwhistell, R. L. *Kinesics and Context.* Philadelphia: University of Pennsylvania Press, 1971.

Bloch, D. A., and Rosenthal, R. A. "Psycho-Social Replication." Paper presented at the First International Congress of Social Psychiatry, London, August 1964.

Bogen, J. E. "The Other Side of the Brain: An Appositional Mind," in R. E. Ornstein (Ed.). *The Nature of Human Consciousness.* San Francisco: W. H. Freeman & Co., 1968, 101–125.

Boszormenyi-Nagy, I. "The Concept of Schizophrenia from the Point of View of Family Treatment." *Family Process.* 1962, 11, 103–113.

Boszormenyi-Nagy, I., and Framo, J. (Eds.). *Intensive Family Therapy: Theoretical and Practical Aspects.* New York: Harper & Row, 1965.

Boszormenyi-Nagy, I., and Spark, G. M. *Invisible Loyalties.* New York: Harper & Row, 1973.

Boulding, K. E. "General Systems Theory—The Skeleton of Science," in W. H. Buckley (Ed.). *Modern Systems Research for the Behavioral Scientist.* Chicago: Aldine Publishing Co., 1968.

Bowen, M. "Family Psychotherapy with Schizophrenia in the Hospital and Private Practice," in I. Boszormenyi-Nagy and J. Framo (Eds.). *Intensive Family Therapy.* New York: Harper and Row, 1965.

Bowen, M. *Family Therapy in Clinical Practice.* New York: Jason Aronson, 1978.

Bradford, L., Gibb, J. R., and Benne, K. *T-Group Theory and the Laboratory Method.* New York: Wiley, 1964.

Brazelton, T. B. *Toddlers and Parents and Development of Independence.* New York: Delacorte, 1964.

Brazelton, T. B. *Infants and Mothers: Individual Differences in Development.* New York: Delacorte, 1969.

Brazelton, T. B. *On Becoming a Family: The Growth of Attachment.* New York: Delacorte, 1981.

Broughton, J. M. "Beyond Formal Operations—Theoretical Thought in Adolescence." *Teachers College Record,* 1977, 79:1, 87–97.

Bruner, J. S. *Toward a Theory of Instruction.* Cambridge, Mass.: Harvard University Press, 1966.

Bruner, J. S. *Beyond the Information Given.* J. M. Anglin (Ed.). New York: W. W. Norton & Co., 1973a.

Bruner, J. S. *The Relevance of Education.* New York: W. W. Norton Co., 1973b.

Bruner, J. S. *On Knowing: Essays for the Left Hand.* 13th ed. New York: Atheneum Press, 1976. (Reprint 1962 Cambridge, Mass. Harvard University Press.)

Bruner, J. S. *The Process of Education.* Cambridge, Mass.: Harvard University Press, 1977.

Buckley, W. *Sociology and Modern Systems Theory.* Englewood Cliffs: Prentice-Hall, 1967.

Buckley, W. (Ed.). *Modern Systems Research for the Behavioral Scientist.* Chicago: Aldine Publishing Co., 1968.

Buzan, T. *Use Both Sides of Your Brain.* New York: E. P. Dutton, 1976.

Cerf, B., and Cartmell, Van H. (Eds.). *Sixteen Famous American Plays.* New York: Garden City Publishing Co., 1941.

Condon, W. S. and Ogston, W. D. "Sound Film Analysis of Normal and Pathological Behavior Patterns." *Journal of Nervous and Mental Disorders,* 143:388–97, 1966.

Constantine, L. L. "Designed Experience: A Multiple, Goal-Directed Training Program in Family Therapy." *Family Process,* Vol. 15, No. 4, December 1976, 373–388.

Constantine, L. L. "Family Sculpting and Relationship Mapping Techniques." *Journal of Marriage and Family Counseling.* 1978, 4(2), 13–24.

Conway, F., and Siegelman, J. *Snapping.* Philadelphia: J. B. Lippincott Co., 1978.

Corsini, R. J. *Methods of Group Psychotherapy.* New York: McGraw-Hill, 1957.

Damude. Quoted in von Bertalanffy, L. *General Systems Theory.* New York: George Braziller, 1968, p. 7.

de Bono, E. *Lateral Thinking.* New York: Harper Colophon Books, 1970.

Deikman, A. J. "Bimodal Consciousness," in R. E. Ornstein (Ed.). *The Nature of Human Consciousness.* San Francisco: W. H. Freeman & Co., 1968, 67–86.

Duckworth, E. "The Having of Wonderful Ideas." *Harvard Educational Review,* 1972, 42:2, 217–231.

Duhl, B. S. "Intimacy: A Dyadic System." Paper presented at Boston Family Institute, May 1973.

Duhl, B. S. "Changing Sex Roles—Information Without Process." *Social Casework,* 1976a, 57:2, 80–86.

Duhl, B. S. "The Vulnerability Contract: A Tool for Turning Alienation into Connection in Individuals, Couples and Families." Paper presented at the First International Family Encounter, Mexico City, November 1976b.

Duhl, B. S. "Piaget, the Boston Family Institute, and Metaphor: An Integrated Approach to Training in Systems Thinking." Unpublished paper presented at Boston Family Institute Conference, May 1978.

Duhl, B. S., and Duhl, F. J. "Differentiation and Integration." Paper presented at the North Shore Hospital Conference, Manhasset, L.I., N.Y., Jan. 1974a.

Duhl, B. S., and Duhl, F. J. "Another Way of Training Therapists." Paper presented at Nathan Ackerman Memorial Conference of Family Process, Cumana, Venezuela, Feb. 1974b.

Duhl, B. S., and Duhl, F. J. "Cognitive Styles and Marital Process." Paper presented at the Annual Meeting of the American Psychiatric Association, Anaheim, Calif., May 1975.

Duhl, B. S., and Duhl, F. J. "From The Inside Out: It's Hard to Kiss a System: A General Systems Approach to Integrative Family Therapy." Paper presented at the American Psychological Association Annual Meeting, Montreal, September, 1980.

Duhl, B. S., and Duhl, F. J. "Integrative Family Therapy," in A. Gurman and D. Kniskern (Eds.). *The Handbook of Family Therapy.* New York: Brunner/Mazel, 1981.

Duhl, F. J. "Intervention, Therapy and Change," in W. Gray, F. J. Duhl, and N. D. Rizzo (Eds.). *General Systems in Psychiatry.* Boston: Little, Brown, 1969.

Duhl, F. J. "A Personal History of Politics and Programs in Psychiatric Training," in G. M. Abroms and N. S. Greenfield (Eds.). *The New Hospital Psychiatry.* New York: Academic Press, 1971.

Duhl, F. J. *Dialogues: The Person in the Therapist.* Videotape series. Boston: BFI 1974-on.

Duhl, F. J. (Ed.). *Perceptions: The Therapist and His/Her Work.* Videotape series. Boston: BFI 1974-on.

Duhl, F. J. "Changing Sex Roles: Concepts, Values, Tasks." *Social Casework,* 1976, 57:2, 87–96.

Duhl, F. J., and Duhl, B. S. "The Uses of the Selves in Co-Therapy and Coupling." Paper presented at the New York Family Institute Conference on: Uses of the Self in Family Therapy, Southbridge, MA., March 1972.

Duhl, F. J., and Duhl, B. S. "Structured Spontaneity: The Thoughtful Art of Integrative Family Therapy at BFI." *Journal of Marriage and Family Therapy,* 1979, 5:3.

Duhl, F. J., Kantor, D., and Duhl, B. S. "Learning, Space and Action in Family Therapy: A Primer of Sculpture," in D. Bloch (Ed.). *Techniques of Family Psychotherapy.* New York: Grune and Stratton, 1973.

Erikson, E. H. *Childhood and Society.* New York: W. W. Norton and Co., 1950.

Ferguson, M. "Karl Pribram's Changing Realities." *Human Behavior,* May 1978.

Flavell, T. H. *The Developmental Psychology of Jean Piaget.* Princeton: Van Nostrand Co., 1963.

Flavell, T. H. *Cognitive Development.* Englewood Cliffs: Prentice-Hall, 1977.

Fox, R. *Kinship and Marriage.* New York: Penguin Books, 1967.

Framo, J. L. "Rationale and Techniques of Intensive Family Therapy," in I. Boszormenyi-Nagy and J. L. Framo (Eds.). *Intensive Family Therapy.* New York: Harper and Row, 1965.

Frank, J. D. *Persuasion and Healing: A Comparative Study of Psychotherapy.* Baltimore: The Johns Hopkins Press, 1961.

Gazzaniga, M. S. "The Split Brain in Man," in R. E. Ornstein (Ed.). *The Nature of Human Consciousness.* San Francisco: W. H. Freeman & Co., 1968.

Ginsburg, H., and Opper, S. *Piaget's Theory of Intellectual Development.* Englewood Cliffs: Prentice-Hall, 1969.

Goffman, E. *Behavior in Public Places.* Glencoe, IL: Free Press, 1963.

Goffman, E. *Relations in Public.* New York: Basic Books, 1971.

Goldstein, K. *The Organism.* New York: American Book Co., 1939.

Gordon, W. J. J. *Synectics. The Development of Creative Capacity.* New York: Harper and Row, 1961.

Gordon, W. J. J. "Connection Making Is Universal." *Curriculum Products Review,* April, 1977.

Gordon, W. J. J., and Poze, T. *The Metaphorical Way of Learning and Knowing.* 2nd Ed. Cambridge, Mass.: Porpoise Books, 1973.

Gordon, W. J. J., and Poze, T. "Toward Understanding The Moment of Inspiration," presented at Creativity Symposium, American Association for the Advancement of Science, Feb. 1977.

Gordon, W. J. J., and Poze, T. "Learning Dysfunction and Connection-Making." *Psychiatric Annals,* March, 1978.

Gray, W. "The System Precursor, System Forming Approach in General Systems Theory." Presented at VIth World Congress in Social Psychiatry, Opatija, Yugoslavia, 1976.

Gray, W. "System-forming Aspects of General System Theory, Group Forming and Group Functioning," in J. E. Durkin (Ed.). *Living Groups: Group Psychotherapy and General System Theory.* New York: Brunner/Mazel, 1981.

Gray, W., Duhl, F. J., and Rizzo, N. D. *General Systems Theory and Psychiatry.* Boston: Little Brown & Co., 1969.

Gray, W., and Esser, A. H. "The Ecopsychiatry of Juvenile Delinquency and Crime." Report prepared for presentation at the National Institute of Mental Health, February, 1980.

Grinder, J., and Bandler, R. *The Structure of Magic*. Vol. 2., Palo Alto: Science and Behavior Books, 1976.

Grinker, R. R. (Ed.). *Toward a Unified Theory of Human Behavior*. New York: Basic Books, 1967.

Gruber, H. E., and Vonèche, J. J. (Eds.). *The Essential Piaget*. New York: Basic Books, 1977.

Gurman, A., and Kniskern, D. (Eds.). *The Handbook of Family Therapy*. New York: Brunner/Mazel, 1981.

Haley, J. "The Family of the Schizophrenic: A Model System." *American Journal of Nervous and Mental Disorders*, 1959, 129, 357–374.

Haley, J. *Strategies of Psychotherapy*. New York: Grune & Stratton, 1963.

Haley, J. *Changing Families*. New York: Grune & Stratton, 1971.

Haley, J. *Uncommon Therapy*. New York: W. W. Norton & Co., 1973.

Haley, J. *Problem Solving Therapy*. New York: Harper Colophon Books, 1976.

Hall, E. T. *The Silent Language*. New York: Doubleday, 1959.

Hall, E. T. *The Hidden Dimension*. New York: Doubleday, 1966.

Hart, J., and Jones, B. *Where's Hannah? A Handbook for Parents and Teachers of Children with Learning Disorders*. New York: Hart Publishing Co., 1968.

Hellman, L. *Scoundrel Time*. Boston: Little, Brown, 1976.

Herink, R. *The Psychotherapy Handbook: The A to Z Guide to More Than 250 Different Therapies in Use Today*. New York: New American Library, 1980.

Hill, J. E. *The Educational Sciences*. Bloomfield Hills, MI.: Oakland Community College Press, 1972.

Hoffman, H. J., and Hoffman, L. W. "Alcoholism: An Evaluation of Intervention Strategy in Family Agencies." Final Report. Project supported by Training Grant 5-T15-AA00041 from the National Institute for Alcohol Abuse and Alcoholism, July 1974.

Hunt, J. McV. *Intelligence and Experience*. New York: Ronald Press, 1961.

Jackson, D. D. "The Question of Family Homeostasis." *Psychiatric Quarterly Supplement*, Part 1, 1957, 31:79–90.

Jackson, D. D. "Family Interaction, Family Homeostasis and Some Implications for Conjoint Family Psychotherapy," in J. H. Masserman (Ed.). *Science & Psychoanalysis, Vol. 2., Individual and Family Dynamics*. New York: Grune & Stratton, 1959.

Jackson, D. D., and Weakland, J. "Conjoint Family Therapy: Some Considerations, Theory, Technique and Results." *Psychiatry*, 1961, 24:30–45.

James, W. *Principles of Psychology* (Vol. I–II). New York: Dover, 1950.

Jefferson, C. "Some Notes on the Use of Family Sculpture in Therapy." *Family Process*, 1978, 17:1.

Jimenez, J. "Synectics: A Technique for Creative Learning." *The Science Teacher*, March 1975, 33–36.

Jimenez, J. "Piaget and Synectics," in *Piagetian Research Abstracts*, C. Mogdil and S. Mogdil (Eds.). Atlantic Highlands, N.J.: Humanities Press, Inc., 1976, 4, 102–119.

Jung, C. C. *Synchronicity*. (From *The Collected Works of C. C. Jung*, Bollingen Series XX, Vol. 8, 1960.) Princeton: Princeton University Press, 1969.

Kagen, J. *Change and Continuity in Infancy*. New York: Wiley, 1971.

Kagen, J. "Do Infants Think?" *Scientific American*, 1972, 226:74–83.

Kantor, D., and Lehr, W. *Inside the Family*. San Francisco: Jossey-Bass, 1975.

Knowles, M. *The Modern Practice of Adult Education: Andragogy versus Pedagogy*.

New York: Association Press, 1972.

Knowles, M. *The Adult Learner: A Neglected Species*. Houston: Gulf Publishing Co., 1973.

Knowles, M. *Self-Directed Learning: A Guide for Learners and Teachers*. New York: Association Press, 1975.

Koestler, A. *Janus: A Summing Up*. New York: Vintage Books, 1979.

Kohlberg, L. "Development of Moral Character and Moral Ideology," in M. L. Hoffman and L. W. Hoffman (Eds.). *Review of Child Development Research,* Vol. 1. New York: Russell Sage Foundation, 1964.

Kohlberg, L. "From Is to Ought: How to Commit the Naturalistic Fallacy and Get Away with It in the Study of Moral Development," in T. Mischel (Ed.). *Cognitive Development and Epistemology*. New York: Academic Press, 1971.

Kohlberg, L., and Mayer, R. "Development as the Aim of Education." *Harvard Educational Review,* 1972, 42:4, 449–496.

Kolb, D. A. "Learning and Problem Solving," in D. A. Kolb, I. M. Rubin, and J. M. McIntyre (Eds.). *Organizational Psychology,* 2nd Ed. Englewood Cliffs: Prentice-Hall, 1974.

Konicek, D. "Marching to a Different Drummer," in T. Timmermann and J. Ballard (Eds.). *Yearbook in Humanistic Education*. Amherst, MA.: Mandala, 1976.

Kramer, C. H. "The Old Pro." *American Association for Marriage and Family Therapy Newsletter,* 1980, 11:4, 1.

Kuhn, T. S. *The Structure of Scientific Revolutions*. Chicago: University of Chicago Press, 1962.

Laszlo, E. *The Systems View of the World*. New York: George Braziller, 1972a.

Laszlo, E. (Ed.). *The Relevance of General Systems Theory*. New York: George Braziller, 1972b.

Levin, S., and Michaels, J. J. "The Participation of Psycho-Analysts in the Medical Institutions of Boston." *The International Journal of Psycho-Analysis,* 1961, 42:3, 271–283.

Lewis, J. M., Beavers, W. R., Gossett, J. T., and Phillips, V. A. *No Single Thread.* New York: Brunner/Mazel, 1976.

Liddle, H. A., and Halpin, R. J. "Family Therapy Training and Supervision Literature: A Comparative Review." *Journal of Marriage and Family Counseling.* 1978, 4:4, 77–98.

Lidz, T. *The Family and Human Adaptation*. New York: International Universities Press, 1963.

Lidz, T., Cornelison, A. R., Fleck, S., and Terry, D. "The Intrafamilial Environment of Schizophrenic Patients: II, Marital Schism and Marital Skew." *American Journal of Psychiatry,* 1957, 114:241–248.

Lilly, J. C. *The Center of the Cyclone*. New York: The Julian Press, 1972.

Lilly, J. C. *Lilly on Dolphins*. New York: Doubleday, 1975.

Lindemann, E., "Symptomatology and Management of Acute Grief." *American Journal of Psychiatry,* 1944, 101:141.

Loevinger, J. *Ego Development*. San Francisco: Jossey-Bass, 1976.

Luce, G. G. *Body Time*. New York: Pantheon Books, 1971.

Luria, A. R. *Cognitive Development: Its Cultural and Social Foundations*. Cambridge, Mass.: Harvard University Press, 1976.

MacDermott, D. *Metametaphor*. Boston: Marlborough House, 1974.

MacGregor, R., Ritchie, A. M., Serrano, A. C., and Schuster, J. P. *Multiple Impact*

Therapy with Families. New York: McGraw-Hill, 1964.

MacLean, P. D. "On the Evolution of Three Mentalities." *Man-Environment Systems,* 1975, 5:213–222.

McLuhan, M. *The Medium Is the Message.* New York: Random House, 1967.

Maslow, A. H. "A Theory of Human Motivation," in P. Harriman (Ed.). *Twentieth Century Psychology.* New York: Philosophical Library, 1946.

Maslow, A. H. (Ed.). *New Knowledge in Human Values.* South Bend, IN.: Regnery/ Gateway, Inc., 1959.

Maslow, A. H. *Toward a Psychology of Being,* 2nd Ed. Princeton, N.J.: Van Nostrand, 1968.

Maslow, A. H. *Religions, Values and Peak Experiences.* New York: Viking Press, 1970.

Masters, W. H., and Johnson, V. E. *Human Sexual Response.* Boston: Little, Brown, 1968.

Masters, W. H., and Johnson, V. E. *Human Sexual Inadequacy.* Boston: Little, Brown, 1970.

Mead, M. *Blackberry Winter.* New York: Pocket Books, 1975. (First published 1972, William Morrow & Co.)

Miller, J. G. "Living Systems: Basic Concepts," in W. Gray, F. J. Duhl, and N. D. Rizzo (Eds.). *General Systems in Psychiatry.* Boston: Little, Brown, 1969.

Miller, J. G. "Living Systems: The Group." *Behavioral Science,* 1971a, 16:4, 302–398.

Miller, J. G. "The Nature of Living Systems," *Behavioral Science,* 1971b, 16:4, 277–301.

Miller, J. G. *Living Systems.* New York: McGraw-Hill, 1978.

Minuchin, S. *Families and Family Therapy.* Cambridge, MA.: Harvard University Press, 1974.

Minuchin, S., Montalvo, B., Guerney, Jr., B. G., Rosman, B. L., Schumer, F. *Families of the Slums.* New York: Basic Books, 1967.

Minuchin, S., Rosman, B. L., Baker, L. *Psychosomatic Families.* Cambridge, MA: Harvard University Press, 1978.

Mischler, E. G. "Meaning in Context: Is There Any Other Kind?" *Harvard Educational Review,* 1979, 49:1, 1–19.

Moreno, J. L. *Psychodrama.* New York: Beacon, 1946.

Napier, A. Y., with Whitaker, C. A. *The Family Crucible.* New York: Harper and Row, 1978.

Ornstein, R. E. *The Psychology of Consciousness.* San Francisco: W. W. Freeman & Co., 1972.

Papp, P. "Family Choreography," in P. Guerin (Ed.). *Family Therapy, Theory and Practice.* New York: Gardner, 1976.

Papp, P., Silverstein, O., and Carter, E. "Family Sculpting in Preventive Work with 'Well Families'." *Family Process,* 1973, 12:2, 197–212.

Parkes, C. M. "Psycho-Social Transition." *Social Science and Medicine,* 1971, 5: 101–115.

Pearce, J. C. *Magical Child.* New York: E. P. Dutton, 1976.

Perls, F. *The Gestalt Approach and Eye Witness to Therapy.* Palo Alto: Science and Behavior Books, 1973.

Perry, W. G. *Forms of Intellectual and Ethical Development in the College Years.* New York: Holt, Rinehart, Winston, 1968.

Piaget, J. *The Origins of Intelligence in Children.* New York: International Universities Press, 1952.

Piaget, J. *The Moral Judgment of the Child.* Glencoe, IL.: Free Press, 1965. (First published in 1932 in French.)

Piaget, J. *Grasp of Consciousness. Action and Concept in the Young Child.* Cambridge, MA.: Harvard University Press, 1976.

Piaget, J. "The Role of Imitation in the Development of Representational Thought," in H. E. Gruber and J. J. Vonèche (Eds.). *The Essential Piaget.* New York: Basic Books, 1977a.

Piaget, J. *The Essential Piaget.* H. E. Gruber and J. J. Vonèche (Eds.). New York: Basic Books, 1977b.

Piaget, J., and Inhelder, B. *The Child's Conception of Space.* F. J. Langdon and J. L. Leinzor, translators. Atlantic Highlands, N.J.: Humanities Press, Inc., 1956. (Originally published in French, 1948).

Piaget, J., and Inhelder, B. *The Growth of Logical Thinking.* New York: Basic Books, 1958. (Originally published in French, 1955.)

Piaget, J., and Inhelder, B. *The Psychology of The Child.* H. Weaver, translator. New York: Basic Books, 1969.

Pittman, F., III. "Managing Acute Psychiatric Emergencies: Defining the Family Crisis," in D. Bloch (Ed.). *Techniques of Family Therapy.* New York: Grune and Stratton, 1973.

Polanyi, M. *Personal Knowledge.* Chicago: University of Chicago Press, 1958.

Polanyi, M. *The Tacit Dimension.* New York: Doubleday, 1966.

Polanyi, M. *Knowing and Being.* Chicago: University of Chicago Press, 1969.

Polanyi, M., and Prosch, H. *Meaning.* Chicago: University of Chicago Press, 1975.

Pribram, K. H. *Languages of the Brain.* Englewood Cliffs: Prentice-Hall, 1971.

Pulaski, M. A. S. *Understanding Piaget.* New York: Harper and Row, 1971.

Rapaport, D. "The Structure of Psychoanalytic Theory." *Psychological Issues,* 1960, 2:2, monograph, 1–159.

Richards, I. A. "The Secret of Feedforward." *Saturday Review,* Feb. 3, 1968.

Rogers, C. P. *On Becoming a Person.* Boston: Houghton Mifflin, 1961.

Rossman, M. "New Age Blues," in *On the Politics of Consciousness.* New York: E. P. Dutton, 1979.

Ruesch, J., and Bateson, G. *Communication: The Social Matrix of Psychiatry.* New York: W. W. Norton & Co., 1968.

Samples, B. *The Metaphoric Mind.* Reading, MA.: Addison-Wesley Publishing Co., 1976.

Satir, V. *Conjoint Family Therapy.* Palo Alto: Science and Behavior Books, 1964.

Satir, V. *People-Making.* Palo Alto: Science and Behavior Books, 1972.

Scheflen, A. E. *How Behavior Means.* New York: Jason Aronson, 1974.

Scheflen, A. E., with N. Ashcraft. *Human Territories. How We Behave in Space-Time.* Englewood Cliffs: Prentice-Hall, 1976.

Schon, D. "Deutero-Learning in Organizations: Learning for Increased Effectiveness." *Organizational Dynamics,* 1975, 4:1, 2–16.

Selvini-Palazzoli, N., Cecchin, G., Boscolo, L., and Prata, G. *Paradox and Counter-Paradox.* New York: Aronson, 1978.

Shannon, C. E. "A Mathematical Theory of Communication." *Bell System Technical Journal,* 1948, 27:3, 379–423.

Shannon, C. E., and Weaver, W. *The Mathematical Theory of Communication.* Urbana: University of Illinois Press, 1949.

Shantz, C. V. *The Development of Social Cognition*. Chicago: University of Chicago Press, 1975.

Singer, M. T. "Family Transactions and Schizophrenia: I. Recent Research Findings," in J. Romano (Ed.). *The Origins of Schizophrenia*, International Congress Series, 1967, 151, 165-78. Amsterdam: Excerpta Medica.

Singer, M. T., and Wynne, L. C. "Thought Disorder and Family Relations of Schizophrenics: III. Methodology Using Projective Techniques." *Archives of General Psychiatry*, 1965a, 12, 187-200.

Singer, M. T., and Wynne, L. C. "Thought Disorder and Family Relations of Schizophrenics, IV. Results and Implications." *Archives of General Psychiatry*, 1965b, 12, 201-12.

Singer, M. T., and Wynne, L. C. "Principles of Scoring Communication Defects and Deviances in Parents of Schizophrenics: Rorschach and TAT Scoring Manuals." *Psychiatry*, 1966, 29, 260-68.

Skinner, B. F. *Science and Human Behavior*. New York: Macmillan, 1953.

Skinner, B. F. "The Flight from the Laboratory," in M. Marx (Ed.). *Theories in Contemporary Psychology*. New York: Macmillan, 1963.

Skinner, B. F. *Beyond Freedom and Dignity*. New York: Knopf, 1972.

Speck, R. V., and Attneave, C. L. *Family Networks*. New York: Random House, 1973.

Sprott, W. J. H. *Human Groups*. Baltimore: Penguin Books, 1958.

Stanislavski, C. *An Actor Prepares*. New York: Theatre Arts Books, Robert M. MacGregor, 1948.

Stein, M. I. (Ed.). *Contemporary Psychotherapies*. New York: The Free Press of Glencoe, 1961.

Szasz, T. "The Myth of Mental Illness." *American Psychologist*, 1960, 15, 113-118.

Thomas, A., and Chess, S. *Temperament and Development*. New York: Brunner/Mazel, 1977.

Umbarger, C., Dalsimer, J., Morrison, A. T., and Bregin, P. R. *College Students in Mental Hospitals*. New York: Grune and Stratton, 1962.

Von Bertalanffy, L. "Some Biological Considerations of the Problem of Mental Illness," in L. Appleby, J. M. Scher, and J. Cumming (Eds.). *Chronic Schizophrenia*. New York: The Free Press of Glencoe, 1960, 36-53, 341.

Von Bertalanffy, L. *Robots, Men and Minds*. New York: George Braziller, 1967.

Von Bertalanffy, L. *General System Theory*. New York: George Braziller, 1968.

Von Bertalanffy, L. "General System Theory and Psychiatry—An Overview," in W. Gray, F. J. Duhl and N. D. Rizzo (Eds.). *General Systems Theory and Psychiatry*. Boston: Little, Brown, 1969.

Von Neumann, J. *The Computer and the Brain*. New Haven: Yale University Press, 1958.

Von Neumann, J., and Morgenstern, O. *Theory of Games and Economic Behavior*. Princeton: Princeton University Press, 1947.

Walsh, F. *Normal Family Processes*. New York: Guilford, 1982.

Watson, J. *The Double Helix*. New York: New American Library, 1968.

Watzlawick, P. *How Real Is Real?* New York: Vintage Books, 1977.

Watzlawick, P. *The Language of Change*. New York: Basic Books, 1978.

Watzlawick, P., Beavin, J. H., and Jackson, D. D. *Pragmatics of Human Communication*. New York: W. W. Norton & Co., 1967.

Watzlawick, P., and Weakland, J. H. *The Interactional View*. New York: W. W. Norton & Co., 1977.

Watzlawick, P., Weakland J., and Fisch, R. *Change.* New York: W. W. Norton & Co., 1974.

Weinstein, G., Hardin, J., and Weinstein, M. *Education of the Self: A Trainers Manual.* Amherst, MA.: Mandala, 1976.

Whitaker, C. A. "Psychotherapy of the Absurd with a Special Emphasis on Psychotherapy of Aggression." *Family Process,* 1975, 14:1, 1-15.

Whitaker, C. A., and Malone, T. P. *The Roots of Psychotherapy.* New York: Blakiston, 1953. (Reissued, New York: Brunner/Mazel, 1981.)

Whitehead, A. N. *Science and the Modern World.* New York: Macmillan, 1925.

Whitehead, A. N., and Russell, B. *Principia Mathematica,* 2nd Ed. Cambridge: Cambridge University Press, 1910-1913.

Wideman, J. W. *Growth and Development in Counselor Education.* Dissertation, Harvard University, 1970.

Wiener, N. *Cybernetics or Control and Communication in the Animal and the Machine.* New York: Wiley, 1948.

Wiener, N. "The Human Use of Human Beings." *Cybernetics and Society.* New York: Doubleday Anchor Books, 1954.

Wynne, L. C. "Schizophrenics and Their Families: Research on Parental Communication," in J. M. Tanner (Ed.). *Developments in Psychiatric Research.* London: Hodder & Stoughton, 1977.

Wynne, L. C., Ryckoff, I., Day, J., and Hirsch, S. "Pseudomutuality in the Family Relations of Schizophrenics." *Psychiatry,* 1958, 21, 205-220.

Wynne, L. C., and Singer, M. T. "Thought Disorder and Family Relations of Schizophrenics, I. A Research Strategy." *Archives of General Psychiatry,* 1963a, 9, 191-198.

Wynne, L. C., and Singer, M. T. "Thought Disorder and Family Relations of Schizophrenics, II. A Classification of Forms of Thinking." *Archives of General Psychiatry,* 1963b, 9, 199-206.

Index